FICTIONS OF TOTALITY

Purdue Studies in Romance Literatures

volume 44

FICTIONS OF TOTALITY

The Mexican Novel, 1968, and the National-Popular State

Ryan F. Long

Purdue University Press
West Lafayette, Indiana

∞ The paper used in this book meets the minimum requirements of American National Standard for Information Sciences—Permanence of Paper for Printed Library Materials, ANSI Z39.48-1992.

Printed in the United States of America
Design by Anita Noble

Library of Congress Cataloging-in-Publication Data

Long, Ryan F.
Fictions of totality : the Mexican novel, 1968, and the national-popular state / Ryan F. Long.
p. cm. — (Purdue studies in Romance literatures ; v. 44)
Includes bibliographical references and index.
ISBN 978-1-55753-487-3 (alk. paper)
1. Mexican fiction—20th century—History and criticism. 2. National characteristics, Mexican, in literature. 3. Politics and literature—Mexico. I. Title. II. Series.

PQ7203.L66 2008
863'.640935872—dc22 2008013001

For Ansel

Contents

Acknowledgments

This book would not exist without the guidance, encouragement, and support of all the friends, teachers, and colleagues who helped me write it over the past several years. Gary Haldeman and Galo González first taught me how to read Latin American literature. Marc Brudzinski, Dawn Fulton, Doris Garraway, Tabea Linhard, and Victoria Lodewick read the earliest versions of this book, and their kind and candid comments set me in the right direction. Among the professors who especially helped me survive graduate school and finish the dissertation are Ariel Dorfman, Danny James, Walter Mignolo, Stephanie Sieburth, and Teresa Vilarós. Special thanks also go to John Kraniauskas, Gabriela Nouzeilles, and Helen Solterer for their work on the dissertation committee as careful, thoughtful, and generous readers. The Duke-UNC Chapel Hill Center for Latin American and Caribbean Studies, and Natalie Hartman in particular, provided space and funding for invaluable intellectual exchange and collective work. John Mraz and Eli Bartra have been important mentors and friends. Jon Beasley-Murray, Tracy Devine-Guzmán, Alessandro Fornazzari, and Freya Schiwy have sustained me with their constant friendship. The doctoral dissertation the book is based on was made possible by a Department of Education FLAS Fellowship that allowed me to live and conduct research in Mexico City. While in Mexico, I was fortunate to receive the institutional support of the Colegio de México, where Rafael Olea Franco, Yvette Jiménez de Baez, Luz Elena Gutiérrez de Velasco, Saurabh Dube, and Ishita Banerjee Dube helped me access archives, make important contacts, and feel at home.

No one helped me develop this project more than Alberto Moreiras. I cannot thank Alberto enough for being such a dedicated mentor, teacher, and friend, who has always encouraged me to work harder, write more carefully, and trust my judgment.

Since arriving at the University of Oklahoma in 2002, I have received generous research funding from the College of Arts and Sciences, the Graduate College, and the Department of Modern Languages, Literatures, and Linguistics. Luis Cortest deserves special thanks for providing invaluable guidance and moral support as an exceptional mentor and close friend. A number of friends have helped make Oklahoma a good home, especially Susan Beaty, José Juan Colín, Rachel Cortest, and Michael and Susan Winston.

Preparing the manuscript and project proposal was made much easier by the careful readings and detailed advice of Alberto Moreiras, Jon Beasley-Murray, and Maarten van Delden. I owe special thanks to the two anonymous readers whose frank and thorough critiques improved the manuscript significantly. Floyd Merrell and Susan Y. Clawson at Purdue Studies in Romance Literatures and Rebecca Corbin at Purdue University Press have been extraordinarily attentive and helpful in every stage of the process.

I would also like to thank the editors of *Casa del Tiempo* for allowing me to reprint a portion of my analysis of *Si muero lejos de ti,* originally published as "La subjectividad olvidada: *Si muero lejos de ti* y la ruptura de historiografía literaria," *Casa del Tiempo* 3.3.2 (Sept. 2001) <http://www.difusioncultural.uam.mx/revista/sep2001/long.html>.

My parents, Fred and Donna Long, have never wavered in their support of my academic and professional pursuits. They and my sister, Sarah Johnson, have always helped me keep things in perspective with patience and good humor. I owe a debt of gratitude to my in-laws, Clint and Elizabeth Baer, for productive conversation and a calm place to write.

Hester Baer not only read every word of this book more than once, but she also helped me through the revisions during a very difficult time in our lives. I could not have finished the project without her intelligence, unfailing honesty, limitless patience, and steady presence. Nothing would be worth it without her or Della, the brightest light.

Introduction

Between the 1950s and the 1980s, Mexico experienced a significant political and economic transition, from a national-popular to a neoliberal state model. Broadly speaking, the first model promoted the development of domestic industries and markets in order to achieve national independence; the second proposes that integration into the global marketplace is the only feasible solution to Mexico's stubborn social inequalities and economic woes (González Casanova; Lustig; Mota; Székely, *Economía*). A significant epistemological consequence of this transition was registered in a specific form of cultural production, the totalizing novel. Through ideological constructions of what the Mexican nation was or was meant to be, both the national-popular state and the totalizing novel in Mexico wrestled with the difficulty of projecting unity and coherence onto an historically heterogeneous social space shaped by legacies of colonialism and dependency. I understand a totalizing novel as a fictional work that aspires to reconstruct a day—as in the paradigmatic example of James Joyce's *Ulysses* (1922)—an event, or even a nation in its totality. Furthermore, this study emphasizes that examples of the genre also consider, implicitly or explicitly, the viability of totalizing representation in general. Over the course of Mexico's recent transition, the incorporative, unifying logic of the totalizing novel unraveled as a consequence of the crisis of ideology suffered by the national-popular state. Traditionally, the national-popular state's hegemony relied upon sustaining the ideology of the Revolution, which cast that event as an unfinished project whose gradual completion was leading the nation—with the state as custodian—toward a future moment of national unity and coherence. When historically determined contradictions came to a head in watershed events like the Tlatelolco massacre of 1968 and the oil bust and subsequent debt crisis of 1982, the national-popular state could no longer maintain its hegemony.

Literary constructions of the Mexican national totality recorded and anticipated this ideological crisis by exposing the violent foundations of the integrative operations that grounded the authority of both state and novel. By revealing the constitutive limits of both nation-state and novel, the bankruptcy of the national-popular state model seriously challenged the viability of two fundamentally important means of organizing and comprehending community in Mexico, and Latin America, whose roots extended back at least to the early nineteenth-century period of independence from Spain (Benedict Anderson; Fuentes, *Nueva*; Mejía Duque; Rama, *Ciudad*; Sommer).

In recent years, many critics in Latin American literary and cultural studies have investigated the connections among neoliberal economic and political reforms, contemporary culture, and the construction of community (Avelar; Franco, *Decline*; Levinson; Masiello). Neoliberalism is both a cause and a symptom of globalization, decentralization, and privatization, processes that have profoundly altered how the nation-state shapes cultural production. As many scholars have pointed out, a general process of political transition that has affected the entire Latin American region in different ways has coincided with the emergence and/or increasing prominence of literary forms, like *testimonio* and the chronicle, that address social and political concerns in ways substantially distinct from those of traditional genres, like the novel (Beverley, *Against*; Gugelberger).

Inspired by recent reappraisals of the Latin American literary "boom" and the critical strength afforded by works that have integrated deconstruction and subaltern studies into their scholarship on cultural production in Latin America, this book is dedicated to improving the general understanding of the Mexican novel in relation to its historical context (Avelar; Beverley, *Subalternity*; Franco, *Decline*; Levinson; Martin; Moreiras, *Exhaustion*, *Tercer espacio*). Both deconstruction and subaltern studies—related fundamentally in the pioneering work of Gayatri Spivak—concern themselves with critiquing the appeal to origins and the exclusive foundations of collective and individual subjectivity. My analysis of the totalizing novel in Mexico thus focuses on the relationship between subject formation and the reproduction or rejection of originary thinking in paradigmatic examples of the genre. This focus guides my inquiry into how the totalizing novel negotiates its necessarily limited ability to contain the radical heterogeneity of the community it strives to represent.

Recent publications on Mexican literature and its historical context have provided valuable insights into hybrid and nonfiction genres, like the *testimonio* and the chronicle, especially in terms of how these genres correspond to contemporary, post-Tlatelolco Mexico (Brewster; Corona Gutiérrez and Jörgensen; Egan). One goal of this study is to provide a better foundation for understanding the increasing prominence of these genres by helping to explain how the novel's privilege as a representative genre began to wane during Mexico's neoliberal transition. Furthermore, a number of scholars have engaged productively with the question of how fictional genres relate to political change in Mexico (Brushwood; Corona Gutiérrez; Franco, "Critique"; Kohut; Sefchovich; Steele). But surprisingly, to my knowledge there is no research that rigorously compares novelistic production from before and after the watershed year of 1968. Addressing that lack was the principal motivation for carrying out this study.

My emphasis on the totalizing novel and its relation to political change situates this book within discussions of the critical category known most commonly as the Latin American "total novel." The viability of this category has been productively challenged on aesthetic grounds (Corral). But most scholarly reflection on the term finds it valid, usefully identifying the genre's roots in order to outline its predominant traits (Mark Anderson; Fiddian, "James Joyce"; Raymond Williams). The key figures to whom critics return time and again are Mario Vargas Llosa and Carlos Fuentes, whose essays from the late 1960s and early 1970s—most notably Vargas Llosa's *Carta de batalla por Tirant lo Blanc* (1969) and *García Márquez: Historia de un deicidio* (1971), and Fuentes's *Nueva novela hispanoamericana* (1969)—established parameters for understanding the genre that remain relevant for contemporary discussions of the Latin American novel. Much more developed and sustained than Fuentes's, Vargas Llosa's observations on the total novel have set out to understand the relationship between a work of fiction and the historical context that inspires it. The successful total novel, in Vargas Llosa's famous terms, commits deicide, supplanting reality with a parallel world of the author's creation.

Not surprisingly for a critic who is also a novelist, Vargas Llosa privileges the creative power of the author, proclaiming that the successful writer can devise formal devices for containing and ordering the chaotic, infinite world that provides the most ambitious novelists with their source material. In his 1969 prologue to a new Spanish-language edition of Joanot Martorell's fifteenth-century chivalric novel *Tirant lo Blanc*, Vargas Llosa concedes that the writer's creation is ultimately illusory in comparison to the reality it supplants:

> En *Tirant lo Blanc* se ve admirablemente esa relación dialéctica entre literatura y realidad, que exige de la ficción un distanciamiento de aquello que expresa para expresarlo vívidamente. La condición de la fidelidad en este caso es la traición. Porque la representación de la realidad total que puede dar una novela es ilusoria, un espejismo: cualitativamente idéntica, es cuantitativamente una ínfima partícula imperceptible confrontada al infinito vértigo que la inspira. (*Carta* 33)

For the author faced with no less than the challenge of representing infinity, Vargas Llosa proposes that the solution lies in sustaining the illusion of totality within the pages of a novel, of creating a work whose appearance of autonomy and coherence are so convincing that readers will forget that the book in their hands is fiction.

What I find particularly interesting in regard to the question of totality and its representation is precisely the limit to which Vargas Llosa refers when he distinguishes the total novel from the "infinite vertigo that inspires it." A writer dedicated to perfecting his craft, Vargas Llosa focuses on how to conceal that limit by creating an illusion of coherence and autonomy. My analysis, by contrast, is based on the presumption that it is more productive to examine how novels, either implicitly or explicitly, *expose* that limit, and second, how this exposure is connected to historical and ideological change. Highlighting this process of exposure suggests that the term *total novel,* which connotes a sense of stasis appropriate for Vargas Llosa's emphasis on completeness, is somehow inadequate. Thus for the purposes of my analysis of how novels work to engage their historical context, I prefer the more active term *totalizing novel.* The point of contact between state and novel that this study emphasizes is a site of open-ended negotiation, a space of overlap that helps explain how a series of Mexican novels respond to a period when the representative authority of both state and novel was challenged by the consequences of contradictory historical tendencies.

It is a well-known fact that the Mexican novel has long been highly critical of the Revolution, the foundational political event of twentieth-century Mexico, as well as of the post-Revolutionary state (Monsiváis, "Notas" and "No con un sollozo"). Less frequently discussed is the common ground shared by novel and state, which is defined by two crucially important assumptions about representation and authority: first, that national experience is comprehensible, and, second, that certain centralized forms are better suited to synthesizing and communicating that experience than others. The national-popular state and the totalizing novel were two especially privileged representational forms of mid- to late-twentieth-century Mexico. In the case of both forms, exclusivity is at the same time foundation and limit of their privileged positions. The political and cultural authority of each depended upon the assumption that access to national totality was necessarily limited to a select few. In a way that was significantly similar to other postcolonial contexts (Amin; Guha, *Dominance*), including everyone else in the processes of political and cultural representation was the ostensible goal in Mexico, but achieving it required that an initial vanguard serve as guide (Bartra, *Jaula*, "Revolutionary Nationalism"; García Canclini; Mallon). In an apparent paradox, a novel like Carlos Fuentes's *La región más transparente* (1958), which criticized the ruling elite for its corruption and lack of transparency, still reproduced an insurmountably exclusionary representation of the nation. But what became increasingly apparent over the years during which the national-popular state lost its hegemony was precisely the reciprocally constitutive, and indeed not paradoxical, relationship between the aspiration to totality and exclusion.

The contradictions that led to the national-popular state's downfall emerged dramatically in the 1960s, 1970s, and 1980s after decades of political centralization forged by the government's efforts to maintain power, which not infrequently relied upon coercion. In the case of post-Revolutionary Mexico, a number of examples come to mind upon considering how the government has employed coercion in order to strengthen and reproduce itself: the often violent negotiation and consolidation of power that eventually led to the formation, in 1929, of the National Revolutionary Party, the early precursor to the still extant Institutional Revolutionary Party; the war and assassination campaign against the Cristeros in the late 1920s and early 1930s; the suppression of the Almazanistas in the 1940 presidential election; the crackdown against the Railroad Workers' Union during their 1958–59 strikes; the massacre at Tlatelolco in October 1968 and further violence against students in June 1971; counterinsurgency campaigns against urban and rural guerrilla movements in the 1970s; and, in general, the impunity that enables the sometimes deadly intimidation of critical journalists, activists, and political dissidents, which persists to this day.

The Mexican state is hardly unique in its recurrence to violence. It is difficult, if not impossible, to identify any contemporary political system that is not ultimately based on exclusion, and which does not employ coercion in order to reproduce itself (Abrams). My discussion of Mexican political change, which serves as context for this study's literary analysis, focuses on two processes particular to the exclusionary foundations of the Mexican post-Revolutionary state: the way in which these foundations became increasingly visible to more and more Mexicans over the course of the national-popular state's struggle to sustain hegemony, and the relationship between this visibility and Mexico's political and economic dependency, which deepened during the same period.

The events of 1968 are emblematic of both of these processes. The state violence perpetrated against students between July and October of that year demonstrated the government's willingness to repress a predominantly middle-class population in the nation's capital. Though state violence had been deadly before 1968, it was typically less extensive and more indirect, such as the co-optation of resistance in organized labor (Aguilar Camín and Meyer). When fatal, it tended to be exercised against populations who were more marginalized, both socially and geographically. The cases of Rubén Jaramillo, a rural resistance leader gunned down along with his family in 1962 in Xochicalco, Morelos, and the summary executions of those who invaded the military barracks in Madera, Chihuahua, in September 1965, are thus exemplary. The year 1968 was indeed different. Hundreds of students were killed in the massacre at Tlatelolco on October 2 in northern Mexico City. At least one thousand more were injured and/or imprisoned. Such massive repression turned out to be impossible to conceal, let alone justify. It also impacted intellectuals (many of whom were also persecuted), who wrote about the violence, inaugurating a more explicitly critical tradition that has changed Mexican journalism, fiction, filmmaking, and other forms of cultural production.

It is important to note that the events of 1968 were also symptomatic of long-term political and economic trajectories, specifically the exclusive nature of the political process in Mexico and the unsustainability of domestic industrial development, which was undermined by dramatic increases in foreign debt (Meyer, "La encrucijada"; Zermeño, *México*). Much of the dissatisfaction expressed by students in 1968 could be traced to the fact that their economic future did not appear as promising as they had been led to believe it would be by the discourse of progress the government propagated. Thus 1968 exemplified, on one hand, the exclusionary tactics of the state and, on the other hand, the dwindling opportunities for productive inclusion into society. Furthermore, it is no coincidence that the Tlatelolco massacre took place just ten days before Mexico City was to host the Olympic Games. Mexico's reputation as a modern nation worthy of performing on the global stage was at stake, and it was not to be tarnished by social unrest. Of course the massacre stained Mexico's image worse than the student protests ever could have, but that does not change the fact that one motivation for carrying out the massacre was to assure that the Games would go on (Aguayo, *1968*). The events of 1968 resulted from the intersection of domestic and international dynamics in such a way as to expose a sharp contradiction between the goal of incorporating Mexicans into the

Revolutionary promise of social and political advancement and the realities of corruption, authoritarianism, and dependency that produced exclusion (Zermeño, *México*).

The contradiction that emerged clearly when the incorporative aspirations of the post-Revolutionary state were revealed to have brutally exclusive foundations produced a profound crisis of national-popular ideology. This ideology, which was based on the promise of gradual, complete incorporation of all Mexicans into a more just and equal nation, serves as the primary point of intersection between novel and state that I examine in this study. The incorporative logic of the state finds a corollary in the incorporative logic that the totalizing novel reproduces, challenges, rejects, or parodies. Throughout this study, I compare state and novel at the ideological level, asking how each discursively constructs the national community. Clearly, the national-popular state has a vested interest in reproducing its hegemony that the novel does not share. Thus I demonstrate how the novel's critique of totality emerges more and more clearly over the course of the period during which the national-popular state gradually lost hegemony. By centering my attention on ideology, I subscribe to the notion that the state is, in large part, an ideological construct (Abrams; Laclau). Like the totalizing novel, state discourse struggles to maintain its representative authority in the face of historical changes. Though it is perhaps impossible to separate history completely from ideology, events like Tlatelolco make it clear that contradictory historical tendencies can outstrip the ability of a particular state form to sustain its ideological coherence and thus maintain its hegemony. In each of the chapters that follow, I provide a section that outlines the historical context that helped produce the novel in question. A clear understanding of this context is essential for comprehending the ideological crisis that grew in Mexico between the 1950s and 1980s, an ideological crisis that challenged the state's authority and registered itself in the totalizing novel's engagement with both its own and the state's capacity to represent the national community.

In order to provide a framework for understanding the relationship between state ideology and the totalizing novel, this study incorporates the ideas of a number of critics and theorists from a broad range of disciplines—including literary criticism, political science, philosophy, and sociology—who concern themselves with the cultural manifestations of political and social change. The following thinkers were especially important to shaping my analysis, whose specific goal is to advance the understanding of how Mexican novels respond to their historical context, and whose general goal is to advance the understanding of the relationship between literary representation and historical change. Roger Bartra's thorough critique of dominant Mexican nationalism and identity discourse is an indispensable point of reference. Regarding political ideology and hegemony, I rely upon the works of Philip Abrams and Ernesto Laclau. The Marxist theories of Fredric Jameson and Pierre Macherey have informed my analysis of literature and context. Deconstructionist and subalternist critics, most notably Jacques Derrida, Brett Levinson, Alberto Moreiras, and Gayatri Spivak, have informed my discussions of subjectivity, exclusivity, and representation. So have Julia Kristeva's feminist work on intertextuality and Spivak's postcolonial feminism.

This book is organized around five novels, whose dates of publication, from 1958 to 1986, correspond to the period that moves from the height of the national-popular state to the beginnings of the neoliberal state. In addition to Fuentes's *La región más transparente* they are Fernando del Paso's *José Trigo* (1966), María Luisa Mendoza's *Con Él, conmigo, con nosotros tres* (1971), Jorge Aguilar Mora's *Si muero lejos de ti* (1979), and Héctor Aguilar Camín's *Morir en el golfo* (1986). I have chosen these specific works primarily because each one addresses the issue of totality in an instructively different way. In addition, they exemplify what I consider to be especially productive when reading a totalizing novel, namely, the combination of the effort to represent totality with a meditation, either intentional or not, on that effort's limitations. These particular texts also respond specifically to social and political problems of their moments of publication with an eye toward how they fit into Mexico's broader history. For example, *José Trigo* recounts the railroad workers' strike of the late 1950s in conjunction with a narrative about the Cristero Rebellion of the 1920s; *Con Él, conmigo, con nosotros tres* frames its portrayal of the Tlatelolco massacre within a story that also returns to the Decena Trágica of 1913; and *Morir en el golfo* contextualizes the oil boom and bust of the 1970s and 1980s in reference to Lázaro Cárdenas's expropriation of the Mexican oil industry in 1938. Finally, this series of novels traces the trajectory of the national-popular state's crisis of ideology. The exclusive foundations of both the state's and the novel's incorporative logic, which emerge through these texts' meditations on the viability of totalizing representation, appear more and more visibly between the years framed by these novels' dates of publication.

Chapter 1 presents *La región más transparente* as a benchmark text against which later novels in the study are measured in relation to their negotiation of totalizing representation and historical context. *La región* is indeed a novel that critiques post-Revolutionary Mexican society in general. But my analysis also proposes that the novel reproduces the epistemological tenets of official discourse that constructs the Revolution as a synthesizing historical promise capable of revealing Mexico's history to Mexicans in a diagnostic vein, announcing a more inclusive future.

Chapter 1 also introduces two examples of incorporative logic that appear as guiding analytical threads throughout this book. The first is Mexicanist philosophy, which, like the totalizing novel and the national-popular state, negotiates means of incorporating all Mexicans into the national project and, also like novel and state, ultimately reveals exclusionary foundations. The visual imagery of historian Emilio Uranga, who imagines Mexicanness as a vault upon which daily life is inscribed and inserted into an explanatory national imaginary, becomes a trope to which I return throughout this study.

The second manifestation of incorporative logic that chapter 1 identifies is the concept of the sublime as formulated by Kant and the critique that Spivak brings to bear on the sublime in her 1999 volume *The Critique of Postcolonial Reason*. In this work, Spivak deconstructs the idea of universality by demonstrating how concepts of universality are, necessarily but paradoxically, historically determined. From historical origins to historical applications, they rely on the construction of a superior consciousness whose mission it is to bring allegedly inferior beings into the fold, thus producing subaltern subjectivities. Kant's sublime and Spivak's critique of it are relevant to my discussion of totalizing aesthetics, since Kant's sublime concerns itself with the representation of the transcendent whole. Taking on the challenge of representing the transcendent whole is a task shared by the national-popular state, the totalizing novel, and Mexicanist philosophy. And, as my study shows, the means by which they tackle this challenge reveal operations of exclusivity similar to those that Spivak elucidates in her critique of Kant.

In its particular manifestation of the attempt to represent the sublime transcendent whole, the structure of Fuentes's novel works to replicate infinity by turning back on itself. It also sets episodes from its own narrative alongside important events from Mexico's past in an effort to demonstrate how the national totality can be contained and communicated within the pages of a work of fiction. The most optimistic and self-assured of the novels I analyze, *La región* corresponds to a time when Mexicanist philosophy was still heavily influential, the national-popular state was enjoying a significant degree of legitimacy based in large part on impressive economic growth, and Mexican and Latin American literature was experiencing a period of innovation that set the stage for the boom. *La región* is without a doubt highly critical of the inequalities that plague mid-century Mexico. But it is also a triumphant example of the representative power of totalizing thought that does not explicitly acknowledge the limits of its own incorporative gesture.

José Trigo is the focus of my second chapter. Unlike Fuentes's novel, which advances a broad social critique, del Paso's concentrates on two specific conflicts, the Cristero Rebellion of 1926–29 and the railroad workers' strike of 1958–59. Its attention to these events produces a tension within the novel around the question of the foundations of the post-Revolutionary state's political power. The violent consolidation of power that demanded the exclusion of the Cristeros is something the novel laments to a degree, but which it ultimately accepts as a necessary step toward national coherence. On the other hand, the novel's portrayal of the railroad workers' strike presents a much more critical look at the state's efforts at consolidation. Written in the wake of the strike, del Paso's text corresponds to a moment in Mexico's twentieth-century history that is less optimistic than the previous decade, which produced Fuentes's text. The railroad workers' union was historically a particularly strong and relatively independent labor organization.

The repression it suffered in 1959 effectively neutralized it as an oppositional force and also prefigured a series of defeats for organized labor and social movements that took place in the 1960s, which affected a number of populations, including teachers, doctors, and most notoriously, students. The tension that arises between *José Trigo*'s portrayal of the two significant social conflicts it represents leads to the novel's explicit recognition of its own limits as a totalizing text. Whereas Fuentes's novel struggles to conceal its limits, del Paso's acknowledges them. *José Trigo*'s critique of political exclusion thus also becomes a critique of the epistemological exclusion that grounds the totalizing novel.

Con Él, conmigo, con nosotros tres appeared shortly after the Tlatelolco massacre, which explains its traumatized narrative perspective. Where *La región* and *José Trigo* found, to different degrees, the nation's history to be a positive explanatory force, *Con Él* finds only an endless stream of blood and death. The national historical synthesis it constructs leaves no room for anyone—even a privileged, middle-class writer —to contribute productively to an understanding of the present, let alone establish a more inclusive future. Mendoza's novel also advances a strong feminist critique of patriarchal society and the history that informs it. In sharp contrast to del Paso's and Fuentes's novels, Mendoza's does not set out to construct a representation of the social totality. Instead, it dedicates itself to identifying the limits of totalizing thought and recognizing its unsustainability. Its critique focuses particularly on originary thinking, arguing that representation never starts from scratch, and when it claims to do so it is concealing its violent foundations. This focus is in direct response to the Mexican government's attempts to distort the facts about what happened at Tlatelolco and to present itself as the pure embodiment of the nation, charged with protecting the Mexican people, even, if not especially, from themselves.

Si muero lejos de ti, like *Con Él*, also tackles totalizing thought head on. Heavily informed by the events of 1968, Aguilar Mora's novel testifies to a pervasive sense of uncertainty about the direction of the nation following Tlatelolco. Coherence and a promising trajectory are completely absent from this text's construction of the social totality. Yet while *Si muero*, an immense and immensely complicated novel, tests the limits of totalizing thought, it acknowledges the difficulty of simply discarding it. In its search for means of imagining individual and collective subjectivities that do not correspond to a national-popular paradigm, the novel recognizes the tenacious appeal of the desire for totality. Its critique of totality is indeed totalizing, and its recognition of this paradox informs its frustrating and frustrated structure and narrative.

The final novel I analyze, *Morir en el golfo*, focuses specifically on the oil boom of the late 1970s and early 1980s, the last great hope of the national-popular state model. Written four years after the petroleum bubble had burst, Aguilar Camín's novel objectifies and parodies totality, condemning efforts to represent it as worthy of little more than derision. A text that borrows a great deal from the detective genre, *Morir* constructs a narrative perspective that distances itself from totality more than any of the other novels included in this study. This separation, which enables parody, owes itself to the text's association of totalizing thought with government corruption, deceit, and incompetence, all of which were exposed dramatically in the oil bust. The oil bust led to an unprecedented debt crisis that, in turn, paved the way for the neoliberal economic reforms that culminated years later in the approval of the Tratado de Libre Comercio, or NAFTA.

Each of these novels approaches totality in a different way that corresponds to the historical moment of its publication. Each tests the limits of totalizing thought that are apparent in that moment. The increasingly widespread repression and ultimately failed economic policies that led to the loss of hegemony of the national-popular state model gradually made representing the social totality into an unviable, unproductive goal. The ideal of the coherent, autonomous nation-state gave way to the market society whose goal is integration into the global economy. A strong cultural consequence of the dissolution of the national-popular ideal in Mexico was the decadence of totalizing thought, a process that becomes increasingly visible during the time period covered between *La región más transparente* and *Morir en el golfo.*

Chapter One

The Revolution Will Be Novelized

Carlos Fuentes's *La región más transparente* Constructs a Compensatory Totality

The principal action of Carlos Fuentes's *La región más transparente* (1958) takes place between 1951 and 1954 in Mexico City. An anonymous omniscient narrator shifts constantly from one story to the next. As a result, the reader gradually becomes familiar with numerous characters spanning the class spectrum who struggle, and almost always fail, to find their place within an unforgiving, rapidly changing society: a *bracero* realizes he cannot easily return home after working in the United States; a taxi driver's accidental death leaves his family in dire financial straits; street performers traverse the growing capital city, scraping by and barely ever stopping to rest; a young prostitute bitterly remembers the home where her brothers raped her. The loosely connected stories of these and other relatively minor characters establish the sweeping social backdrop against which the central figures' lives unfold. These tend to represent the upper and middle economic classes, and they include the characters who have received the most attention by the novel's critics. The first to appear introduces himself in a first-person passage that begins with the novel's famous opening line: "Mi nombre es Ixca Cienfuegos" (9).[1] Cienfuegos is the novel's most enigmatic character, a rather eerie urban ethnographer of sorts who traverses the vast urban landscape with remarkable speed, all the while persuading, and sometimes coercing, almost everyone he meets to reveal their innermost secrets.[2]

Through Cienfuegos's and the anonymous narrator's efforts, the reader learns what motivates the novel's main characters as they seek power, meaning, or simply stability. Ambition drives both Federico Robles, a ruthless land speculator and banker, and his wife, Norma Larragoiti, an unscrupulous social climber. Robles eventually goes bankrupt and weds his humble indigenous lover, Hortensia Chacón, whereas Larragoiti dies in the fire that destroys her luxurious mansion. Manuel Zamacona, an intellectual with sincere reformist goals, contemplates Mexico's past and speculates about its future, only to suffer an absurd fate of his own when a stranger shoots him in cold blood in a roadside cantina.[3] And insecurity and opportunism cause Rodrigo Pola, a failed writer, to resign himself to writing screenplays for B movies.

Though the principal action of the narrative takes place during the early 1950s, the novel portrays past events through several characters' memories, which take them and the reader back to a number of different historical moments: the pre-Revolutionary rural childhood of Robles; the disinheritance, self-imposed exile, and eventual return to Mexico of the aristocratic Ovando family; the execution by firing squad of the duplicitous Gervasio Pola, Rodrigo's father, and his fellow Zapatistas in 1913; and the corrupt and at times deadly business transactions of the 1930s that helped establish a new social elite. These spatial and temporal shifts enable the narrative to expand its scope while revealing a tightly interconnected web of relationships among dozens of characters whose destinies become inseparable from one another's and converge in the fate of the nation. The structure of Fuentes's text clarifies the nature of these shifts and relationships by dividing the narrative into three parts and identifying the dozens of sub-sections that comprise them with various titles, many of which refer to characters' names, such as "Pimpinela de Ovando," "Feliciano Sánchez," and "Gladys García."

Two strong narratives of redemption also help organize the novel's complex structure, and they focus on four characters, who will also be the focus of my analysis: Zamacona, Robles, Cienfuegos, and Gladys García, a seemingly minor character who works as a prostitute and private dancer. Zamacona and Robles redeem the Revolution, and Cienfuegos and García work on redeeming the present, which is also the novel's task. These redemptive narratives appear concentrically within the novel, and the Revolution story grounds and develops inside the story of the present. In short, the novel works on the past before moving on to the present. In both redemptive narratives the ultimate goal is access to totality, a goal the Revolution story attains but that remains just beyond the reach of the story of the present. Significantly, the stories of both Cienfuegos and Robles rely upon the construction of marginalized female characters, including Larragoiti, Chacón, and García. The way in which these characters are either expelled from or incorporated into the lives of the male characters and the society they are meant to redeem, especially in the case of Gladys García, plays a central role in the novel's ability, or failure, to access totality.

This chapter proposes that *La región* intends to save the ideals of the Mexican Revolution from the corruption that has defined its legacy by constructing a compensatory totality, a coherent, all-inclusive social space capable of reconciling long-standing personal and national-historical contradictions. The novel's appeal to totality is a product of its context, which is defined predominantly by three discursive structures that also mobilize totalizing thought: the ideology of the Mexican national-popular state, Mexicanist philosophy, and the Latin American literary "boom."[4] Within the text itself, García appears as at once the goal, and thus legitimation, of the incorporative totalizing gesture and its excluded limit. García's character is essential to the conclusions I draw from my analysis of Fuentes's novel. First, the text not only reproduces the exclusive character of the post-Revolutionary ideology that it critiques, but it also reveals the exclusivity of Mexicanism. Second, *La región* demonstrates how exclusivity and the desire for totality are necessarily constitutive of one another.

Thus my conclusion aims to explain how García's importance to Fuentes's novel reveals the intrinsically exclusive character of all totalizing representation. This general critique of totality incorporates the critical analysis that postcolonial feminist critic Gayatri Spivak brings to bear on Kant's concept of the sublime. Kant's meditations on the sublime as an aesthetic, ordering totality provide a uniquely useful point of reference for understanding how Fuentes's novel, which like any representation must be finite in size and scope, attempts to contain and communicate the infinite totality of Mexico's past, present, and future. Spivak's critique of Kant is a convincing description of the exclusive character of his ostensibly universal philosophy, and thus an important means of understanding the exclusivity that grounds Fuentes's construction of totality in *La región*.

Throughout this book, Kant's sublime and Spivak's critique of it stand as essential reference points for comprehending how totality functions within and as an object of critique of the novels in question. Chapter 1 thus sets the stage for the remaining chapters, which establish a trajectory of the decline of totalizing thought in the Mexican novel of the national-popular period. The exclusive foundations of totality that Fuentes's novel does not explicitly acknowledge become more visible over the years as the Mexican state must rely more on violence and coercion than consensus in order to sustain its legitimacy.

I

La región más transparente practically bursts at the seams. Its complex structure corresponds to and tries to contain the tensions among national, regional, and global tendencies that shaped the mid-twentieth-century Mexican context within which Fuentes produced it. A novel whose aesthetic qualities owe at least as much to national predecessors like Agustín Yáñez's *Al filo del agua* (1947) and Juan Rulfo's *Pedro Páramo* (1955) as to the works of James Joyce, John Dos Passos, and William Faulkner, *La región* is also a founding text of the boom. Indeed, Fuentes's text strives to isolate, rescue, and mobilize that which can be defined as properly Mexican during a formative moment of that country's national political trajectory and its relation to the rest of the world, especially the United States. The urgency of the novel's task, which focuses on the Revolution of 1910 and what it could still mean for Mexico in the 1950s, is laid out clearly by Manuel Zamacona when he protests, "No puedo pensar que el único resultado concreto de la Revolución Mexicana haya sido la formación de una nueva casta privilegiada, la hegemonía económica de los Estados Unidos y la paralización de toda vida política interna" (273). Zamacona seems to challenge the novel to imagine the Revolution as something different from what it has indeed already become. The text responds by casting itself as a privileged means of transforming the Revolution from a historical event with undeniable sociopolitical consequences into a redemptive epistemology capable of recasting the present and saving it from the injustice, corruption, and exploitation that threaten to define it. The text's treatment of the Revolution ultimately reveals at least as much about that event's lasting consequences as it does about the limitations of this ambitious, totalizing novel. Specifically, the incorporative gesture established through the text's Revolutionary epistemology fails to avoid perpetuating the exploitation the novel explicitly condemns.

La región más transparente defines a successful literary engagement with Mexican society as one that reproduces the nation's history as a totality whose uniqueness explains who Mexicans are by revealing where they have been. The totality that Fuentes's novel attempts to construct can be understood, in Fredric Jameson's terms, as the "hypothesis of a historical moment of plenitude or completion against which [...] other historical stages are judged and weighed" (*Marxism and Form* 38). Jameson's analysis foregrounds the evaluative nature of positing totality, which suggests that one moment stands as an ideal to which others are compared and revealed to be more or less sufficient. Corresponding to the period of its production, Fuentes's novel portrays the Mexican Revolution as the key to imagining totality. Significantly, it grants the same status to the moment of the novel's completion as experienced by its readers. Thus *La región* ultimately privileges the novel form as a means of imagining totality in an ambitious effort to close the gap between historical reality and national-communitarian desire.

La región posits that a literary text—in no small part by presenting itself as a prime example—is capable of guiding the reader toward imagining a national community that is more coherent and inclusive than the fractured, unequal society the novel critiques through mimesis. The gap that separates the society Fuentes portrays and the society Zamacona and the novel itself desire is the result of a general failure of modernity in Latin America that Alberto Moreiras describes in terms of "narrative fissure," or the "contrasts between expectations of modernization and the realities of the course of events" (*Exhaustion* 49).[5] According to Moreiras, an adequate response to the contention that "macronarratives of modernity" have failed has not yet been formulated (49). What is certain, Moreiras contends, is that a certain "negative globality" persists as the product of narrative fissure, and that it "must be culturally figured in the various impossibilities, everywhere observable, of narrative closure and cultural self-understanding" (50). By contrast, Fuentes's first novel represents a moment in the history of Mexican and Latin American literary production when both narrative closure and cultural self-understanding were presented as goals that could be achieved in tandem with one another. What is useful about Moreiras's reflections, published more than forty years after Fuentes's novel, is that they highlight the impossibility of sealing the connection between narrative and cultural definition; and identifying this impasse explains more about the novel than does praising the text for exemplifying a successful construction of Mexican totality.

The novel's failure to sustain a coherent, reproducible representation of community productively reveals the limits of the totalizing imaginary and points toward something different from it, something that resists appropriation. In the case of *La región*, the entity that resists appropriation is Gladys García, who represents Mexico's most marginalized and vulnerable population. Fundamentally excluded from the novel's incorporative gesture, García is the text's limit. Even though she is a construct of the novel itself, she exemplifies the inability of any literary text to sustain a coherent and stable representation of reality. This failure is thus an important type of success, since first, it alludes to a community whose necessary incompleteness and openness to the future can never be contained, and second, it identifies an important driving force of literary production, namely, the constant reference—either intended or unconscious, explicit or implicit—to something that lies beyond the text's attempt at narrative closure. In Brett Levinson's terms, this constant reference to something different is a product of the endless possibility of "novel articulations" that function within a text and between text and reader. For Levinson, "literariness is the condition of novel articulations (the "in the name of" that makes a political affirmation possible), hence of novel communities and communal projects" (27). A paradigmatic total novel, *La región* is a text that desires completeness and self-sustaining coherence. But its inability to achieve that desire, highlighted through the emblematic García, attests to the debt the novel owes to other discourses of completeness and coherence that inform it.

In *A Theory of Literary Production* (1978), Pierre Macherey insists that a writer is "not a subject centred in his creation, [but] an element in a situation or system" (67), thus emphasizing the extent to which a literary work, regardless of the author's prowess, relies upon the historical context that helped produce it. The principal characteristic of *La región* that ties it significantly to its context is its desire to establish and sustain a totalizing representation, a desire that corresponds to the epistemological foundations of post-Revolutionary state ideology and Mexicanist philosophy. All three discourses—literary, political, and philosophical—base their totalizing ambitions on the notion that understanding Mexico's past is necessary for comprehending the present and shaping the future.

II

The Revolution is the national past's most powerful incarnation in *La región* and, arguably, in the discursive context of the novel's production. Zamacona's take on the Revolution echoes that of Mexico's mid-century philosophers and writers, most notably Octavio Paz. Zamacona's philosophy of the Revolution, in fact, may have come straight from the pages of Paz's *El laberinto de la soledad* [The Labyrinth of Solitude] (1950). For like Paz, he argues that the Revolution revealed, all at once, all of Mexico's contradictory history to all Mexicans:[6]

> en la Revolución aparecieron, vivos y con el fardo de sus problemas, todos los hombres de la historia de México. Siento [...] sinceramente que en los rostros de la Revolución aparecen todos ellos, vivos, con su refinamiento y su grosería, con sus ritmos y pulsaciones, con su voz y sus colores propios. Pero si la Revolución nos descubre la totalidad de la historia de México, no asegura que la comprendamos o que la superemos. (Fuentes, *La región* 271)

Thus Zamacona clarifies the nature of the challenge he lays before Fuentes's text, which is to "understand or transcend" the Revolution in an effort to comprehend totality. Furthermore, Zamacona explains, Mexicans must rescue the Revolution from the ongoing betrayal it has suffered at the hands of corrupt politicians, greedy capitalists, and opportunistic ideologues, because, "al recoger todos los hilos de la experiencia histórica de México, nos propuso metas muy claras: [...] por sobre todas las cosas, superando el fracaso humano del liberalismo económico [...] la necesidad de conciliar la libertad de la persona con la justicia social" (273). Here referring to the economically liberal policies of the Porfiriato, Zamacona wishes to save the Revolution from becoming merely one more step along a long-term trajectory of economic liberalization and global integration that began in the nineteenth century.

Notably, the text's appeal to totality and its juxtaposition of certain characters' stories, which aim to redeem the Revolution, share important traits with the political system that built itself upon the corruption of whatever ideals the Revolution was simultaneously, and cynically, defined as embodying. These traits are first, an appeal to totality, and second, the foundational construction of subaltern subject positions, which I will discuss in greater detail when I look at the story of Ixca Cienfuegos and Gladys García.

The post-Revolutionary Mexican state, one of whose primary functions was to conceal the capitalist trajectory that the political and economic upheaval produced by the Revolution ultimately reconstituted, sustained its legitimacy upon the illusion of its privileged access to totality.[7] It maintained this illusion through a dual operation that appealed first to its own autonomy and self-sufficiency, and second to a future moment of always-deferred plenitude, in a gesture that, as Ernesto Laclau has theorized, forms the basis of a particular political form's hegemony.[8] During the transformative years of the 1940s, 1950s, and 1960s in Mexico, the increasingly strengthened centralized state, whose power was practically synonymous with the Partido Revolucionario Institucional (PRI), constantly constructed itself as an authority capable of guiding Mexico's rapid economic growth and diversification.[9] The state established and circulated a national-developmentalist ideology that coincided with and reinforced how Mexico's past and present were portrayed as coming together in any number of political and cultural representational structures.[10] The two words that make up the phrase "national development" immediately suggest the predominant characteristics of how Mexico's identity was constructed and consolidated from above. First, reference to the nation implies unity and centralization.[11] Second, the emphasis on development reflects the dominant, ultimately Hegelian vision of Mexican history as a process leading toward the perfection of a national ideal, an ideal whose custodian and incarnation was the Mexican state.

When Philip Abrams proposes that ideology's specific function is to "mis-represent political and economic domination in ways that legitimate subjection," and that, as an ideological project, the state "is the distinctive collective *mis*representation of capitalist societies" (75; original emphasis), his observations resonate with Roger Bartra's work on how domination, particularly the subjection of impoverished rural and urban populations, becomes culturally justified—that is, concealed as such—in elite circles of Mexican society.[12] Describing the development of the nation-state as the establishment and consolidation of a fundamental "estructura de mediación," Bartra explains how social antagonisms, like class conflict, are stripped of their disruptive potential through a process of mediation, like the state's construction of its role as the people's redeemer (*Jaula* 191). Elucidating the quasi-religious character the nation-state often radiates, Bartra refers to the way in which the Mexican national-popular state's work of legitimation managed to incorporate the commonly accepted notion, the currency of mid-century intelligentsia, that the Mexican people needed to be rescued from themselves and their cultural maladies (197).[13] This redemptive narrative obscures the actual historical roots of domination, perpetuates the real causes and effects of repression, and bolsters the state's legitimacy. As Bartra argues, "la historia es disuelta y los eslabones concretos entre pueblo y poder son una conexión estructural que sólo la Divina Providencia o la Razón del Estado son capaces de inventar. En el interior de la imaginería nacionalista sólo las conexiones [...] que convergen en el Estado, son significantes" (198).[14]

Carlos Fuentes's novel constructs Manuel Zamacona as a character who wants to wrest the past, most importantly the Revolution, from the elite who control and benefit from its official interpretation. Zamacona condemns the ruling party for having excluded the majority of Mexicans from the political process, once again highlighting the similarities between the 1950s and the Porfiriato:

> Lo que rechazo es la somnolencia que el "partido único" ha impuesto a la vida política de México [...]. ¿O estará dispuesto el PRI a sancionar un statu quo sin solución alguna? Esto equivaldría a decirle al pueblo de México: "Estás bien como estás. No es necesario que pienses o hables. Nosotros sabemos lo que te conviene. Quédate allí." Pero ¿no es esto lo mismo que pensaba Porfirio Díaz? (274–75)

While Zamacona emphasizes the social and political failures of the Revolution's official legacy, his interlocutor in this conversation, the wealthy investor and land speculator Federico Robles, has a very different idea about the Revolution and its redemption. He dismisses attempts to save the Revolution as much as he endorses efforts to cash it in. An unabashed capitalist, Robles does not flinch when he identifies the human cost of economic development. As he explains to Ixca Cienfuegos earlier in the novel, "La pura verdad es que para tener capital hay que pagarlo con vidas, como la de los niños que murieron en las salas de tinte de Río Blanco, y después hacer leyes del trabajo" (96). For Robles, the children of Río Blanco, who died during a pre-Revolutionary period of primitive accumulation, are as expendable as the ideals of the Revolution, which must be sacrificed in order to achieve national development. Robles, who under the command of Obregón helped defeat Villa's División del Norte in the battle of Celaya, has little patience for abstract discussions of the Revolution's potential outcomes. Describing the early 1920s to Cienfuegos, he says, "Aquello fue el momento de crisis de la Revolución. El momento de decidirse a construir, incluso manchándonos las conciencias. De sacrificar algunos ideales para que algo tangible se lograra" (109). Later, when he meets Zamacona, Robles mocks the intellectual's concern for the past, declaring it "lo muerto" and something that "se acabó para siempre" (266). For Robles, economic concerns are primary: "A ustedes los intelectuales les encanta hacerse bolas [...]. Aquí no hay más que una verdad: o hacemos un país próspero, o nos morimos de hambre. No hay que escoger sino entre la riqueza y la miseria. Y para llegar a la riqueza hay que apresurar la marcha hacia el capitalismo, y someterlo todo a ese patrón" (268).

Though completely stripped of ideologically fueled niceties, Robles's position concurs with the dominant economic policies of the time, which centered around state support of key domestic industries and the development of internal markets, and which ultimately transformed the Revolution into a discursive entity that sustained inequality and discouraged popular political participation.[15]

As historian Lorenzo Meyer observes, even the relatively progressive administration of Lázaro Cárdenas (1934–40)—which enacted two major policies that temporarily disrupted the economic power of domestic and foreign elites: land reform that redistributed 18 million hectares (Meyer, "El primer tramo" 1241) and the expropriation of the oil industry—paved the way for Mexico's capitalist trajectory. For example, large landowners who lost land because of reforms eventually recouped their economic power. In fact, Meyer surmises, a significant source of the wealth that fueled Mexico's industrialization came from landowners who adapted to post-Revolutionary economic changes ("El primer tramo" 1244). Speaking in general terms, Meyer identifies a dominant tendency that coincides almost exactly with Fuentes's portrayal of Federico Robles's ideas about Mexico's development:

> Simplificando, puede decirse que a partir de ese momento la Revolución dio por terminados sus proyectos de reforma social y política y sus dirigentes lanzaron de lleno al país a una nueva empresa: propiciar por todos los medios el crecimiento económico y cambiar materialmente en unas cuantas décadas al país. ("La encrucijada" 1276)

During and after World War II, Mexico gained unprecedented access to export markets, and its industrial base grew dramatically. Before the war, different administrations enacted protectionist measures to spur domestic economic growth, which meant that the demand created during the war was met by an industrial base that was prepared to satisfy it (Meyer, "La encrucijada" 1277). Government involvement in Mexico's economy grew apace.[16] In summary, the post-war period witnessed the development of an industrial economy strongly supported by the state, whose benefits were enjoyed primarily by capitalists, "mientras que el poder adquisitivo de la mayoría de los obreros y campesinos se mantuvo estancado y en algunos casos disminuyó" (Meyer, "La encrucijada" 1278). In fact, by 1975, the richest 5 percent of Mexico's population owned the same share of the nation's wealth as it did in 1950, while Mexico's poorest lost ground during the same period of almost uninterrupted economic expansion (Aguilar Camín and Meyer, 194, 200, 209).

While Mexico's economic and political elite redeemed the Revolution in order to fill their pockets and gain power, fictional intellectuals like Zamacona and actual intellectuals like Paz and Fuentes attempted to redeem the Revolution by defining it as the key to understanding Mexico and guiding the nation toward a more inclusive and just future, when the success of a few would not come at the price of widespread misery. Inequality is in fact a major theme of *La región*, and it appears emblematically during the scene that portrays Zamacona and Robles's conversation. When he arrives at Robles's mansion, Zamacona sees a group of beggars waiting outside the gates, expecting their weekly allotment of surplus household goods. The narrator's description of the beggars, as seen through Zamacona's eyes, reinforces a typical dichotomy that determines who participates in directing Mexico's historical course:

> Al fondo, detrás de la reja cochera, se apiñaban una docena de caras morenas, algunas oscurecidas por sombreros de petate, otras cubiertas hasta la boca por rebozos, todas inmóviles. Manuel trató de distinguir algún sentimiento particular en ellas: cada una no revelaba otra cosa que su muda e inmóvil espera: labios cerrados, ojos negros despojados de brillo, pómulos altos. Manuel los imaginó, idénticos, en todas las épocas, en todas las vidas. Como un río subterráneo, indiferente y oscuro, que corría por debajo de cualquier cambio o idea. (265)

Zamacona fails to discern anything individual about the beggars who wait on the other side of Robles's gate and the other side of history, who are "identical, in every age, in every life." Zamacona's previous observation about the Revolution and totality suggests that, at that historical moment, all Mexicans, including the beggars, emerged, living and able to speak ("alive [...] with their voices"). By the 1950s, they are silent once again, and they occupy an unchanging space isolated from efforts to incorporate them into the stream of history. It is important to note that the novel constructs the beggars' silence as silence *for* Zamacona.

The reader never gains access to their thoughts, and perceives them only through the filter of the intellectual. The text tries to overcome this barrier, especially through its portrayal of Mexico City's most marginalized, like Gabriel, the *bracero*, his friend Beto, and Gladys García. But Zamacona's inability to see beyond impassive faces and the novel's attempt to give voice to the voiceless do not reveal a tension between two discrete, self-sustaining social spheres, but instead they trace a constitutive relationship, within which the projection of silence onto the other founds the intellectual's epistemic privilege.

III

This asymmetrical relationship is, paradoxically, a necessary, foundational component of Mexicanist discourse, whose prescriptive tenets proposed communitarian fullness, to use Laclau's term, as the ultimate goal. Mid-twentieth-century Mexicanism forms part of a long and well-established intellectual tradition. The political events that shaped it go back to the Conquest, and continue through Independence from Spain, nineteenth-century US influence and invasion, the Porfiriato, and the Revolution of 1910. Influential philosophical trends include eighteenth-century humanism; the positivism of the late nineteenth century; a neoromantic and nationalist reaction that mitigated positivist tendencies during and after the Revolution; José Ortega y Gassett's perspectivism; and the influence of contemporary German thinkers, such as Simmel and Heidegger, whose ideas were disseminated throughout Spain and Latin America through the work of Ortega y Gassett in the 1920s and 1930s.[17] Some notable Mexican thinkers who have contributed to the Mexicanist tradition since Independence are Servando Teresa de Mier, Lorenzo de Zavala, José María Vigil, and Justo Sierra.[18]

Fuentes's novel places Zamacona within this trajectory when it describes how he views himself as engaged in a "búsqueda, cerrada, ciega, marginal, del punto de encuentro entre lo que realmente somos y las formas que han de expresar una sustancia, en sí, muda" (58). The dichotomy of form and substance reinforced by the contrast between Zamacona's thoughts and the beggars' stereotypically indigenous faces, recalls the imagery employed by two prominent Mexicanist texts whose dates of publication correspond to the Revolutionary period and the 1950s: *Forjando patria* (1916) by Manuel Gamio, and the short essay by Emilio Uranga titled, "Optimismo y pesimismo del mexicano" (1952).[19] Gamio, an anthropologist trained at Columbia University, initiated archaeological investigations at Teotihuacán.[20] *Forjando patria* represents his efforts to guide Mexico toward more developed self-understanding through anthropological and sociological analysis, which, according to Gamio, must consider the incorporation of Mexico's diverse indigenous populations.[21] Gamio's text looks forward to a moment of national unity and collective self-recognition, and reaching this moment requires the "conocimiento y caracterización etnográfica de los diversos grupos sociales" so that "sus actividades y características converjan y se desarrollen armónicamente y se prepare un futuro estado de cohesión social que es inherente a toda nacionalidad definida y consciente" (58–59).

Gamio's text defines Mexico's more European(ized) populations as possessing privileged knowledge of the nation's potential communitarian fullness and of the paths that lead to it. Indigenous populations appear in *Forjando patria* as elements necessary for completing a system they do not imagine. Even though the national project still stands unrealized, Gamio identifies an already existing basic framework:

> Cuando [...] hayan sido incorporados a la vida nacional nuestras familias indígenas, las fuerzas que hoy oculta el país en estado latente y pasivo, se transformarán en energías dinámicas inmediatamente productivas y comenzará a fortalecerse el verdadero sentimiento de nacionalidad, que hoy apenas existe disgregado entre grupos sociales que difieren en tipo étnico y en idioma y divergen en cuanto a concepto y tendencias culturales. (27–28)

Gamio presupposes an already established entity into which indigenous populations will be inserted. The "latent and passive forces" that their integration promises to awaken are essential to a "true feeling of nationality," but not in any substantial way different from it.

In his argument with Federico Robles, Zamacona proposes that the Revolution challenged Mexicans to "descubrir la totalidad de México a los mexicanos. Rescatar el pasado mexicano del olvido y de la mentira," and to reject the unreflective importation of European ideas that dresses "México con un traje confeccionado por Augusto Comte" (*La región* 272). Like Zamacona, Uranga implores his readers to know Mexico's own history and rely less on foreign models and intellectual traditions: "Abandonados a nosotros mismos, 'encerrados' en nosotros mismos, ¿bajo qué horizonte ideológico hemos de militar? ¿Cuál es esa noción clave, verdadera bóveda, en cuya concavidad hemos de inscribir nuestra acción cotidiana?" (408). Uranga soon answers his own question when he writes that "lo mexicano es la idea que nos dirige, aquella idea que presta unidad a nuestros quehaceres" (409). His subsequent definition of "idea" demands a lengthy citation:

> Una idea es una atmósfera, y una atmósfera es un sentido o una significación en cuyo seno, advertida o inadvertidamente, nos movemos, y a que referimos, para que adquieran inteligibilidad, todas nuestras experiencias. Lo mexicano cumple justamente estos requisitos indispensables para erigirse en idea histórica. [...] Vivimos inmersos en un mundo de sentido o de significación sin que sea necesario precisar, definir, cuál es ese sentido. Pero llega un momento en que el sentido se hace tema consciente de reflexión, de interpretación, en que percibimos dónde estaba ubicado el centro de nuestras coordenadas. [...] Nuestra secular autognosis toca por fin un fondo y lo ilumina conscientemente. (409)

Uranga's striking imagery conceives of the unifying force of cultural self-knowledge as horizon, vault, atmosphere, and finally, "world of meaning." These delimiting figures circumscribe spaces within which Mexican lives are carried out, inscribed, and understood. Significantly, it is not necessary to know the exact nature of the organizing principle of the Mexican space. But it is important to meditate deliberately on that principle, to accept that it exists as a preliminary step toward identifying it, and continue with philosophical reflection "hacia zonas más luminosas" (410). Thus, like Gamio, Uranga subordinates essential parts to a preconceived whole in his mid-century meditations on Mexico's identity.

The title of Fuentes's novel merits consideration. A reference to Alfonso Reyes's *Valle de Anahuác (1519)* (1915), it clarifies the relationship between the text's form and content when it is compared to the images Uranga and Gamio use to theorize the search for *lo mexicano*.[22] Uranga's "true vault" and Gamio's "true feeling of nationality" establish a surface and a framework upon and within which different components—Uranga's "daily actions," Gamio's "latent and passive forces"—appear and make sense as partially pre-determined elements of a whole. Fuentes's *La región más transparente* can be read as expressing the desire for a completely visible totality within which the different elements of the novel become meaningful. Zamacona, like Gamio, argues that the completion of this sense-making process requires incorporating those populations who remain excluded, "Una verdadera integración de los miembros dispersos del ser de este país" (*La región* 272).

IV

The claim to authenticating and integrating powers that Fuentes's novel makes—a gesture similar to those that legitimized the national-popular state and Mexicanist philosophy—helps explain its status as a founding text of what came to be known as the "boom" of Latin American literature.[23] Its incorporation of modernist narrative techniques, like the juxtaposition of expressive fragments and the elaboration of a complex, fugue-like structure, also contributes to this status.[24] Both traits work together in Fuentes's novel, and in many other boom novels, to elevate the position of the genre as a whole.[25] Two prominent examples of boom criticism, written by consecrated boom novelists, argue strongly for the novel's privileged expressive capacity: Fuentes's *La nueva novela hispanoamericana* and Vargas Llosa's *García Márquez: Historia de un deicidio*. As mentioned in the introduction to this study, these works are also, and not coincidentally, founding meditations on the concept of the total novel. For Fuentes, successful writers exhibit special language skills that enable them to represent their community completely and authentically, to expose long-standing falsehoods, and to challenge those whose power feeds on deception:

> El escritor, simplemente, está más poseído por el lenguaje y esta posesión extrema obliga al lenguaje a desdoblarse, sin

> perder su unidad, en un espejo comunitario y otro individual. [...] Esta función [...] es posible con particular intensidad en Hispanoamérica porque nuestro verdadero lenguaje está en proceso de descubrirse y de crearse y, en el acto mismo de su descubrimiento y creación, pone en jaque, revolucionariamente, toda una estructura económica, política y social fundada en un lenguaje verticalmente falso. (*Nueva* 94–95)

Though some critics and writers of the time were skeptical of Fuentes's exuberant appraisal of the written word's revolutionary potential, his emphasis on aesthetic innovation was generally shared by his contemporaries, many of whom, like Vargas Llosa, saw the boom as an opportunity to reformulate Latin American culture and society.[26] In what at first appears a paradoxical assessment, Vargas Llosa argues that the Latin American novelist actually benefited from what he identifies as a "falta de una tradición cultural," which signified "un vacío que es también suprema libertad" (*Historia* 208).[27] For Vargas Llosa, writers exercised their freedom most completely by manipulating form, as opposed to shaping content. This distinction establishes the image of the novelist as a sculptor who transforms the content of history and everyday life: "La creación literaria consiste no tanto en inventar como en transformar, en trasvasar ciertos contenidos de la subjetividad más estricta a un plano objetivo de realidad" (104). The successful boom writer's craft helped produce what contemporary writers and critics considered a general, region-wide elevation of consciousness: according to Julio Cortázar, "la más extraordinaria toma de conciencia por parte del pueblo latinoamericano de una parte de su propia identidad" (qtd. in Rama, "El 'Boom'" 61); for Fuentes, a literature able to "actualizar y darle orden a muchas lecciones del pasado" (qtd. in Anadón 621); and for Jaime Mejía Duque, the arrival of Latin American literature to "la edad de la razón" (25).[28]

La región más transparente helped inaugurate a general feeling of optimism among intellectuals regarding Latin America's cultural trajectory, a sense of having arrived on the global stage with expressive forms adequate to the global projection of Latin America's substance. Mejía Duque wrote in 1974, in a reflection that attests to a regional community of thinkers, "Como dijera Octavio Paz, *por primera vez somos contemporáneos de todos los hombres*" (25; original emphasis). In a discussion with Manuel Zamacona, Ixca Cienfuegos makes a similar observation about Mexican, and perhaps by extension, Latin American, universality: "La salvación del mundo depende de este pueblo anónimo [...]. El pueblo de México, que es el único contemporáneo del mundo" (367). Cienfuegos's observation raises an important question: upon what does the salvation of the Mexican people depend? The main answer the novel offers is the redemption of the Revolution, which it represents by redeeming Federico Robles, the character who has most egregiously betrayed the Revolution's ideals.

V

Despite the ease with which he describes sacrificing people and ideals to produce a better material future for Mexico, Robles eventually realizes that he must reckon with the ghosts who haunt him. Financial ruin obliges Robles to reflect on his personal past, which produces a feeling of remorse that leads to renewal. Instead of seeking revenge against those who helped perpetrate his financial downfall, Robles turns inward and acknowledges his long-repressed guilt: "en una zona sin articulación en su mente, brillaba el rostro de Feliciano Sánchez, acribillado y blanco; y más atrás, en el último estanque de la memoria, el de Froilán Reyero [...] embarrado de polvo junto al paredón" (381). Early in his career, Robles killed Sánchez as a favor to a general, who, in return, awarded him with property bound to increase in value as Mexico City grew. Reyero was Robles's cousin, and he believed ardently in the ideals of the Revolution, ideals that Robles has consistently betrayed.

Fuentes's novel imagines Mexico as a totality through the lens of the Revolution, which it constructs as an event that bears heavily upon Mexico's mid-century present. Robles's downfall clarifies the compensatory nature of the totality the novel imagines. It provides a space within which individual characters pay their debts to the national community. Robles's transformation begins during a conversation with Zamacona and Cienfuegos in a Mexico City café. Zamacona brings along a copy of Octavio Paz's *El laberinto de la soledad*, a text that describes the Revolution as "una portentosa fiesta en la que el mexicano, borracho de sí mismo, conoce al fin, en abrazo mortal, al otro mexicano" (294). Fuentes's novel portrays Robles as reenacting that encounter, which is a recognition of communal responsibility that permeates *La región.* When Levinson describes literary articulation as possessing a political valence, he emphasizes how it is capable, through novel tropes, of constructing new communities, of obliging the subject to encounter the other. Fuentes's novel structures and mobilizes communal responsibility around two central tropes. The first, the image of the subterranean river [*río subterráneo*], corresponds to Zamacona and Robles's redemption narrative. And the second, the image of one person's hand reaching out to another's, corresponds to the story of Cienfuegos and García. The *río subterráneo* comes to Zamacona's mind when he sees and thinks about the beggars at the gate of Robles's mansion. When he is arguing in the café with Cienfuegos about how to overcome Mexico's past, the trope becomes more directly associated with Robles. Zamacona asks:

> ¿Pero a quién se hará responsable de ese dolor y esa traición? [...] por cada mexicano que murió en vano, sacrificado, hay un mexicano responsable. Y regreso a mi tesis: para que esa muerte no haya sido en vano, alguien debe asumir la culpa. La culpa por cada indígena azotado, por cada obrero sometido, por cada madre hambrienta. Entonces, sólo entonces, ese hombre singular de México será todos los mexicanos humillados. Pero ¿quién acarrea los pecados de México, Ixca, quién? (368–69)

The reader does not wait long for the answer. It is Robles who is affected profoundly by Zamacona's words: "Viejo, cada minuto, cada palabra más viejo, montaña inmóvil y río subterráneo, sus ojos corriendo como lava entre lagunas petrificadas, Federico Robles sentía y tocaba las palabras de Manuel Zamacona" (369). Zamacona's words dislodge something sclerotic within Robles, compelling him to remember, for the first time in years, the name of Feliciano Sánchez. Lost inside himself, he no longer hears Cienfuegos and Zamacona's conversation; instead he hears "un nombre olvidado, cancelado por el éxito y el poder [...]. Un hombre muerto en vano; un hombre culpable" (369).

Sánchez's name has been "canceled," a term that, like the trope of the *río subterráneo*, recalls Zamacona and Robles's earlier conversation, a conversation that begins while the beggars' faces continue to disturb Zamacona's thoughts. In this earlier conversation, Zamacona asks Robles to help him understand Mexico's troubled past, to help him find "la palabra mágica o la simple justificación que me expliquen una historia tan teñida de dolor como la nuestra" (267). Robles responds that Mexico's pain hardly compares to Europe's recent sufferings: "Pregúntele usted a un europeo si esto no es el paraíso. Dolor es haber pasado dos guerras mundiales, bombardeos y campos de concentración" (267). Zamacona's rebuttal expresses his desire to formulate a way of understanding Mexico that is properly Mexican, different from Europe's historical trajectory, which, for Zamacona, follows an identifiable logic. But the key to Mexico's historical reason is still missing:

> —No, no, no me entiende usted [...] —Porque esos hombres que sufrieron el bombardeo y el campo de concentración, como usted dice, pudieron al cabo asimilar sus experiencias y cancelarlas, dar una explicación a sus propios actos y a los de sus verdugos—. Quería representarse muchas, dos, sólo una cara de un hombre torturado, desplazado, marcado con la estrella amarilla. Sólo podía recrear las caras del minuto anterior, las anónimas y pedigüeñas. —La experiencia más terrible, Dachau o Buchenwald, no hizo sino destacar la fórmula agredida: la libertad, la dignidad del hombre, como guste llamarla—. Como un río subterráneo, pensó, indiferente y oscuro. —Para el dolor mexicano no existen semejantes fórmulas de justificación. ¿Qué justifica la destrucción del mundo indígena, nuestra derrota frente a los Estados Unidos, las muertes de Hidalgo o Madero? [...]
>
> ¿Dónde está nuestra clave, dónde, dónde? [...] Hay que resucitar algo y cancelar algo para que esa clave aparezca y nos permita entender a México.
>
> [...] No, no se trata de añorar nuestro pasado y regodearnos en él, sino de penetrar en el pasado, entenderlo, reducirlo a razón, cancelar lo muerto —que es lo estúpido, lo rencoroso—, rescatar lo vivo y saber, por fin, qué es México y qué se puede hacer con él. (267–69)

The processes of repetition, substitution, and exchange that structure Zamacona's thoughts also organize Fuentes's novel. For example, the repetition of images and phrases like "subterranean river" and "indifferent and dark" emphasizes how thoughts and experiences from the past constantly disturb the present inhabited by the novel's characters. The novel gradually develops a compensatory epistemological system through the process of reviving old thoughts and impressions by placing them in new contexts. This passage also emphasizes the symbolic importance of the face, recalling Zamacona's encounter with the beggars whose faces impose themselves on his thoughts as he tries, and fails, to imagine the face of just one person who perished in the Holocaust. The victims of Mexico's as yet unexplained history implore Zamacona to justify their suffering. Finally, Zamacona's thoughts suggest the importance of exchange, of balancing the living and the dead, resuscitating or rescuing one, and canceling the other. Relating these processes to Zamacona's belief that the Revolution simultaneously revealed all of Mexico's history highlights the connection between totality and reason. The Revolution exposes everything, but leaves to those who inherit its legacy the task of ordering it, of "reducing it to reason."

Robles tries to reduce Mexico's historical experience to economic reason, but his discourse of progress and the absolute primacy of the future is interrupted by faces from his past that cannot be contained by the logic of exchange. The memory of Sánchez and Reyero obliges Robles to recast their faces as signs of Mexico's total, subterranean history:

> Los dos rostros se aliaban y confundían en esa zona última de la memoria: rostros asesinados, decorados de pólvora y sangre, ambos idénticos en la reproducción mental, no querida, de Robles. [...] Las dos cabezas muertas, en los ojos perdidos de Robles, se unían en un solo cuerpo de mil brazos acribillados, picoteados de plomo. Froilán Reyero, Feliciano Sánchez, los dos nombres que él recordaba, no eran sino una manera singular de nombrar a todos los muertos anónimos, a todos los esclavos, a todos los hambrientos. La tristeza y desolación de todas las vidas mexicanas cruzó, en ese instante, por la sangre de Robles. (381–82)

Robles's guilt-ridden relationship to the Revolution binds together an endless chain of Mexicans within the confines of a singular, totalizing historical event. Renamed and resignified, Sánchez and Reyero return, unwanted, to Robles, forcing him into a historical communion whose importance he had previously dismissed as so much intellectual blather. The Revolution's persistent presence transforms Robles's understanding of his place in the order of things.

The section of the novel titled "Feliciano Sánchez" immediately follows this description of Robles's memory, and it explains how Robles betrayed the man who haunts him. The way Robles recalls Sánchez's name suggests a chain of guilt made visible once his power and success are canceled. Robles's surplus capital ("lo muerto" in the terms of Zamacona's search for balance), augmented by killing Sánchez, is finally canceled. Following Zamacona's equation, this cancellation resuscitates life. Robles appeases his guilty conscience and starts life over again. He renews himself by leaving his wife, Norma Larragoiti, and deciding to spend the rest of his days with his lover, Hortensia Chacón, a blind, predominantly indigenous woman who stands in stark contrast to the more European-featured and ambitious Larragoiti.[29] Economically speaking, Robles trades investment banking and real estate for cotton farming on a modest scale. Racially speaking, he returns to his own modest, indigenous roots and makes a peaceful future for himself and Chacón. Finally, Chacón's blindness sustains the cliché that those who cannot see often understand more about themselves and their destinies than those who can. The narrator's final description of Robles portrays him with Chacón. In a gesture that prefigures the trope that concludes the novel, she takes his hand: "La sangre le pulsaba en las puntas de los dedos, ligeros sobre las yemas de Federico" (424). In a way that connects both Chacón and Larragoiti to another of the novel's female characters, Gladys García, both of Robles's lovers remain essentially static characters. More than developed individuals, they serve as guides to measure the extent to which male characters are redeemed. Robles's final proximity to Chacón reinforces her position within the novel as little more than a bellwether of his moral progress. Robles returns to himself through Chacón, whom the novel constructs as purely authentic, a woman who has remained true to her own, albeit two-dimensional self throughout the text.

The economic exchange Robles justified earlier in the novel is outstripped by personal and collective history at the moment of his downfall. Before Robles enters the café where Zamacona and Cienfuegos are arguing, Zamacona wonders aloud about his character: "Quisiera saber si su personalidad depende de esos elementos de poder que hoy le han sido arrebatados, o si hay algo más, una fuerza verdadera, algo que no permita reducir a Robles, pese a una quiebra" (361). This supplemental identity, which subsumes Robles's economic standard of measuring success, appears for the reader as Robles's conscience, the transformative guilt he experiences when he remembers Sánchez. Significantly, before he falls into the silence that allows him to recall Sánchez's name, Robles returns to the Revolution:

> Sí, la Revolución. Ustedes saben cómo empezó, y yo lo viví. Sin programa, sin ideas, casi sin metas —aunque el amigo Zamacona aquí piense lo contrario. Con jefes improvisados y pintorescos. Sin táctica ni pensamiento revolucionario auténticos. De acuerdo: mucho se perdió o fue traicionado. Pero algo se salvó, y lo salvamos nosotros.... (362–63)

That which was saved was not planned either. It interrupts Robles from within and forces his return to the past with no regard for his theory of economic reason, which is now as bankrupt as Robles himself.

Zamacona does not escape the unpaid debts of the Revolution either. He is shot and killed in a bar near Acapulco by a stranger who could have belonged to the group of beggars outside Robles's gate, and who seems to pay Zamacona back for the degrading descriptions of faces the narrator transmits through his gaze: "—A mí nadie me mira así— dijo el hombre con ojos de canica" (380), just after he shoots Zamacona. Zamacona's death becomes more clearly related to the novel's narrative of redemption, its own system of balancing life and death, when the reader realizes that Zamacona is Robles's son, who, the novel suggests, must be sacrificed to help cleanse the sins of his father. Zamacona's absurd death, which shocks the reader with its absolute lack of prelude or justification, points to an existentialist strain in Fuentes's novel, which is also characterized by the trajectory of Rodrigo Pola, whose transformation from a seemingly earnest, aspiring literary figure to a peddler of subpar screenplays reveals a deep-seated sense of alienation. He, unlike Robles, only finds meaning in making money. However, Pola's cynicism is balanced in the end by his final appearance in the novel, which occurs just before Cienfuegos's encounter with García. The epistemological triumph embodied in this last encounter, which I elaborate below, effaces Pola's ennui. And Zamacona's death ultimately functions within an economy of redemption, since his filial connection to Robles, unknown to both characters, represents yet another *río subterráneo* that ties together different individuals' stories within a system of collective redemption.[30]

VI

Having defined the memory of the Revolution as the primary historical source of redemption, Fuentes's novel then exalts itself as an even more powerful redemptive force. The logic of redemption and sacrifice that completes a cycle with Zamacona's death continues to the novel's conclusion. This time it is carried out by Ixca Cienfuegos, who, aside from Zamacona's reclusive mother, Mercedes, is the only character in the novel who knows that Zamacona is Robles's son, an awareness that exemplifies the omniscience Cienfuegos gradually attains over the course of the novel. Charged earlier in the novel by his mother, the widow Teódula, to find a sacrifice for her so that she can help return Mexico to its indigenous past, Cienfuegos ultimately names Robles's wife. Teódula then carries out the task herself, engulfing Larragoiti in the flames of her burning mansion. Before Larragoiti's death, Cienfuegos is already skeptical of his mother's plan, which intends to strike its own kind of balance with history. As Teódula communicates to Cienfuegos: "—Nos acercamos a la división de las aguas. Ellos morirán y nosotros resucitaremos al alimentar. Hemos pagado nuestro tributo de sueños; la ciudad lo pagará por nosotros" (333). Cienfuegos's doubts about the usefulness of the sacrifice prefigure his ultimate transformation. Referring to the indigenous voices from the past that Teódula hopes to reawaken, Cienfuegos says, "Mira que he querido escucharlas, mira que he pasado los años con los ojos cerrados esperando su rumor. Es como si un viento de palabras nuevas se lo hubiera llevado todo" (331). This storm of words—like the new language Fuentes advocates in *Nueva novela*—concludes the novel, elevating Cienfuegos to the level of consciousness that the novel itself enjoys, revealing how he knows everyone's stories from every moment of Mexican history. But his inability to reach one particular person suggests the need, and ultimately the promise, of a future balance. That person is a character who is sorely understudied in the vast bibliography of secondary literature on *La región*: Gladys García.

García, a young woman forced to leave her home after one of her brothers raped her, survives in Mexico City by working as a prostitute and a dancer in a city-center cabaret.[31] She appears only three times in the novel, but these appearances are important, not only for their content, but also for their positions within the text: at the beginning, the middle, and the end. In each of these episodes, García is portrayed as encountering a force external to and more powerful than her, which, unbeknownst to García, either descends upon, looks down upon, or envelops her. This force operates within the novel as the text's own epistemic privilege. Over the course of García's appearances in the novel, its transcendent power signals the gradual realization of the totality to which the text aspires. Its function in relation to García also mirrors the ultimately exclusive nature of Mexicanism and national-popular state ideology as discourses of asymmetrical incorporation.

García's structural and thematic prominence is revealed in the novel's opening pages. Though the first section of the novel is listed in the table of contents as "Mi nombre es Ixca Cienfuegos," this designation does not appear in the text proper. The first section that is named within the text immediately follows, and it is titled "Gladys García." The first action the novel attributes to García is taking a breath. After being ejected from the cabaret where she works, she "respiró la mañana helada" (11). This reference to the air García inhales connects her emergence into the text with the previous section, the one Cienfuegos claims for himself when he appears as first-person narrator. Introducing himself as a tour guide of sorts, Cienfuegos invites the reader to follow him down into Mexico City's urban maze: "Ven, déjate caer conmigo en la cicatriz lunar de nuestra ciudad, ciudad puñado de alcantarillas, ciudad cristal de vahos y escarcha mineral, ciudad presencia de todos nuestros olvidos" (10). In their descent, Cienfuegos and the reader encounter García before anyone else, presenting her as that which has been forgotten, establishing an association between prostitution and abjection, and, at the same time, casting her in an integral role of the space Cienfuegos describes. The use of the term *vahos* to describe the city's air connects Cienfuegos's dominant perspective to García's first action, since *vahos* means "breath," as well as "steam" or "vapor." García's name corresponds to the first titled section of the novel, but at that point she is already framed by Cienfuegos's powerful narrative presence.

García's second appearance occurs when her erstwhile lover, Beto, finds her, to his surprise, in the brothel where she works. The narrator's description of this encounter reinforces the difference between dominant and inferior narrative presence that the text sets up in its introductory juxtaposition of Cienfuegos and García. Beto and García are described as barely able to speak to one another. Their fragmentary, nearly incoherent sentences contrast sharply to the complex, articulate observations of characters, like Zamacona and Robles, who belong to more privileged social classes. For example, Beto's speech is interrupted by ellipses, "—[…] Te acuerdas cuando me pelé con la güera esa, y ya no nos vimos… No fue cosa mía, Gladys, de que yo quisiera; era que así nos tocó, a los tres. Dizque hay gentes muy voluntariosas, que se les hace lo que se les antoja. Pero tú y yo…" (195).

The content of Beto's observation attests to his and García's feelings of powerlessness, and the narrator's description of García's response further affirms this perception through what it describes, and, at the formal level, because it does not appear in García's own words: "Gladys se tapó los ojos con las manos y quiso decir algo; oraciones, palabras, un profundo temor al sueño le temblaban entre los senos" (195). The words and feelings trapped inside her body mark García as a material presence less aware of her situation than someone like Zamacona or Cienfuegos, who are characters able to transcend materiality and talk about the "forms that are bound to express a substance, by itself, mute." The novel adopts such a form when it shifts from García and Beto's halted speech to their silent thoughts, which, described in detail over the novel's following pages, are much more perceptive and sophisticated than their words but imperceptible to one another and only visible to the reader.[32] For example, García reflects, in what becomes a very ironic observation in light of the novel's narrative perspective, "*te has fijado en la gente igualita a nosotros* [...], *que no dejan que la voz se les oiga?*"(195).[33] Clearly, the novel aims to give a voice to Mexico's most marginalized, like García, who, as a prostitute, exchanges her body for survival and explicitly represents the exploitation and dehumanization that ground economic reason. And, her connection to the logic that Robles once espoused adds to her status as the ultimate goal of narrative redemption. But García's third appearance, when she encounters Cienfuegos once again, reveals why that goal is unattainable. Before she appears, however, Cienfuegos changes significantly.

Zamacona argues that the Revolution exposed all of Mexico's history all at once. Robles's redemption suggests a chain of identification between him and every betrayed Mexican. The compensatory totality the novel describes through its characters' thoughts and narrative trajectories unites with the text's structure at its conclusion, when Cienfuegos undergoes a transformation. Until the novel's ending, Cienfuegos functions as a narrative device, an ethnographer of sorts who collects and ties together the stories of practically every single one of the dozens of characters who inhabit Fuentes's novel. In the text's final pages, Cienfuegos becomes the novel itself as his thoughts combine seamlessly with the voices and memories of everyone he has encountered. His body disappears and he is able to adopt multiple perspectives simultaneously.[34] Cienfuegos also becomes Mexico's national history over a pages-long stream of consciousness that enumerates dozens of events from the pre-Conquest period to the post-Revolutionary era:

> El frío viento de diciembre arrastró a Cienfuegos, con pies veloces, por la avenida, por la ciudad, y sus ojos—el único punto vivo y brillante de ese cuerpo sin luz—absorbían casas y pavimentos y hombres sueltos de la hora, ascendían hasta el centro de la noche y Cienfuegos era, en sus ojos de águila pétrea y serpiente de aire, la ciudad, sus voces, recuerdos, rumores, presentimientos, la ciudad vasta y anónima. (443)

Able to absorb Mexico City and eventually the nation's past through his eyes, Cienfuegos transmits what he sees with his voice. He becomes a focal point through which Mexico's total reality, past and present, emerges as novelistic representation. Thus he executes what the Revolution had done, but this time as an integral structural element of a foundational boom novel, which attempts to "reduce to reason" that previous totalizing event.

The novel, which ends with the description of Cienfuegos's transformation, comes full circle in its final page. Cienfuegos's—and the novel's—trajectory, his process of becoming Mexico, is interrupted by García, who stands alone on a bridge in northern Mexico City and looks down upon the shack where she grew up. The last action the novel attributes to her is the same as the first. She takes a breath. After a series of quotations from earlier in the novel, which have now become part of Cienfuegos's ethereal, all-encompassing presence, the following passage concludes the text. García appears within the swiftly moving maelstrom of thoughts, feelings, words, and events that Cienfuegos embodies, described here as a dust storm:

> y sobre el puente de Nonoalco se detiene Gladys García, veloz también dentro del polvo, y enciende el último cigarillo de la noche y deja caer el cerillo sobre los techos de lámina y respira la madrugada de la ciudad, el vapor de trenes, la somnolencia de la carne, los tufos de gasolina y alcohol y la voz de Cienfuegos, que corre, con el tumulto silencioso de todos los recuerdos, entre el polvo de la ciudad, quisiera tocar los dedos de Gladys García y decirle, sólo decirle: Aquí nos tocó. Qué le vamos a hacer. En la región más transparente del aire. (459–60)

This kind of contrast between form and mute substance not only permeates but frames the novel, a frame established by the trope of two hands desiring contact. On the first page, after naming himself, Cienfuegos announces his desire for contact with someone who has no name, who will help him affirm a collective identity through a process of communion that recalls Paz's reflections on the Revolution in *Laberinto*. Cienfuegos narrates: "Jamás nos hemos hincado juntos, tú y yo, a recibir la misma hostia; desgarrados juntos, creados juntos, sólo morimos para nosotros, aislados. Aquí caímos. Qué le vamos a hacer. Aguantarnos mano. A ver si algún día mis dedos tocan los tuyos" (10). The reference to García at the novel's conclusion suggests that she is the missing piece of Cienfuegos's narrative, yet his fingers never reach hers.

The failure to make contact with García interrupts Cienfuegos's transformation, but it also reinforces her status as a goal of appropriation, the ultimate step necessary to realize the self-recognition of Cienfuegos and the collective identity he embodies. The novel endlessly postpones this appropriation by virtue of its self-referentiality, exemplifying what Joseph Frank once attributed to Joyce's *Ulysses*, which "cannot be read [but] only reread." Frank continues, "A knowledge of the whole is essential to an understanding of any part" (19). García frames *La región más transparente* in such a way that the beginning edge of the frame emerges as such only once the "ending" has been reached. At its conclusion, the novel enacts formally the desire for totality that it thematizes. The self-referentiality that occurs during Cienfuegos's transformation is a detailed repetition of several events that transpire in the novel, and it creates the need to return to the text's previously outlined parts to see how they fit into the gradually revealed whole. A rereading of *La región* must highlight García's importance, but the fact is that she remains stubbornly outside of, or excluded by, the collective subject that Cienfuegos's transformation produces.

VII

At face value, García stands for the need to recognize injustice and to incorporate Mexico's most marginalized into the national imaginary. But naming García as the ultimate goal of Cienfuegos's longing for contact does not *identify* a preexisting subject previously excluded from representations of Mexican society, but instead it *produces* the subaltern as the limit upon which the text constructs itself. The novel remains unfinished by referring back to its beginning at its ending, a return that consolidates García's role as the elusive goal of the completion of the text and the nation of which it constructs an allegorical, totalizing representation. Still, García's itinerary remains, in Gayatri Spivak's terms, "the limited access to being human" (*Critique* 30). García's limited subjectivity grounds Cienfuegos's universal subjectivity. Thus the failure to make contact with García is, by this measure, not a failure at all. Instead, it reinforces the exclusive character of the desire for a representation able to contain all of the contradictions that constitute the construction of community. The contradiction the novel cannot contain lies at the heart of its appropriative project: positing the goal of García's humanization demands her *a priori* dehumanization.

García is most profoundly dehumanized at the moment when Cienfuegos reaches out to her. Cienfuegos is the totality of which García can, at best, become a component, part of an essence that is perpetually unfolding, like the national-popular state and the Mexicanness that serves as ground and horizon for thinkers such as Gamio and Uranga. This desire to represent the forever evolving yet already defined nation is akin to Kant's conception of the sublime, that which contains and helps comprehend what the imagination must fail to grasp, a failure that, negatively, reassures rational human beings of their capacity for reason. Regarding the infinite, Kant writes that it "is absolutely (not merely comparatively) great. [...] the point of capital importance is that the mere ability even to think it as a *whole* indicates a faculty of mind transcending every standard of sense" (102; original emphasis). Transcending sense defines Cienfuegos's final aim. Postponed contact with García holds out the promise of a future moment of completion that stands on the horizon but that cannot be represented. *La región* expresses the nation as infinite but ultimately comprehensible; and the difference between infinity and comprehension, according to Kant, can only be appreciated as aesthetic:

> Hence it must be the *aesthetic* estimation of magnitude in which we get at once a feeling of the effort of imagination for mentally grasping the progressive apprehension in a whole of intuition, and, with it, a perception of the inadequacy of this faculty, which has no bounds to its progress, for taking in and using for the estimation of magnitude a fundamental measure that understanding could turn to account without the least trouble. Now the proper unchangeable fundamental measure of nature is its absolute whole, which, with it, regarded as a phenomenon, means infinity comprehended. But, since this fundamental measure is a self-contradictory concept, (owing to the impossibility of the absolute totality of endless progression,) it follows that where the size of a natural Object is such that the imagination spends its whole faculty of comprehension upon it in vain, it must carry our concept of nature to a supersensible substrate (underlying

> both nature and our faculty of thought) which is great beyond every standard of sense. Thus, instead of the object, it is rather the cast of the mind in appreciating it that we have to estimate as *sublime*. (103–04; original emphasis)

Fuentes's novel's aesthetic charge emerges precisely from Cienfuegos's failure to make contact with García. The promise of her appropriation is graspable, like Uranga's vault or Gamio's "true feeling of nationality." The realization of that promise, though, exists beyond representation, beyond sense, but still within reason.

But who reasons? Certainly some do and others do not, a distinction the novel establishes as separating Cienfuegos from García. The aesthetic appeal of the novel's conclusion comes from its representation of a positive encounter with the sublime. As Spivak emphasizes in her analysis of Kant's *Critique of Judgment*, a positive encounter with the sublime requires, for Kant, the "*development* of moral ideas," without which, that "which we, prepared by culture, call sublime presents itself to man in the raw merely as terrible" (qtd. in Spivak, *Critique* 12–13; Spivak's emphasis). For the uneducated, the sublime is a fearsome abyss. But for Cienfuegos and the novel he becomes, the sublime reassuringly reveals the gap between sense and reason that posits the necessary existence of a supersensible order, like the totality to which the state, Mexicanist philosophy, and Fuentes's novel all appeal. Kant argues that the subject aware of its limits becomes the moral being, and becomes a final purpose that gives meaning to the totality of experience: "Since now it is only as moral being that we recognize man as the purpose of creation, we have in the first place a ground (at least the chief condition) for regarding the world as a whole connected according to purposes and as a *system* of final causes" (qtd. in Spivak, *Critique* 32; original emphasis from Kant's text).

García, constructed as part of an already-unfolding system, does not recognize the limits of her perception. The forces that envelop her are external and beyond her awareness. Cienfuegos wants to be her guide, but his mission produces her as the necessary consequence of the epistemological violence that separates those who learn from an encounter with the sublime and those who fear it, those who redeem and those who are subjected to redemption. This asymmetry is reinforced by the connection established between García, standing alone at the end of the novel, and Cienfuegos's desire for communion at the beginning. Her character motivates a rereading and suggests the text's infinite nature, further approximating it to the sublime. The novel's aesthetic power, produced by the effort to allude to the supersensible, depends upon the subalternization of García, the figure around whom the novel defines itself as a totalizing, redemptive vision of history's explanatory operation on the present, which aims to inaugurate a promising future.

Carlos Fuentes's first novel articulates a complex narrative of redemption around the story of the national-historical event *par excellence* of twentieth-century Mexico, the Revolution. It interweaves the stories of Manuel Zamacona and Federico Robles to create a narrative that incorporates a number of characters—Feliciano Sánchez, Froilán Reyero, and the beggars outside of Robles's mansion—just as Uranga's vault incorporates the inscriptions of daily life. This narrative constructs a compensatory totality around the trope of the *río subterráneo*, an image that ties Robles's guilt and renewal to all other Mexicans. The novel's reading of the Revolution sets the stage for a reading of the mid-century present, which centers around the narrative that juxtaposes Cienfuegos and García, and that is reinforced by the trope of the hands desiring contact. The inner concentric circle formed by the Zamacona-Robles redemption story casts the Revolution as the totalizing moment and still vital force, left to be "understood or transcended." The outer concentric circle formed by the Cienfuegos-García redemption story casts the novel itself as the totalizing incarnation of the present. The novel's work on the Revolution rehearses its work on the present. I propose that the novel's conclusion reveals that, in order for the novel to sustain its redemptive force in the present, as a defining and evolving representation of the present, it must remain open and posit an outside, Gladys García, as the goal of a promise always left unrealized. This operation demonstrates that Fuentes's novel shares foundational similarities with the political, philosophical, and aesthetic discourses of its time. The novel's ground for the inclusionary promise of national fulfillment is exclusion. This fact helps reveal the limit of these other discourses as well.

Identifying the limit of the incorporative totalizing gesture is an operation I will employ in my analyses of the other novels that I consider in this study. *La región* posits the appropriation of all Mexicans as a necessary step toward representing a compensatory totality. Thus Gladys García emerges as the constitutive outside of the novel's appropriative foundation. I contend that García is the ever-excluded marginal figure, and thus the ever-constructed subaltern. At the same time, she marks the novel's limit, its failure to appropriate all difference, to subsume alterity within a coherent vision of the Mexican national community and its trajectory. As with the man of "eyes of marble" who kills Manuel Zamacona, it is possible to read García as just another example of Fuentes's denigrating portrayal of Mexico's popular classes.[35] On the other hand, it is possible to read both characters as interruptions of the redemptive narratives the novel establishes through its reconstruction of Mexico's past and its work on Mexico's present and future. García is the ground and limit of Fuentes's novel, a paradoxical fictional construction that reveals how *La región* operates, to borrow a phrase from Moreiras's critique of Latin Americanism, as the paradoxical "ceaseless capture [...] of the unmasterable excess of the social" (97). Able to employ the Revolution as a device for constructing a closed redemptive narrative, which results in the salvation of Robles through the sacrifice of Zamacona, *La región* feeds off of the force of national history, a force that, I propose, is less accessible to later novels, which appear during the gradual decline of the national-popular state's hegemony. *La región* founds itself upon the fissure between appropriation and its limit. Later novels bear witness to the widening of this constitutive gap.

Chapter Two

Animating the Popular

Fernando del Paso's *José Trigo* and the Ruins of Totalizing Thought

José Trigo (1966), Fernando del Paso's first novel, relates fictional accounts of three significant historical moments of post-Revolutionary Mexico: the Cristero Rebellion of 1926–29, the railroad workers' movement of 1958–59, and, to a lesser but still important degree, the 1964 urban renewal project that transformed Mexico City's northern district of Nonoalco-Tlatelolco. The novel recounts these events within a framing story that tells the tale of an anonymous first-person narrator who visits the train yards of Nonoalco-Tlatelolco on at least two occasions, January 11 and December 26 of an unspecified, long-ago leap year.[1] It is unclear whether he is referring to 1960, 1964, a year projected into the future, or a combination of different moments. But when the narrator first arrives, hundreds of railroad workers still inhabit the train yards, living in ramshackle houses, sheds, and reclaimed railroad cars. Their struggle has ended in defeat, and the narrator is seeking information about what took place in Nonoalco-Tlatelolco during the months that led up to the climactic moment of the labor dispute, when on December 12, 1960, thousands of workers gathered at the Church of Santiago Tlatelolco only to be dispersed violently by soldiers and riot police.[2] Of particular interest to the narrator is the story of José Trigo, who arrived in Nonoalco-Tlatelolco on April 1, 1960, and who fled the train yards on the night of December 12 of the same year. The novel's title character, whom the narrator never finds, is constructed over the course of the text as a witness to events that helped determine the fate of the railroad workers' strike. In the novel's final pages, the workers identify themselves with Trigo as the latter becomes a symbol of their struggle to perceive and shape their own destinies. Thus José Trigo functions as an important missing piece to the puzzle of what transpired in Nonoalco-Tlatelolco in 1960. Significantly, the narrator's search for him also reveals a great deal about the area's storied past.[3]

Asking about José Trigo, the narrator is directed toward the railroad car that serves as the home of Buenaventura, an ancient, Celestina-like figure who becomes the narrator's primary source of information about José Trigo, the strike, the train yards, and the people who live there.[4] Presumably, the histories that Buenaventura communicates to the narrator provide the basis for the novel he writes, a heterogeneous text that combines, among other things: first- and third-person narrative alongside heavy doses of indirect free style; poetry, prose, and song; chapters that range from realistic, chronological narratives to fantastical theatrical pieces; a middle chapter that rewrites the novel's main plot in terms of Christian and Aztec eschatological narratives; and fragments from a railroad worker's manual about intersections and switches.[5] The narrator's text thus records and transforms the stories told by Buenaventura and a handful of others, most prominently Bernabé, Anselmo, and Guadalupe, three switch operators, and Pedro, a carpenter. Many years after these conversations the narrator returns to Nonoalco-Tlatelolco. By this time, the train yards are gone, replaced by high-rise housing projects as part of the urban-renewal campaign that also produced the Plaza of the Three Cultures when it added modern residential and office buildings to the square that already contained Aztec ruins and the colonial-era Church of Santiago Tlatelolco.[6] Thus the narrator finds himself sealed off from the source of the story his novel communicates.

The framing device that describes the narrator's search for José Trigo and what he learns about the train yards structures the content that comprises the majority of del Paso's text, which follows a number of plots whose dominant shared trait is that they trace different characters' itineraries through spaces imbued with symbolic meaning. For example, two of the novel's chapters relate the story of how Buenaventura, her husband Todolosantos, and nine of their twelve children left Nonoalco-Tlatelolco in late 1927 to join the Cristero Rebellion and fight invading federal forces near the Volcano of Colima, a battleground whose features are given religiously significant names by its defenders, such as the Meseta de Cristo Rey.[7] A chapter about the history of Mexican railroads provides a taxonomy of locomotives, passengers, cargo, and the cities they pass through, like Celaya and Ciudad Juárez, place names that recall the battles fought there during the Revolution. The most symbolically important space the novel constructs is Nonoalco-Tlatelolco, where all of the novel's characters eventually converge.[8] The novel obsessively details the history that has shaped this part of Mexico's capital, from the founding of the Aztec city of Tlatelolco in 1337, through events of the colonial and post-Independence periods, and up until the 1960s. For a number of different reasons, characters like Eduviges, the woman who shares her home with José Trigo; Luciano, the uncorrupted labor leader and grandson of Buenaventura; and José Trigo himself come from communities spread out across Mexico. Thus Nonoalco-Tlatelolco, with its watchtowers, roundhouse, railroad cars, *pulquerías*, oyster bar, brothel, billiards hall, and gypsy encampment, becomes a nationally important space whose landmarks acquire special meaning as they witness the trajectories of the characters who walk among them. The fact that the train yards contain and transmit an extensive network of historical signification makes their disappearance a serious loss.

Two trajectories become especially important over the course of the novel, those of José Trigo and Luciano. Luciano is the novel's most ardent and articulate defender of the railroad workers' efforts to improve their standing. Two chapters focus on his journeys across the encampments, which take him from his house to a number of places, including meetings with other laborers, the brothel, a strip-tease in the big-top of an itinerant carnival, and a rousing speech he delivers before an assembly of workers. Luciano eventually goes into hiding as he fears for his life when he is threatened by turncoats determined to sabotage the striking union's efforts. José Trigo also traverses the encampments, heading from east to west, across the Puente de Nonoalco, which divides the camps, and back again. Trigo's most fateful journey through Nonoalco-Tlatelolco takes him to the place where Manuel Ángel, who has participated in sabotage and accepted government bribes, murders Luciano, who had earlier challenged Manuel Ángel to tell him the truth about his attempts to undermine the striking workers' solidarity. In the first of four such escapes, José Trigo, who has witnessed the murder, evades Manuel Ángel's pursuit. The night of December 12, during the massive demonstration at the Church of Santiago Tlatelolco, marks the last encounter between Manuel Ángel and José Trigo, which ends when José Trigo disappears forever, his fate unknown. The novel closes with the narrator's meditations on the destruction of the train yards and the history they embodied.

José Trigo constructs the train yards as a space privileged for its unique ability to produce popular history. The people who live there recount, discuss, and debate the stories of their past in a process whose end result is a collective understanding of the events, both personal and historical, that have shaped a working-class community with roots that extend across the nation. In this chapter I focus on the fact that by the novel's conclusion, the train yards are gone, leaving an insurmountable abyss that separates the narrator from the story he wishes to tell. This aspect of the novel establishes a relation to totality that sets *José Trigo* apart from *La región*. Fuentes's novel mobilizes the promise of the Revolution by casting itself as a text capable of accessing the sublime order of Mexican national identity as this identity reveals itself through time. By contrast, *José Trigo* does two things that are notably different. First, it is a novel that enacts the *animation* of total national experience more than it does *access* to that experience. Second, the spaces and people *José Trigo* animates no longer exist. They were *once capable* of accessing the sublime order of Mexicanness that *La región* helped construct and reproduce, an order now inaccessible to the present of del Paso's novel's conclusion.

This chapter's focus on the concept of animation aims to identify *José Trigo*'s guiding theory of representation, whose principal tenet is that authorial control over creation is inherently limited. The stories and actions of the novel's characters are always only understood as collective, dialogic products of language, and not discreet, positive, fixed phenomena. Their veracity and communicability are constantly negotiated and questioned. Furthermore, the distance between the narrator and the train yards is an explicit admission of the novel's limit, of its inability to transmit the history of Nonoalco-Tlatelolco from the present to the future. *José Trigo* also rejects the notion of stable, verifiable origins of meaning. This rejection appears most clearly in the novel's radically ambivalent depiction of Luciano's apparent resurrection, which relates how his cadaver is animated by his fellow workers. The passage that describes Luciano's resurrection is also significant for being an allegory of the narrator's animation of the train yards. Finally, the novel's rejection of origins dovetails with its critique of presence and access to it, a critique that informs both the scenes of Luciano's resurrection and the railroad workers' evocation of José Trigo in their final demonstration. In this climactic moment, the workers access sublime totality, but only for an instant, and only as the result of their collaboration with one another. The monologic perspective of the sole narrator who closes the text cannot transmit the totality the workers glimpsed. The novel's final focus on the narrator's limitations reinforces its assertion that making meaning is an ambivalent, always negotiable process.

Understanding meaning and creation as processes always open to change does not in any way deny the important, real consequences they produce. Instead, it is a way of thinking that conceives of history as radically contingent, leaving meaning and experience open to new interpretations and incarnations in a necessarily uncertain future. This theory of representation not only undermines any claims *José Trigo* could make to ultimate narrative authority, but it also allows the reading of history to continue in a way that is more open and less prescribed than in the dominant, totalizing discourse that characterizes Fuentes's novel, Mexicanist philosophy, and national-popular state ideology.

José Trigo mounts a strong critique of how totalizing discourse produces subaltern subjectivity because it identifies the way such discourse appeals to static, officially authorized definitions of popular classes. This identification appears most clearly in the novel's portrayal of the railroad workers' strike, which, notably, contrasts sharply with its portrayal of the Cristero Rebellion. *José Trigo* roundly condemns the Cristiada, defining its participants in terms very similar to the way the Mexican state defined them, thus reinforcing the epistemological hierarchy that privileges the intellectual and produces subaltern subjectivity. On the other hand, the text's construction of the railroad workers' movement and its narration of the search for José Trigo acknowledge a lack of ontological superiority. *José Trigo* is a text that thus challenges the notion—sustained by many writers and critics of the boom and exemplified by *La región*—that the novel is privileged in its ability to represent national and/or regional identities. I propose that the difference between the representation of the Cristiada and the strike in *José Trigo* reveals how the novel acknowledges, first, its ultimate incapacity to capture popular experience and, second, the violence implicit in that gesture. In the end, *José Trigo* undermines the sustainability of not only the substance of hegemonic conceptions of Mexican experience, but also the epistemology that grounds them.

I

The general way in which *José Trigo* animates popular experience can be introduced by turning briefly to Jorge Luis Borges's story "Las ruinas circulares" (1942), which ends when its protagonist, the man who dreamed life into another man, learns a terrible secret about his own provenance. As fire threatens to destroy the ruined temple where he completed his creation, Borges's magician decides not to flee: "Por un instante, pensó refugiarse en las aguas, pero luego comprendió que la muerte venía a coronar su vejez y a absolverlo de sus trabajos" (455). The fire has already overtaken the man he created, who had moved to another temple in the North. Aware that his creation could not be harmed by fire, the magician speculates: "Temió que su hijo meditara en ese privilegio anormal y descubriera de algún modo su condición de mero simulacro. No ser un hombre, ser la proyección del sueño de otro hombre ¡qué humillación incomparable, qué vértigo!" (454). Welcoming death, the magician succumbs to the conflagration only to discover that his time has not yet come: "Caminó contra los jirones de fuego. Éstos no mordieron su carne, éstos lo acariciaron y lo inundaron sin calor y sin combustión. Con alivio, con humillación, con terror, comprendió que él también era una apariencia, que otro estaba soñándolo" (455).

The magician's ambivalence toward his newfound awareness communicates a degree of ambiguity typical of Borges's fictions. Why is the man relieved, humiliated, and terrified? One could easily imagine that he is relieved not to die and humiliated to realize he is another's projection. But his terror exposes something more complex. In the same instant the magician realizes he will not yet reach his life's conclusion, he is forced to recognize that he has forever misunderstood his life and its beginning. Any claims he may have made to originality have been undermined. Borges's parable raises the question of whether there is an original magician, a master creator. But it cannot be reduced to a tale that simply provides the alternative of either existentialist *anomie* or faith in the existence of an ultimate higher power. For the protagonist of "Las ruinas circulares" indeed creates something, a person who is as much a reflection of himself as he is a reflection of another. And this web of reflections generates affect—feelings for the other and feelings for oneself—that may form the basis for a community of animated beings who persist somewhere between autonomy and determinism.

José Trigo also contemplates origins, destinies, and creation. And as in Borges's story, it portrays apocalyptic moments as epiphanies that raise many questions and provide few answers. It traces processes of animation, of different people and things imbuing other people and things with life, and their potential as foundations of community. Significantly, the novel questions its own origins and creative capabilities by explicitly thematizing the ambiguities of language, the medium through which it breathes life not only into Mexico's past but also into itself as a means of constructing the past. Like Borges's magician, del Paso's novel finds itself in an intermediate space, certain of neither its provenance nor its fate.

The idea of granting agency to a novel, of attributing active verbs to it, may seem unsound. Yet Borges's story is an allegory of this very gesture because it asks what happens when a dream—"pensado entraña por entraña y rasgo por rasgo, en mil y una noches secretas" (454)—is left to its own devices. Similarly, Fuentes's *La región más transparente* demonstrates how an author creates the appearance of a novel's agency within its very pages when Ixca Cienfuegos embodies Mexico's past, which includes words, phrases, and scraps of dialogue from previous sections of the text. *José Trigo* is a novel much less sure of its ability to embody the past, let alone to construct, contain, and communicate the sublime totality of Mexican experience. In fact, *José Trigo* embodies what can be termed a second-order totalizing vision of Mexico's past. It is one step removed from a system of representation that could contain everything.

On the one hand, I use the term "second order" to describe *José Trigo*'s construction of the relationship between novelistic representation and sublime totality in order to clarify the gap between the present and the past that del Paso's novel exposes vis-à-vis access to a supersensible order of Mexicanness. On the other hand, my use of the term refers to Alberto Moreiras's discussion of "second-order Latin Americanism" in *The Exhaustion of Difference* (2001). Of course I do not suggest that Fernando del Paso deliberately undertook a disciplinary analysis of Mexico while he spent seven years writing *José Trigo*.[9] But his novel does engage with fundamental tenets of Mexicanism and national-popular state thinking, including the desire to delimit a specifically national history and to define the "people," two operations necessary for the legitimation of state authority and philosophical discussions of Mexican cultural singularity. In his work on national-popular state formation in Latin America, Gareth Williams identifies a connection between the concepts of totality and the people that also informs my analysis of *José Trigo*: "The idea of the people and, along with it, the concept of the popular, came to be construed as a potentially hegemonic formation designed to suture the totality of the nation's demographic and cultural differences to the formation and expansion of the nation-state" (4–5). The sutures that structure Mexico's totality in del Paso's novel become more visible than they were in Fuentes's *La región*, and this process of exposure is related to the way *José Trigo* questions its ability to sustain a totalizing vision of Mexico's historical experience, its present, and its future.

I find that Moreiras's analysis of second-order Latin Americanism also helps elucidate the particularities of *José Trigo* and the historical context from which it emerged. In short, Moreiras draws a distinction between two instances of Latin Americanism: the first insists stubbornly on the validity of Latin Americanism as a discipline whose roots lie in the post–World

War II Area Studies programs of US universities; the second acknowledges the profound limitations of the first and seeks a Latin Americanism that refuses to reproduce them. The two Latin Americanisms are distinguished in Moreiras's argument by their relationships to cultural difference. The first "works as an instantiation of global agency, insofar as it ultimately wants to deliver its findings into some totality of allegedly neutral, universal knowledge of the world in all its differences and identities" (32); the second, Moreiras proposes, would function as a means of "arresting the tendential progress of epistemic representation toward total articulation" (45). Citing Michael Hardt and Antonio Negri's *Empire* (2000), Moreiras continues by proposing that "this second Latin Americanism emerges as a critical opportunity through the metacritical realization that the first, or historical, Latin Americanism has come to a productive end with the end of the disciplinary paradigm of rule that understood the progress of knowledge as the panoptic search and capture of 'positions, fixed points, identities'" (45). But it is not as simple as opposing difference to identity, of proposing that singularity can resist homogeneity. Instead, Moreiras argues, second-order Latin Americanism

> works primarily not as a machine of epistemic homogenization but potentially against it as a disruptive force [...] whose desire does not go through an articulation of difference or identity but instead goes through their constant disarticulations, through a radical appeal to an epistemic outside, to an exteriority that will not be turned into a mere fold of the imperial self. (33)

Del Paso's novel ultimately resists totalization through its self-reflexive critique of the novel's ability to fold difference into itself and into a dominant, homogenizing, national teleology. Furthermore, *José Trigo* progresses along a track that shifts from the capture of difference to a thorough acknowledgment of the disarticulations that disrupt the potentially totalizing force of a conception of identity and difference that presupposes the ultimate goal of sameness.

Brett Levinson's discussion of literary articulation, which bears on my reading of *La región más transparente*, is also relevant to my analysis of *José Trigo*. For Levinson, literature's "charge" is "the invention of an articulation for the relationality of beings, which no existing semiotics or common sense can supply" (26). Both Fuentes's and del Paso's novels integrate schemes of relationality into their elaborate constructions and reconstructions of Mexico's history and contemporary society. In its portrayal of the Cristero Rebellion, *José Trigo* articulates connections between characters, events, and places that can be folded into the already existing semiotics of the Revolutionary state's ideological foundations. On the other hand, what distinguishes *José Trigo* from Fuentes's novel is the way it explicitly and self-consciously exposes the limits of that incorporating gesture. The disarticulations that del Paso's novel leaves for the reader at its conclusion allude to the integrative failure of the totalizing novel, an allusion that arises not only from the critique of the Revolution as political praxis—a critique *La región* also advances—but also from the critique of Revolutionary ideology and its integrating operations. The type of relationality that *José Trigo* does propose, then, is one that rejects the epistemological hierarchy that elevates the allegedly superior creator to a position above and separate from the beings he or she creates.

II

Borges's magician thought that his originality distinguished himself from his creation. When he realized that they were significantly the same, the magician was obliged to recognize that he no longer knew what "the same" actually meant, an acknowledgment that he and his creation were forced to negotiate. *José Trigo* exhibits a similar process of recognition, the disturbance of a notion of original and originary subjectivity, and the awareness of persisting in a liminal, disarticulated space. The anonymous narrator's search for José Trigo in the train yards of Nonoalco-Tlatelolco typifies how del Paso's novel traces its characters' trajectories through ambiguously comprehended spaces and experiences. The search narrative also establishes the absolute break between the dialogic, history-producing space the train yards once exemplified and the monologic, sterile space the narrator occupies at the novel's end.

Early descriptions of the narrator's arrival at the train yards emphasize how intersecting gazes, overlapping moments, people, and objects work in concert and piece together whatever they can about what happened to José Trigo and the train yards he traversed. The following passage is worth citing at length because, in addition to introducing the complex network of reflections, both mental and physical, that characterize the narrator's search and what he finds, it is emblematic of the novel's formal characteristics, including style, perspective, and structure:

> ¿José Trigo? [...] Él me vio llegar desde lejos, en el amanecer de un once de enero de un año bisiesto de hace muchos años. Me miró o no me miró porque el sol —¿o la luna?— le daba en los ojos y yo estaba en sus ojos caminando entre las vías oxidadas de durmientes podridos donde hacía mucho tiempo no corrían los trenes de carga [...] yo cada vez más grande en sus ojos, él cada vez más grande en los míos, y los dos que nos miramos y yo que le pregunto: ¿José Trigo? Y él como mirando más arriba de mi cabeza, donde el humo de las chimeneas de las fábricas de jabón, de vidrio y de cerveza se confunde con el humo de la vieja locomotora de maniobras [...] y con el humo del fuego de un basurero donde hace muchos años yo vi, cuando pasaba por los llanos de Nonoalco preguntando ¿José Trigo? un cráneo de conejo en un cerro de cáscaras de naranja [...]. —¿José Trigo? No, no conozco a nadie que se llame José Trigo —dijo como si dijera estación, trabajo, ferrocarrilero, garitones. [...] y no sé nada de torres de vigilancia y de entronques y de los ojos redondos y rojos refulgentes de las ménsulas de señales que vieron a José Trigo guiñándole la muerte y lo vieron llegar desde lejos, vagar por estos llanos de Nonoalco [...]. (5–7)

The passage portrays moments in time as confused as the smoke that becomes intermingled as it rises from factory smokestacks, locomotives, and burning trash. It could be day or night. At one point the trains no longer run; at another, they still operate. The narrator has been here before, but it is not clear when. Thus the train yards function as a container of the past that enables a simultaneous vision of the different moments that have transpired there. The text not only intertwines different instances in time, but also different perspectives. The narrator and the man he approaches see one another reflected in each other's eyes. Objects also have stories to tell, like the signals that watched when José Trigo barely escaped death at the hands of Manuel Ángel. The passage also communicates the fungibility of things and words, like the different streams of smoke and the nouns the man could have said instead of saying "José Trigo." Finally, *José Trigo*'s opening pages challenge the notion of narrative reliability when they reveal that the man who claims ignorance about José Trigo is able to describe in very specific detail that which he supposedly does not know.

In a manner consistent with the novel's persistent turning back upon itself, *José Trigo* closes with the same question that opens the text:

> ¿José Trigo? y mientras tanto, en balde y para qué, poniendo todas o casi todas las palabras: (palabras más, palabras menos) abajo, las palabras tierra, campamentos. Arriba, las palabras cielo, estrellas. Y entre la mañana, por la tarde, además, y con la noche, las palabras nada y nadie. Porque todo esto, y esto es un decir, fue la mañana, la tarde, la noche en que soñé o creí soñar que buscaba a José Trigo por cielo y por tierra: bajo todos los cielos habidos, sobre todas las tierras por haber. Y no vi nada ni a nadie. Nada bajo el cielo. Y sobre la tierra, nadie. (536)

As in the opening pages, the narrator calls attention to how words are selected. Language's arbitrary and at times absurd relationship to the experience to which it refers is a constant theme of *José Trigo*, as exemplified in the following description of the narrator's encounter with Buenaventura: "Manzanas incircuncisas, rosario, jaula, zancos: con éstas y otras palabras que sacó de su baúl mundo, comenzó la madrecita Buenaventura la historia" (19). The image of the word-filled "world trunk" aptly describes the novel's conception of language as a set of building blocks people use to assemble their experiences and stories.

At the novel's conclusion, the narrator appears to see words more than the things they are meant to describe. Thus it is unclear whether he actually sees nothing or no one, or the words *nothing* or *no one*. The narrator's final emphasis on words is consistent with the novel's general portrayal of language, but the context in which the narrator places the *sky* and the *earth* and the *nothing* and the *no one* that lie between them is different from the contexts within which words are employed in the other passages cited above and throughout most of the text. What distinguishes the conclusion is the narrator's isolation from the train yards and the dialogue between people and objects that once took place there. On his own, the conclusion suggests, the narrator is left literally disheartened, not only facing frustrated resignation but also crushed by the train yards' disappearance: "Vi cómo cercenaban los campamentos, cómo los antiguos moradores batieron tiendas y se fueron. Y detrás de ellos se fue mi corazón atijereado que se desbarató en palabras" (527). The narrator's language is not the same now that the train yards are gone since it no longer participates in a collective storytelling process. Buenaventura's active role in this process contrasts her to Gladys García, who plays a passive role in legitimizing Ixca Cienfuegos's integrating gesture. Del Paso's novel does not hold out the promise of capturing Buenaventura's independent contributions to the production of knowledge about Nonoalco-Tlatelolco's history. Whereas García becomes the subaltern who is constructed at and as the excluded foundation of totalizing identity, Buenaventura persists as the non-integrated other who founds nothing sustainable.

A final pair of contrasting images further reinforces how the novel opposes the productive dialogic space of Nonoalco-Tlatelolco to the sterile monologic space the narrator is condemned to occupy forever ("on all of the earths still to come"). In the chapter titled "Una oda," *José Trigo* constructs a history of the Mexican railroad that explains how the train transports the totality of the nation. The central image that relates this chapter to the novel's framing narrative is the train whistle: "Al llegar al campamento escuché, a lo lejos, el silbato de una locomotora" (229). For the narrator, the sound of the whistle carries the entire nation along with it. It is an ephemeral net that transforms itself as it gathers up the history it contains:

> El silbatazo suena como un golpe de mar que se quiebra en los farallones, como un trueno, como una profunda nota de órgano en el interior de un altísimo templo. [...] Qué animal, qué hombre, qué piedra, qué árbol, qué río no ha escuchado alguna vez el silbato de una locomotora: el silbato cargado de mar, de tierra, de tiempo, y la locomotora cargada de carros y los carros cargados de frutas, de sal, de especias, de hombres, y los hombres cargados de años, de recuerdos, de sueños, de otros hombres. [...] Porque el silbato de un tren es el tren mismo. Y es todo lo que lleva el tren. Y es todos los lugares que conoce el tren. [...] Preguntad quién no ha oído el silbato

> de un tren y quién que lo haya oído no se ha ido un poco con él [...] Porque no hay lugar que no haya recorrido. Así como no hay hombre que no lo recuerde. (229–30)

The whistle even has the power to resurrect the dead: "Cuando el tren silba, sus recuerdos llegan en tropel. Y ellos vuelven a ser los hombres que en los talleres del ferrocarril de Topolobampo repararon el cañonero Tampico. Los mismos que en Mapimí crearon la fuerza obrera que se unió a la Revolución. [...] Los que murieron en los combates [...]" (234–35). By the time the narrator stands alone, mourning the loss of the train yards, however, the whistle is not the same, since it no longer carries "como antes, toda esa carga de mar y de recuerdos" (526). Just as the whistle once capable of raising the dead is now irrevocably transformed, so are the narrator's words. Though they breathe life into the history of Nonoalco-Tlatelolco, they can no longer emerge from within that since-vanished space to communicate new experiences and stories.

III

Regarding the construction of Mexico's popular classes, *José Trigo* is not consistently as ambiguous and cautious about its authority as it is during the search narrative. In fact, its portrayal of the Cristiada, which dismisses the Cristeros' motivations and condemns them to obscurity, represents an integration of the people into a dominant vision of the nation that practically mimics official strategies of defining the conflict.[10]

The Cristero Rebellion of the late 1920s was fundamentally important to the consolidation of the nascent Revolutionary state, which used its opposition to the Cristeros to help ground its authority.[11] Jean Meyer concludes that the dominant motivating force behind those who fought against the government during the Cristero Rebellion was the belief that the state had overstepped its bounds (184), a perception that provoked tens of thousands of Mexicans to take up arms against their government, and against the ideological institutionalization of the Revolution that "was trying to take the priest away from them" (187).[12]

The anti-Revolutionary character of the Cristero Rebellion raised a serious challenge to the emerging state, whose legitimacy relied upon the construction of the Revolutionary masses. In defeat, the Cristeros were expelled from the dominant historical record in order to sustain a homogenous notion of the Mexican people. As Jean Meyer notes, "writers have denied [the Cristeros'] numbers, their strength, and their nature, in order to avoid having to say that the peasants were counter-revolutionary" (213).[13] Of course, the suppression of the Cristeros' legacy was not only discursive. After the last Cristeros gave up their weapons in September 1929, the Federal Army initiated a campaign to hunt down the leaders of the Cristero Army, assassinating some 5,000 between 1929 and 1935 (Jean Meyer 201–02). On the non-military front of state expansion, the government intensified its efforts of "morally integrating" Mexico's diverse populations through construction projects, mass-media information campaigns, federal education policy, and a détente between Church and state (Jean Meyer 217).[14] Writing in the 1970s, Jean Meyer sums up the consequences of the Cristero War as "crucial as regards the crystallisation of the present-day political, economic, and social system" (217). The impact on those who fought against the formation of this system, in addition to the material consequences enumerated above, was serious: "The peasants were decisively crushed, and this was the last insurrection of the masses. Henceforth they were conscious of their weakness [...] and the peasants resigned themselves to their violent and prejudicial integration into the regime, which was now firmly established" (Jean Meyer 216).

Though Jean Meyer's conclusion is somewhat sweeping, he accurately portrays the top-down, centralized, and sometimes violent integration of Mexico's diverse populations as a hallmark of the national-popular state.[15] The military leaders who emerged victorious from the chaos of the Mexican Revolution—most significantly two who would serve as president, Álvaro Obregón (1920–24) and Plutarco Elías Calles (1924–28)—oversaw the transitional years that transformed the Revolution from a multifaceted armed conflict into an ideological force underpinning a new system of government.[16] Of course the unification of the Mexican nation under the banner of the Revolution was more illusory than real. Social inequalities, for example, were often not confronted at their roots, but were instead smoothed over with populist rhetoric or only incompletely addressed through reform (Córdova 320).[17]

During the tumultuous post-Revolutionary period, unity and capitalist development became the primary political and economic goals of Mexico's ruling elite. An important step toward achieving those goals was the creation of the Partido Nacional Revolucionario (National Revolutionary Party, or PNR) in 1929, whose official program, in Lorenzo Meyer's words, emphasized "la necesidad de la conciliación nacional, conciliación entre individuos, facciones y clases" ("Primer tramo" 1197). The rhetoric and construction of social unity that was demanded by the political unity embodied in the foundation of the official party in 1929 coincided temporally and discursively with the consequences of the government's war against the Cristeros, which revealed how defining the people sometimes meant violently shaping them to fit an allegedly preconceived notion of who they were supposed to be.

IV

José Trigo's depiction of the Cristero Rebellion does not challenge the validity of this type of popular integration, which is similar to the paternalistic Mexicanism of thinkers like Gamio and Uranga, discussed in the previous chapter. In fact, the two chapters of the novel that focus on the Rebellion, titled "La Cristiada (I)" and "La Cristiada (II)," reproduce hegemonic discourse in that they delegitimize the Cristeros and symbolically erase them from history.

Formally speaking, the chapters that focus on the Cristiada represent an exception to the novel's predominantly fractured, dialogic, and ambiguous style. These chapters are primarily realist. They are not presented by the anonymous first-person seeker of José Trigo, but instead by an omniscient third-person narrator who recounts events along a strictly linear chronology, and who employs devices of suspense, plot-development, and characterization that convey a sense of narrative coherence and readability that is mostly absent from the rest of the novel.[18] Notably, both "Cristiada" chapters adopt an authoritative narrative structure that departs significantly from how the novel portrays the railroad workers' strike and the narrator's search for José Trigo.

Similarities do exist, however, such as the Cristiada narrative's emphasis on how words imbue places with symbolic meaning. Another trait this section shares with the rest of the novel is its use of framing devices. At the beginning and end of each chapter that treats the Rebellion, there are two sections set off from the main narrative, titled "Ficción geográfica" and "Noticia histórica." Del Paso's text introduces the Cristeros to the reader in the first of these sections, which conducts a toponymic tour through the area surrounding the Volcano of Colima where the novel's Cristeros have established their base. As the narrator describes it with a series of active verbs, Colima's landscape wanders as well:

> La Meseta de Cristo Rey desbordábase, hacia el Oriente, en la Barranca del Divino Cordero. Por el Poniente, la limitaba el Acantilado de la Divina Providencia, accesible tan sólo por la Quebrada del Calvario, la cual subía por el Noroeste de la Meseta hasta perderse en las Crestas de la Asunción, donde el aire se enrarecía, y que servía de base al Culmen de la Trinidad, suntuoso como un catafalco. (92)

The other three "Ficciones geográficas" continue the narrator's description of the area, a map of which appears inside the novel's back cover. The sense of motion the narrator lends to the landscape underscores the ephemeral nature of the parallel nation the Cristeros attempted to establish, which, in Jean Meyer's words, was an attempt to refound "the rural world on [...] family and religious bases" (143). The narrator's detailed attention to the religious place names, which is repeated in the map, produces a baroque sense of exaggeration that becomes comical, for example, in the narrator's reference to the "Valle de la Circuncisión" (126), or in the following redundancy that describes how a peak was "bautizado con el nombre del Peñón de los Ángeles" (408).[19] Here, the term *baptized* is excessive within the context of a naming ceremony whose religious nature is already overly emphasized. But the comic is balanced by the tragic in the passage cited above when the narrator employs the equally baroque simile "sumptuous like a catafalque," whose reference to the funereal foreshadows the Cristeros' defeat.

Such attention to language and its often comical excesses appears throughout del Paso's novel, and reinforces the idea that words animate experience. The exceptional trait of the novel's Cristiada chapters, however, is its explicit delegitimization of the way in which the Cristeros told their own story. In addition to parodying the Cristeros' use of religious place-names, the narrator condemns their cause at the end of the first Noticia histórica as senseless civil war: "Quien estaba por Dios no se detendría en matar a su hermano, su amigo y su pariente: negarse a ello hubiera sido pecado indispensable" (93). The conclusion to the Cristero narrative—which recounts how Buenaventura, her husband, and their surviving children and grandchildren retreated and spent seven years wandering the countryside before returning to Nonoalco-Tlatelolco—is no less strident, and it seems to revel in its own apocalyptic language and tone:

> Nadie volvió [...] al Volcán. La tierra no dio a sus muertos. Los huesos nunca reverdecieron. Los hombres cambiaron sus armas por instrumentos de labranza: destrales, espadas, carabinas, se transformaron en hoces, coas. [...] Volvieron así a sus originales labores rurales y geórgicas. Y las fuerzas naturales se desencadenaron. Un centellón destrizó y convirtió en chamizo la parota que otrora sirviera para la confesión auricular. Pronto se escucharon ruidos soterraños y la tierra del Volcán, que había permanecido intrépida por largo tiempo, se conmocionó en forma tremebunda y cayó para no levantarse. El santoscali quedó bañado en cardeñas y arenas volcánicas, y tesoros de granizo barrieron el campamento, refugio de la mentira. (439)

The land the Cristeros had animated with religious significance now lies buried under volcanic ash, its survivors spread far and wide, "como el viento solano por los montes" (441). Declaring the Cristeros' stronghold a "sanctuary of deceit," the narrator echoes statements by Mexican government officials who also dismissed the Cristeros' motives. For example, in a speech he delivered during the Cristiada, General J. B. Vargas railed against the Church and those whom he considered to be its blind followers: "The evil clergy [...] is harmful because its mission is to brutalise the ignorant people so as to exploit it and make it fanatical to the point of idiocy" (qtd. in Jean Meyer 29).[20] The tragically ironic aspect of Vargas's sentiment, and the policy it justified, is that the Mexican army hardly fought the clergy during the Cristero Rebellion.[21] Instead, it waged war against the people Vargas presumably wished to protect, most of whom were among Mexico's poorest.[22]

José Trigo's portrayal of the Cristero Rebellion does not challenge the official story. Instead, it reinforces the hegemonic understanding of who the Cristeros were as it employs a narrative style that dominates its subject matter, thereby reproducing the hierarchical, monologic interpretation of experience and history that bolstered the Revolutionary state's claims to legitimacy in its efforts to construct a unified nation. Of course, the two chapters that recount the Cristiada in *José Trigo* are parts of a fictional whole. They contrast with how del Paso's novel portrays the other historical events that concern it, and thus they represent the problems that arise upon desiring and/or maintaining the illusion of the seamless integration of the popular into a coherent national totality.

Jean Meyer calls the government's response to the Rebellion a "colonial war," which was "carried on by a colonial army against its own people" and defined by "the harshness of the repression, the execution of prisoners, the systematic massacre of the civilian population, scorched earth, looting, and rape" (51). Another aspect of this war is the power of language to define the terms of the event and how it is understood for posterity. In her discussion of the discursive colonial legacies that persist in postcolonial India, Gayatri Spivak calls for "a critique of political culture, political culturalism, whose vehicle is the writing of readable histories, mainstream or alternative" ("Who Claims Alterity?" 271). That the chapters "Cristiada (I)" and "Cristiada (II)" are the two most readable sections of *José Trigo* seems to me emblematic of the way, in this instance, the novel mobilizes a colonizing narrative, one that demonstrates how certain populations are cast as less capable of interpreting their own experience and contributing actively to the construction of the nation-state. As Florencia Mallon puts it in her analysis of a government-managed commemorative festival in Xochiapulco, Puebla, where the famous battle of May 5, 1862, was waged victoriously against the French, "only those who march to the right music and the right beat can participate. Such is the nature of the hegemonic impulse" (283). For *José Trigo*, the Cristeros were marching down the wrong path.

V

Though not so grave a threat as was the Cristero Rebellion,[23] the railroad workers' movement of 1958–59 indeed challenged the national-popular state's hegemony. Furthermore, the movement demonstrated the persistence of crucial contradictions in the state's efforts to integrate popular classes that dated back to the 1920s. In one of the conversations that the novel narrates (and which the first-person narrator presumably records), Pedro, the carpenter, asks Buenaventura, Nonoalco-Tlatelolco's matriarch, if she remembers certain workers' struggles of the past, including "la huelga del veintisiete" (460). In his analysis of the historical roots of the movement of 1958–59, Antonio Alonso outlines how the post-Revolutionary consolidation of Mexican labor and its integration into state structures undermined workers' independence. As an example, Alonso mentions the same event that del Paso's fictional character does, the 1927 strike of the Confederación de Transportes y Comunicaciones (CTC). Through the authority of the newly founded government institution known as the Junta Federal de Conciliación y Arbitraje, President Calles declared the CTC strike illegal (Alonso 29). One year later, President Portes Gil began the discussions that led to the establishment of the Ley Federal del Trabajo, which would become "la cristalización de los gobiernos posrevolucionarios en materia laboral" and into which "se depositaron la soberanía y voluntad de los obreros, a fin de que los gobiernos de la Revolución Mexicana pudieran adecuar los momentos a su estrategia y fines y llevaran adelante la defensa de sus intereses" (Alonso 30). To provide an important example of the official discourse surrounding the establishment of the Federal Labor Law, Alonso cites Emilio Portes Gil, whose rhetoric is remarkably similar to the language employed by Uranga and Gamio in their philosophical discussions of the emergence of Mexicanness:

> Cuando todos los [...] trabajadores de la República estén organizados, la industria prosperará y tendrá su mayor desarrollo. Mientras imperen los caprichos y se vaya por caminos diversos, la industria estará a merced de grupos contradictorios. Por eso abogamos por la creación de núcleos de resistencia y de previsión económica y pedimos a las industrias que, sin desconocer los derechos de los trabajadores, se organicen para que juntos contribuyan al desarrollo de la industria mexicana. (31–32)[24]

Portes Gil predicts a future of unity and prosperity based upon the organization of Mexican workers into a whole as yet non-existent but whose bright prospects already appear on the horizon. In 1936, another milestone of the government's incorporation of labor was reached with the formation of the Confederación de Trabajadores de México (CTM), an organization whose power over Mexican workers was to grow in the following decades, especially under the rule of its most notorious leader, Fidel Velázquez.[25]

Founded in the winter of 1932–33, the Sindicato de Trabajadores Ferrocarrileros de la República Mexicana (STFRM) was to follow a rocky path in its association with the CTM, from which it removed itself in 1948 (Alonso 72–74). Alonso summarizes the overall context of Mexican labor by the late 1940s as marked by the division between those who supported the CTM and those who struggled for more independent unions, like many members of the STFRM (79–81). The fictional conflict portrayed in *José Trigo* corresponds to the actual conflict between the STFRM and the predominant railroad concern, Ferrocarriles Nacionales de México (FNM), which took place between summer 1958 and spring 1959. Disputes arose around a number of issues, including salaries, benefits, and housing. But perhaps the most stubborn sticking point was the independence many union members desired, particularly regarding their ability to elect local and national leaders who were not beholden to the government's or the FNM's interests, or, in the common Mexican term for corrupt labor leaders, those who were not *charros* (Alonso 110–21).[26]

The violence exercised by the state against the members of the STFRM who demanded independent union leadership was reinforced by the CTM's discursive delegitimation of the resisting workers. For example, in a speech he delivered to the 59th National Congress of the CTM on August 28, 1958, Fídel Velázquez appeals to Revolutionary unity while denouncing those who do not tow the line. Referring to the CTM's active role in public policy, he states:

> Nuestra intervención [en la política nacional] se efectúa en función de un compromiso solemne en condiciones de dignidad y decoro con el propósito de fortalecer las instituciones nacionales y con el mejor deseo de servir a la causa que representa la Revolución Mexicana, que es la misma que

> sostiene el proletariado.[…] La maniobra parte de distintos puntos, pero con un sólo objetivo: crear el caos y la anarquía en todos los aspectos de la vida nacional. […] los que figuran como cabecillas de esos movimientos carecen de autoridad moral para realizar [sus propósitos de depuración sindical]. (qtd. in Alonso 130–31)

Velázquez's cynical appeals to unity and the common cause that the Revolution and the proletariat allegedly share were echoed months later in the spring of 1959 when government officials justified their repression against striking workers, which effectively ended the STFRM's movement by April (Alonso 151–52). Using language similar to the discourse that, less than a decade later, would attempt to justify the government's murderous suppression of the Student Movement of 1968, a political leader who would also figure prominently at that time as mayor of Mexico City, Alfonso Corona del Rosal, condemns the STFRM as a grave threat to national stability:

> Es indiscutible que los paros ferrocarrileros, que se venían realizando fuera de toda ley y de todo derecho, en perjuicio a la nación, fuesen reprimidos. Como revolucionario lamento sinceramente que gentes que obran diciendo que sostienen ideas profundamente revolucionarias y enarbolan la bandera de la depuración sindical hayan obrado tan torpemente en perjuicio del ideal revolucionario. (qtd. in Alonso 155)

For Alonso, the repression and its justification stemmed naturally from a by-then deeply rooted political system structured around the ideology of the Revolution. Those who stepped off of "cauces institucionales" became a threat that the state would have to "encauzar" or "suprimir" "para que el orden constitucional no se debilitara o quebrara" (155).

Yet, as Alonso argues, the repression against the STFRM's movement actually exposed a weakness in the national-popular state's hegemony. The movement made dramatically public the deep roots of labor corruption and the lengths to which the state would go to maintain order. In Alonso's words, "los gobernantes mexicanos aceptaron que *se había roto el orden legal para mantener el orden político*, lo cual habla por sí solo de la magnitud que llegó a cobrar la movilización oficial contra el movimiento independiente de los ferrocarrileros" (152–53;

original emphasis). Although the years just after the railroad workers' conflict transpired without producing a serious challenge to the government (Aguilar Camín and Meyer 221), the combination of repression and bombastic discursive delegitimation that characterized the government's response foreshadowed the events of 1968, which would indeed challenge and even undermine state hegemony.[27]

The claims to unity made by official leaders like Fidel Velázquez and Alfonso Corona del Rosal justify repression in the name of protecting Mexico and "the collectivity," and of preserving order in "all facets of national life." Though perhaps not surprising, their rhetoric is emblematic of how individuals within the government help construct the state they serve as an entity with privileged access to totality, which is an effort to legitimize the power the government exercises in order, ostensibly, to direct national life toward the stated goals of "strengthening national institutions" and carrying out the "Revolutionary ideal."

VI

The official discourse that ultimately justified state violence in both the Cristero Rebellion and the STFRM strike constructs history by inserting events into an all-encompassing narrative whose actual goal is to legitimize domination. The portrayal of the railroad workers' strike in *José Trigo* resists this kind of history, even while the novel's depiction of the Cristero Rebellion fosters a readable version of events that bolsters the hegemonic understanding, and consolidation, of post-Revolutionary Mexico. An insistence on coherent, readable narratives produces subaltern stories and means of ordering the past. For example, successfully animating the past and contributing to how history remembers them is a capability denied the Cristeros in dominant Mexican historiography and in del Paso's novel.[28] In *José Trigo*, their efforts to create a Kingdom of Heaven on Earth fail, and, in the third-person narrator's words, the area surrounding the Volcano of Colima "did not give up its dead" and "the bones never came to life again."

Resurrection is a well-developed theme in *José Trigo*, and a topic often treated by the secondary literature.[29] The novel's railroad worker narrative begins its climactic sequence with a scene of popular resurrection that could hardly be described in more different terms from those used to portray the Cristeros' defeat. This description of a popular success is emblematic of the novel's sympathetic portrayal of the railroad workers' strike, especially when compared with its portrayal of the Cristiada. Furthermore, the strike narrative, through both form and content, reiterates the value of dialogic, collective processes of narration, which also structure the novel's framing narrative.

Fernando del Paso began writing *José Trigo* in April 1959, the month when the railroad workers' movement was finally defeated. As stated earlier, his novel shifts the events of the movement from 1958–59 to 1960. Furthermore, del Paso fictionalizes the movement's conclusion by depicting the government's repression as culminating in a massacre inside the Church of Santiago Tlatelolco.[30] Del Paso's fictionalization of the movement focuses on one of its actual, principal conflicts, namely, the question of independent leadership. *José Trigo* contrasts Luciano, the honest local union leader, to the corrupt Manuel Ángel. Forced to go into hiding for fear of being killed by those who are betraying the union, Luciano emerges to confront Manuel Ángel, who murders him. No one but Manuel Ángel and José Trigo, who witnessed the murder, knows what has happened to Luciano, and many workers begin to doubt his integrity. The novel's support for the movement and its rejection of the government's repression are structured around the reappearance of Luciano's body, which leads the workers to acknowledge his honesty and which strengthens their resolve to resist the government. Luciano is collectively resurrected in a scene that portrays how people animate their own experience and stories in a very different way from how the novel depicts the Cristeros' overwhelming defeat and erasure from history.

A few days after his murder, a group of workers discovers Luciano's body, hidden in an abandoned blue car. They immediately begin spreading the news, shouting Luciano's name. A crowd gathers around the car. It grows quickly, and eventually covers the encampments, extending from either side of the railroad tracks that run next to the car and through Nonoalco-Tlatelolco. For a moment, Luciano comes alive, animated by the workers' hope that he is not dead. His name, in turn, animates the crowd:

> la palabra [Luciano] cayó en el centro como una piedra en el agua, y todos la fueron repitiendo, cada vez más alto, y la multitud que se había reunido alrededor del viejo automóvil azul se empezó a ondular, y cada onda fue cada vez más grande, cada grito más fuerte, cada voltear de rostros para decírselo a los de atrás, más violento y alegre. (505)

The power of Luciano's name overrides the realization that he has been dead for days. At first, only the workers close to the blue car know they have found a cadaver, but this knowledge expands through the crowd after Luciano, somehow, has been transferred from the car to a blue handcar that rolls down the railroad tracks.[31] The growing acknowledgment of Luciano's death infuses the crowd gradually with silence: "Pero nadie supo por qué, si allí venía Luciano [...] el grito se fue colando en la tierra, [...] por qué [...] el silencio se dejó venir desde la torre y despacio, muy despacio, fue devorando al grito" (509). The silence consumes the crowd's jubilation and signals the need for a dual process of reconstruction and invention as the workers acknowledge the fact that at the foundational center of their community lies an absence. They undertake this task collectively as each person gathers up a memory along with a piece of Luciano's body: "Todos se fueron repartiendo a Luciano. A unos les tocó un ojo. A otros les tocó un dedo. [...] Y cada uno de todos los hombres [...] se fueron repartiendo sus pedazos, se los fueron llevando poco a poco. Porque nadie pudo verlo entero" (509–10). The workers dismember Luciano's cadaver in order to re-member it later as the foundation of their political identity.

The bits and pieces of information that the narrator learns about José Trigo and the train yards eventually form a whole as well, but only through a collaborative effort—a gathering of testimonies—that animates it. The way the workers reconstruct Luciano is actually an allegory of how the narrator reconstructs the train yards and the events that occurred there. For instance, just as Luciano's death leaves an absence at the center of the whole the workers form, José Trigo, whom the narrator never finds, remains the primary absence that motivates the novel. The value of intermediacy, of negotiation and dialogue, is another trait shared by the workers' resurrection of Luciano and the narrator's resurrection of Nonoalco-Tlatelolco. For the narrator, intermediacy emerges from the network of objects and people that comprise the novel's landscape, like reciprocal gazes, watchtowers, and their reflections. For Luciano's fellow workers, intermediacy is produced by their conversations and, in the moment of Luciano's resurrection, by the railroad tracks and the specific speed of the handcar that carries Luciano through the crowd.

The pace of Luciano's handcar is described in a complex sentence that is paradigmatic of the density of most of the novel's use of language. It moves "demasiado aprisa para darse cuenta que todo el cuerpo de Luciano estaba muerto, y demasiado despacio para darse cuenta que nada vivía ya en Luciano" (510). Suspended between limits of speed and slowness, Luciano now exists in the space between two kinds of death, one defined positively ("Luciano's body was dead") and one defined negatively ("nothing lived anymore"). The workers perceive Luciano's persistent existence as two forms of negativity: not death and not not-living. This perception is contradicted by what the narrator and the readers know to be a fact, that Luciano is indeed dead. Yet to those who witness Luciano's journey in the handcar, his actual death is meaningless. He exists to them, literally, in a state of suspended animation. More meaningful to the workers is their perception of his state of non-death and non non-living, an intermediacy reminiscent of Borges's magician, who does not die when flames engulf him, who does not live in the way he imagined himself to live, but who also does not non-live, who persists as a member of the affective community of animated beings. In this episode, del Paso's novel radically rejects the construction of a positive, empirically identifiable, and thus capturable foundation of community. Instead, it proposes a community based on the dialogic negotiation of lack, which results in the animation of a being gradually acknowledged to be absent.

The workers animate Luciano in a process that ultimately animates them, a process of community-building that begins when their gazes intersect, forming a network of perspectives and intermediate spaces that organizes all they know about Luciano. After the carriage passes between them, the workers "sólo se encontraron con los ojos de los hombres que estaban en la otra valle, al otro lado de las vías, y que también habían visto a Luciano, y callaban, y los miraban" (510). Eventually, Luciano is made whole through the memories that the workers communicate amongst themselves: "Y así fue con los labios y con la nariz y con la gorra azul y con los dedos de los pies. Todos se los fueron llevando adentro. Todos fueron recordando cómo era Luciano" (511).

Yet the workers determine less about how Luciano actually was than they project their needs and desires on his absence. Luciano is conjured by the collective will to resurrect him, which in turn is fueled by his indeterminate return to the train yards. The way the workers make sense of Luciano's appearance can be understood as functioning like a Derridean trace, that site "where the relationship with the other is marked" (*Grammatology* 47), and whose instability makes signification possible. In Derrida's view, traditional metaphysics relies on the notion of fully accessible presence, which conceals the radical heterogeneity of meaning and turns the relationship with the other into a relationship of sameness. By transforming heterogeneity into homogeneity the imposition of presence legitimizes fixed meaning, capture, and violent definition. In *José Trigo*, Luciano is presented explicitly as an entity whose meaning is negotiated and never fully determined. It is precisely his suspended existence that allows his fellow workers to make meaning out of him. Luciano's indeterminate return allows the workers to animate him as he, in turn, animates them.

The collective realization of Luciano's death suggests the foundation of a new community when it does not discourage the workers, but instead proves to them that Luciano was a trustworthy figure. "Si lo mataron es prueba que no nos traicionaba" (513), proclaims one railroad worker. A martyr, Luciano is endowed by death with more political power than he had while alive, grounding the workers' faith in him and in themselves. In a clear allusion to biblical resurrection, the collective embodies this faith three days later. The reference to a three-day period is hardly the only Christian reference that informs the novel's portrayal of Luciano's reappearance. For example, his body parts become relics as the workers construct a hagiography around his absence.[32] As this construction continues, however, Luciano's specificity fades and it is gradually replaced by the workers' collective identity, which ultimately emerges as primary.

When the workers begin to talk about Luciano, they slowly put him back together through dialogue. Their discussion eventually leads to political activism in the form of a massive demonstration, which includes all of the train yards' inhabitants.[33] As they reach an agreement about Luciano's loyalty, the workers continue talking, and gradually become aware of their political power and what they can achieve if they reconstruct Luciano by remembering him: "Y todos fueron hablando así, uno por uno. No hubo una sola vez que una voz se mezclara con otra. Lo fueron haciendo por turno [...] Entonces fue cuando apareció Luciano. Cuando cada quien fue poniendo el pedazo que había guardado" (513). Each worker contributes words and a piece of Luciano to a dialogic process that does not reconstruct Luciano so much as it constructs the strikers' collective subjectivity through Luciano's suspended existence.

VII

The subjectivity the workers construct through dialogue exists only briefly, as an ephemeral ideal constructed around its association with Luciano, and also with the elusive José Trigo. Significantly, this collectively constructed subjectivity permits the workers brief access to a totalizing order akin to the sublime. In fact, the strongest allusion to the sublime feeling in *José Trigo* occurs during the railroad workers' final demonstration, when they become José Trigo in a transformation that takes place amidst the delirium of activity that leads up to the charged, climactic finish to the strike narrative.[34] The content of these pages—the rapid access to totality and that vision's violent and sudden destruction—represents a rush to present everything at once, transmitted in passages remarkable for their accelerated pace and condensed language:

> Y nosotros que éramos José Trigo, nosotros estábamos allí, en el atrio del templo de Santiago [...] fuimos un hombre bañado por la luz; así nos vieron, así nos viste tú, tú que tenías mil caras también bañadas por la luz de las antorchas, y así nos vimos nosotros, reflejados dos veces en tus ojos y mil veces despedazados en los cristales de sudor que cubrían tu piel. (514)

This dialogic process of auto-construction continues as the crowd describes how it follows its own tracks in a process that recalls the narrator's search for José Trigo, pursuing his vanishing trail through the encampments. Like the crowd's cohesion, the footprints it follows last only an instant: "sobre la tierra de este campamento, sobre esta tierra nuestra de José Trigo [...] cada uno, cada dos dejan huellas cada paso, cada dos, huellas que duran lo que un parpadeo" (515). The crowd follows itself and comes to know itself in a process that leads to an apotheosis of totalizing vision: "hombro con hombro fuimos llevado *casi en vilo* nosotros José Trigo que vimos: con nuestros grandes ojos al tamaño de todo lo que se puede mirar de una vez" (517; my emphasis). Now it is the workers who appear in a state of suspended animation, from which they are afforded a glimpse of the historical totality of which they have become a part.

Immediately after, however, their totalizing vision is destroyed by the army: "en el atrio del templo del Señor Santiago, se derrumba el mundo, se desmorona en luces, piedras, polvo y estrellas: llegó el ejército, llovió sangre, se apagó el canto de los escogidos [...] y el fuego, el olor a azufre, el humo de la pólvora, una inmensa nube blanca ...." (523). The narrative then moves abruptly from the destruction of the world the workers had established inside the temple to a seemingly strange admission, which exposes the narrator's inability to communicate the access to totality the workers, so briefly, gained: "Y yo no he contado todavía tu historia" (523). In this way, *José Trigo* refuses to posit itself as enjoying privileged, sustainable access to sublime order, which is a gesture fundamental to the representative authority that *La región más transparente* attempts to sustain.

VIII

José Trigo's portrayal of the railroad workers' movement rejects the reason of state to which the novel appeals in its depiction of the Cristero Rebellion. The workers' defeat in the Church of Santiago is anything but victory over an "encampment of lies," as the third-person narrator characterized the destruction of the Cristeros' base at the Volcano of Colima. It is instead a violent repression of popular knowledge and popular access to history;

and it is also a prelude to the destruction of the encampments where the workers lived. The new Nonoalco-Tlatelolco no longer communicates the past. The train whistles that reverberate through its sterile spaces carry nothing with them.

But is it true that the narrator has "still not told [their] story"? First, the processes of reciprocal animation that occur when the workers discover themselves through Luciano's cadaver and during the demonstration that evokes José Trigo, are processes that also describe the dialogic construction that goes on between the narrator and the train yards. Nonoalco-Tlatelolco is a community animated, but not contained, by the novel. And it is in fact the community's absence—not the presupposition of its presence, which would enable its capture—that continues to produce effects for the narrator and the novel's readers, effects that suggest potential relations and communities that are not prescribed by totalizing, homogenizing impulses.

It is worth returning to the novel's final pages in order to elucidate further the allegorical relationship between Luciano's resurrection and the narrator's reconstruction of the train yards. The novel's final two sentences read "Nada bajo el cielo. Y sobre la tierra, nadie" (536). Clearly, the footsteps the demonstrating workers left on "our land of José Trigo" have long since vanished, as they endured for so little time. But what does lie in this space of bound absence, defined by two negatives? It is not absolute death, nor is it positive life, but instead it is something intermediate, like the rate of Luciano's speed on the handcar. Fernando del Paso's novel animates the popular in a way similar to the operation carried out by Borges's magician. *José Trigo*'s narrator can make no claim to originary authority. Instead he chronicles absence, filling in gaps but only ephemerally. The novel's conclusion attests to the rejection of positivity and it embodies once again an explicit acknowledgment of the function of the trace, the absence at the heart of signification, and thus the illusory nature of presence. In the end, *José Trigo*'s totalizing vision of Mexico's history stops short of fixing identities and capturing the popular. The novel gradually constructs the decadence of the national-popular state and its corresponding epistemology, which is based on the projection of an access to a positive, identifiable totality. The novel does not challenge the state's violent foundations through its portrayal of the Cristero Rebellion, but it rejects their corrupting legacy, as demonstrated by the repression of the railroad workers' strike.

The novel's condemnation of the Cristero Rebellion and its legitimizing representation of the railroad workers' movement present contrasting views of popular identity formation. The Cristeros' attempts to establish a Kingdom of Heaven on Earth fail, and the novel's third-person narrator obliterates the space that could have served as a site of resurrection. The workers who mobilize themselves around Luciano's reappearance are presented as engaging in a productive, dialogic process of animation with the potential to challenge the state, a process that also poses a challenge to the kind of hierarchical state thinking that *José Trigo* ultimately refuses to reproduce. I conclude that *José Trigo*'s ambivalence toward popular mobilization—reflected in the contrasting ways it defines the Cristero Rebellion and the workers' movement—corresponds to the way that the novel gradually undermines its own claims to epistemological superiority. Its animation of the past undergoes a shift that suggests an increasing awareness of originary violence and its negative effects on the production of knowledge; it is as if *José Trigo* were wrestling with itself, which seems to me an apt metaphor for such a heterogeneous text. *José Trigo* moves from a first-order totalizing construction of the Cristero Rebellion to a second-order totalizing vision that negates the forced articulation of the popular with the national. An emphasis on disarticulation informs the novel's conclusion, when the narrator is left to pick up the words that have sprung from his shattered heart, his own signifying absence. Because it animates, and does not capture, the train yards, *José Trigo* keeps Nonoalco-Tlatelolco alive without claiming to have the last word. In fact, the novel rejects the very concept of the last word, and leaves the future open by not engraving its reconstruction of the past on something like Uranga's vault, by not fixing history's trajectory within a preconceived future.

Chapter Three

The Stained Plaza

María Luisa Mendoza's *Con Él, conmigo, con nosotros tres* and the Origins of the Mestizo Nation

María Luisa Mendoza's first novel, *Con Él, conmigo, con nosotros tres* (1971), is one of the earliest literary interpretations of the Tlatelolco massacre. A fictionalized, multi-perspective, semi-autobiographical account subtitled "*cronovela*," *Con Él* combines narrative and chronicle by telling the story of its protagonist, Delfina Zebadúa Latino, alongside journalistic and poetic descriptions of October 2 and its immediate aftermath.[1] Delfina, a young woman who lives in an apartment overlooking the Plaza of the Three Cultures during the Student Movement and on the night of the massacre, responds to Tlatelolco by trying desperately to write down her thoughts about Mexico and the violence that has characterized its history. Frustrated by her inability to capture contemporary events, let alone her feelings of impotence about them, Delfina reflects on the historical trajectory of her paternal ancestors, the Zebadúa family, whose decline and fall the novel traces in tandem with three bloody historical events: President Benito Juárez's defense of his power in 1871, the "Decena Trágica" of 1913 when General Victoriano Huerta ordered the assassination of Ignacio Madero, and Tlatelolco.

The earliest period the novel relates, which extends from the 1870s to the final years of the nineteenth century, centers around the story of Delfina's paternal grandmother, Altagracia Albarrán de Zebadúa, who, like Delfina, also speaks in the first person. Altagracia is unhappily married and sick of bearing her hated husband's children. When giving birth to her twelfth child, she refuses to open her legs in an act of resistance that grants her the terrible refuge of death from the miserable life she has suffered under her husband's rule. As a consequence, Altagracia does not appear in a portrait taken in 1901 of Delfina's paternal grandfather (Altagracia's husband), his mother, and his twelve children. This particular photograph triggers Delfina's memory and attains tremendous symbolic significance when, fantastically, it is restaged almost seventy years later in Delfina's Tlatelolco apartment. The series of violent events that leads to Delfina's present continues, following Altagracia's death, when Altagracia's tenth child, Manuel Zebadúa Albarrán, who is also Delfina's father, finds himself driving a makeshift ambulance and collecting the dead and wounded left scattered on Mexico City's streets during the Decena Trágica. Manuel's story, recounted by Delfina in the first person, eventually leads to Delfina's occasionally second-person reflections on her childhood and early adult life, which emphasize her troubled relationship with her mother, Angustias Latino Ceballos, her early education at a Catholic school in Guanajuato, the summers she spent with her aunts in their crumbling, colonial-era Mexico City home, and her inability to bear children. The novel's roundabout approach to the present concludes, chronologically speaking, with the third-person description of Delfina's cousin, Juan Ruvalcaba Zebadúa, a student who dies in the massacre. The narrative ends when Delfina's dead relatives, including Juan, enter her apartment, pose for one last family portrait and prefigure Delfina's death as well.

In contrast to *La región* and *José Trigo*, *Con Él* is profoundly affected by a single historical event, the Tlatelolco massacre. Though the novel connects Tlatelolco to previous moments of violence in Mexico's history, the 1968 massacre frames the narrative and forces Delfina to ask the text's most pressing and relevant question: how does one narrate such a trauma? The novel itself stands as a response. Its ironic use of language and pronounced intertextuality help to produce a portrayal of people and events that refuses to insert them into a dominant vision of national history. The Mexican state attempted to construct Tlatelolco as a tragic but necessary guarantee of public order and collective progress and, perversely, an opportunity for Mexico to renew itself. In specific terms, *Con Él* contests the state's construction of events. As a result, in general terms, it reveals and refuses to engage in the kind of originary thinking that pretended to legitimize Tlatelolco. This chapter proposes that Mendoza's novel combines reflections on violence, language, writing, gender roles, and sexuality in order to reject a patriarchal social order not only capable of carrying out a massacre like Tlatelolco, but also of integrating it into the national narrative.

The novel's wholesale rejection of the national narrative is another trait that distinguishes it significantly from Fuentes's and del Paso's novels. Even though *José Trigo* ultimately undermines the dominant totalizing vision and its exclusive epistemology that Fuentes's novel reproduces, its portrayal of the Cristero Rebellion gives some credence to the hegemonic vision of Mexico's post-Revolutionary history. The characters in *Con Él*, by contrast, find no refuge whatsoever in the vault of integrative, totalizing historiography. The novel assembles a strong feminist critique of Mexican society that exposes the connections between state violence and patriarchal understandings of women's roles and family structures. *Con Él* also reflects upon the degree to which the process of writing is implicated in the perpetuation of dominance over women and other marginalized groups, like students. In particular, the novel introduces the term *pleonasm*, which denotes redundancy, into a number of different contexts with the result of deconstructing socially formed distinctions between what is "necessary" and "superfluous." The novel often associates these distinctions with sex and violence, emphasizing their real, sometimes deadly, consequences.

Manipulating different uses of the term *pleonasm*, which implicitly calls into question the relevance of any word, reinforces the novel's ironic style. The distance afforded Delfina by irony and wordplay allow her to separate her experience from dominant narratives of history and society, but only to a limited degree. The novel does not propose that Delfina can achieve total independence from the discursive structures that shape her and her family's lives. Unlike the female characters in Fuentes's novel—Hortensia Chacón, Norma Larragoiti, and Gladys García especially—Delfina is actively engaged in constructing her own subjectivity. Even though Delfina's resistance to dominant discourse only achieves limited results, Mendoza's novel's feminist critique of history and language strikes at the heart of processes of signification that reproduce domination and justify different types of socially legitimated and state-sponsored violence, including the subjection of women and the murder of students.

The main target of the novel's critique is originary thinking, which grounds narrative authority. My analysis thus identifies the different forms this critique adopts in *Con Él*. To that end, this chapter moves from a discussion of feminism and intertextuality—which incorporates the observations of feminist critics Julia Kristeva, Rosario Castellanos, and Luz Elena Gutiérrez de Velasco, among others—to a thorough exposition and deconstruction of the discourse leaders of the Mexican government employed in their attempts to justify Tlatelolco. In light of the massive, and ongoing, cultural response to Tlatelolco, with the aim of better contextualizing Mendoza's text this chapter also provides a brief synopsis of other representations of the Student Movement and the massacre. Regarding pertinent examples of intertextual reference in Mendoza's novel, I focus on Octavio Paz's poem "Intermitencias del oeste (3)" (1968), which he wrote in response to the massacre, and the plaque proclaiming the birth of Mexico as a mestizo nation that dedicated the Plaza of the Three Cultures in 1964.[2] After discussing the relationships between oppression, writing, and childbirth that inform Delfina's narrative, the chapter concludes by looking at the family photograph that inspires Delfina to write.

I

According to the *Oxford English Dictionary* a pleonasm is a statement that uses more words than necessary. Thus the term aims to designate which words are essential and which are superfluous. In Mendoza's novel, pleonasm also takes on a sexual connotation when it distinguishes between allegedly "productive" sexual activity, i.e., intercourse that results in pregnancy, and so-called redundant sexual activity, such as female orgasm and masturbation. The association of the central trope of pleonasm with intercourse, birth, and masturbation in Mendoza's novel connects linguistic expression—i.e., deciding which words are necessary and which words are not—with pleasure and procreation, either of a child or, in Delfina's case, her novel. For Delfina, who, like Mendoza at the time, is an aspiring woman writer, both linguistic and sexual expression help her establish a degree of independence. But Delfina fails to wrest herself completely from the constraints of the personal and collective histories that have shaped her life and her understanding of it.

The feminist critique of Mexican society in *Con Él* focuses in particular on the expectation that women are to be mothers charged with reproducing the patriarchal family structure.[3] The novel's response to this expectation is the text itself, which can be understood in line with the following observation Julia Kristeva makes about writing: "When a woman novelist does not reproduce a real *family* of her own, she creates an imaginary story through which she constitutes an identity" (Marks and de Courtivron 166; original emphasis). And as the author of her text, Delfina produces a type of motherhood that is involved in contesting signification, a suitable task for this novel that resists state ideology, patriarchy, and how both discursive constructs reproduce dominant narratives of the nation.[4]

Though Mendoza herself rejected the label of feminist in an interview that followed the publication of *Con Él*,[5] her novel's critique of patriarchy enacts what Rosario Castellanos, writing shortly after *Con Él*'s publication, calls: "La osadía [por parte de la mujer] de indagar sobre sí misma; la necesidad de hacerse consciente acerca del significado de la propia existencia corporal [...] la inaudita pretensión de conferirle un significado a la propia existencia espiritual, [esfuerzos que son] duramente reprimida y castigada por el aparato social" (*Mujer* 15). In her analysis of *Con Él* from 1995—more than twenty years after the novel was published—Luz Elena Gutiérrez de Velasco rightly condemns the undeserved, scholarly disregard for Mendoza's practically forgotten text. She argues that it deserves further consideration for its innovative take on literary genre, its critique of the patrilineal family history, and its use of language, which calls attention to the constructed nature of social norms through its struggle against historically ingrained dominant narratives (327). Gutiérrez de Velasco concludes that *Con Él* ultimately portrays Delfina's regeneration through writing, which leads her to attain a mature, stable identity (327). But the novel presents a process that is more defined by unresolved tensions than a positive step toward renewal. *Con Él*'s critique of writing and its relation to history does not allow so easily for the kind of originary thinking that an evocation of renewal necessarily presupposes.

The novel's critique of originary thinking is developed through its rich intertextuality. For example, the novel's final description of the crucially significant portrait of Delfina's ancestors includes the following allusion to Tlatelolco: "En la plaza los empleados municipales lavan con cepillos la sangre seca" (185). By referring to the bloodstains on the Plaza of the Three Cultures as part of the description of a family portrait whose matriarch, Altragracia, is absent because she fought to the death against bearing her last child, Mendoza's text connects Delfina's ancestry to that of the nation through its association of violence and origins. Furthermore, the novel foregrounds different surfaces upon which personal and national histories are inscribed: the photograph, the plaza, and the written page. Finally, *Con Él*'s reference to bloodstains also exemplifies its intertextual character, as the phrase about municipal workers is borrowed from Paz's poem "Intermitencias." Other intertextual references in the novel include nursery rhymes, children's songs, and additional literary texts. The title of Mendoza's novel, for example, is taken from José Gorostiza's *Muerte sin fin* (1939).

Intertextuality, in Kristeva's terms the "transposition of one (or several) sign system(s) into another" (59–60), presupposes the incompleteness of a given sign system. The production of meaning, according to Kristeva's analysis, never emerges from a pure origin. Instead, Kristeva writes, making sense is a "signifying practice," whose "'place' of enunciation and its denoted 'object' are never single, complete, and identical to themselves, but always plural, shattered, capable of being tabulated" (60).

The critique of coherence that Mendoza's novel advances corresponds to what Kristeva has also argued regarding writing and subjectivity, a relationship that bears on the limited independence that *Con Él* ultimately grants Delfina. In a 1974 interview originally published in *Tel Quel*, Kristeva proposes that

> Women who write are brought [...] to see sexual differentiation as interior to the praxis of every subject. [...] If women have a role to play in this on-going process [of production of symbolic meaning] it is only in assuming a *negative* function: reject everything finite, definite, structured, loaded

> with meaning, in the existing state of society. (Marks and de Courtivron 166; original emphasis)

Observing that this negative "feminine" position—which is neither essential nor absolute in Kristeva's thought—can be subsumed into a dominant "phallic" process of signification, Kristeva continues and explains that this position's critical potential is a function of its rejection of coherent subjectivity: "No 'I' is there to assume this 'femininity,' but it is no less operative, rejecting all that is finite and assuring in (*sexual*) *pleasure* the life of the concept. 'I,' subject of a conceptual quest, is also a subject of differentiation—of sexual contradictions" (Marks and de Courtivron 167; original emphasis). Mendoza's novel assembles revealing connections among the experiences of sexual pleasure, writing, and the violence of dominant subjectification that, like Kristeva's analysis of feminist subjectivity, resist coherent definition.

Con Él mobilizes these connections in its critique of the way the state justified Tlatelolco. In order to understand how Mendoza's text dismantles dominant discourse in the case of Tlatelolco, it is necessary to turn now to that event and the state's attempt to incorporate the massacre into a totalizing narrative of the Mexican nation by appealing to definite and finite processes of establishing meaning. Within the context of the government's totalizing appeals to Mexico's past and its future, the most sinister of such appeals was the deadly decision regarding who was and who was not a Mexican citizen, or, in reference to the novel's use of the term *pleonasm*, who was essential and who was redundant.

II

On a rainy Wednesday evening on the second day of October 1968, a bright green flare appeared in the sky over Mexico City's Plaza de Tlatelolco. Thousands of people were assembled below, about half of them soldiers, police, and other members of diverse and in some cases clandestine security forces. The remainder, some 8,000,[6] were either striking students or their sympathizers, participants in a movement that began in late July and gathered strength in ebbs and flows through August and September. Many recall seeing the flare, or *luz de bengala*. Although this sign's meaning was obscure to almost everyone there, to a select few its message was clear. For officers in the secret service and the judicial police, and for snipers hired by officials in the highest levels of the government to position themselves in various places around the Plaza, the *luz de bengala* was their signal to begin firing. A particularly sinister detail of the operation was that the snipers—whose presence was known to only a handful of government officials—fired deliberately on José Hernández Toledo, a general in the Mexican Army. As soon as Hernández Toledo was wounded, his troops responded by firing on the crowd of demonstrators, and terrible chaos ensued.[7] Whatever the purpose of the government's violent crackdown, its meaning was quickly lost in translation. As an effort to end what has come to be known as the Mexican Student Movement of 1968, it succeeded. As an effort to legitimize the government's authority, it failed. An important consequence of this failure was that it opened spaces from which Mexicans began to criticize their government in a manner unprecedented for its breadth, its longevity, and its origins in the country's privileged intellectual classes. The shots the flare cued, intended to close the book on a period of social conflict, instead initiated a process of interpretation of that conflict and its revelations about Mexican politics that continues to reverberate almost 40 years after the shots were fired. In the end, the government's totalizing appeal to the nation's past and future in its explanation of Tlatelolco exposed the cynicism and bankruptcy of post-Revolutionary ideology.

Before and after Tlatelolco, Mexico's government leaders and institutions attempted to sustain the state's legitimacy by constructing its recourse to violence as necessary for preserving the social order, and as cathartic for providing Mexico with an opportunity to renew itself. The government-controlled mass media generally portrayed the massacre as a fight between student snipers and a besieged military.[8] Official statements helped establish and legitimize this scenario.[9] On October 12, the Olympic Games began, burying the massacre under the celebration of Mexico's so-called entrance into modernity.[10] Survivors were imprisoned for months and even years, their testimonies suppressed and discredited. Not until the 1990s were there investigations into what happened.[11] No government official has ever stood trial, let alone been convicted, though recent efforts have been made to prosecute Luis Echeverría Álvarez, the secretary of *gobernación* (a position similar to Britain's Home Secretary) in 1968 who would become president in 1970.[12]

Before the massacre, the government laid the foundation for justifying whatever repressive acts it might determine to be necessary. Its predominant strategy was to delegitimize the Student Movement, as it had the striking members of the STFRM a decade earlier. Government officials portrayed adherents to the Movement as either aggressive delinquents or confused ingénues; either powerful actors who threatened Mexico's national security or weak puppets controlled by insidious foreign interests.[13] Radically vacillating portraits of perceived enemies were common in the discourse of the hysterically paternalistic national-popular state, embodied in the late 1960s by the particularly rigid Díaz Ordaz.[14] Exaggerating either the weakness or strength of students legitimized two of the state's central roles: the stern yet worried teacher who helps misguided youth or the merciless father who punishes traitors. The distinction between these roles ultimately traced a bright line that determined who did and who did not deserve to be called a Mexican citizen. In his study of Mexican educational ideology, historian Héctor Aguilar Camín cites a speech in which Díaz Ordaz responds to student unrest in 1966. His words reveal a Manichean understanding of the nation's youth and establish the parameters that determine what "Mexico"—described here as somehow both separate from and comprised of the youth—must encourage and what it must reject:

> Nos decepcionaría una juventud conformista o resignada, pero México tampoco quiere una juventud irresponsable que abrace con incauta pasión todas las causas, que se tome como instrumento dócil al servicio de intereses bastardos o como caja de resonancia de estériles desahogos. México necesita una juventud atenta a los rumbos que sigue la Patria y actuando apasionada, pero racionalmente, para beneficio del pueblo del que forma parte entrañable. ("Desde" 104)

Two years later, young Mexicans felt the true weight of Díaz Ordaz's words when the consequences of crossing the lines between resignation and irresponsible behavior and between reason and passion became absolute.

The symbolic importance of where the government carried out the massacre is as overwhelming as it is obvious.[15] When the state sponsored the construction of modern high-rise apartment and office buildings to complement the Aztec ruins and colonial-era cathedral that had stood there for centuries, it made a deliberate effort to inaugurate the Plaza of the Three Cultures as a monument to Mexico's mestizo heritage and its national unity. This intention is stated explicitly on a large stone tablet erected at Tlatelolco when the Plaza project was officially dedicated by then-President Adolfo López Mateos in 1964 (Fowler 234). The tablet reads,

> El 13 de agosto de 1521
> Heróicamente defendido por Cuauhtémoc
> Cayó Tlatelolco en poder de Hernán Cortés
> No fue triunfo ni derrota
> Fue el doloroso nacimiento del pueblo mestizo
> Que es el México de hoy.

The massacre added another layer of inaugurational meaning to Tlatelolco Plaza by embodying Díaz Ordaz's restrictive notion of citizenship, refounding and cleansing the nation by excluding those accused of failing to fulfill their obligations as productive citizens and threatening national security. Government speeches and documents of the time described a nation suspended between the past and the future.

Adding to the symbolic weight that the conflict between the Student Movement and the government garnered, students also portrayed the national community at a crossroads, with one path leading to an inclusive and effective democracy, and the other to a more repressive consolidation of state power.[16] Initiated primarily as a reaction to government oppression, the Student Movement gradually developed a competing vision of national politics, thus challenging the government's legitimacy.[17] This challenge provoked a shockingly disproportionate government response, which, as a brief look at official statements from 1968 reveals, was justified by appealing to the Constitution and executive authority, and which cast the Student Movement as a potentially devastating threat to the nation's future.

On September 1, 1968, President Díaz Ordaz delivered the fourth annual *informe de gobierno*, or address to the nation, of his six-year term. The speech warns the participants in the Student Movement against continuing their struggle, and it justifies the use of military force as necessary to maintain national security. Reminding Mexicans of Article 89 of their Constitution, Díaz Ordaz emphasizes that it is the responsibility of the executive branch to: "Disponer de la totalidad de la fuerza armada permanente o sea del ejército terrestre, de la marina de guerra y de la fuerza aérea para la *seguridad interior* y la defensa exterior de la Federación" (Ramírez 2: 204; original emphasis).[18] A few paragraphs later, utilizing the same significantly ambivalent "we" that appeared in his 1966 speech, he all but predicts Tlatelolco: "No quisiéramos vernos en el caso de tomar medidas que no deseamos, pero que tomaremos si es necesario; lo que sea nuestro deber hacer, lo haremos; hasta donde estemos obligados a llegar, llegaremos" (205).

Díaz Ordaz's language is as frightening as it is ambiguous. His use of the future and subjunctive tenses emphasizes that he does not specify which measures he—speaking in the name of Mexico—will take nor when he is obliged to take them. He reserves the right to define the moment when the decision to use force is necessary, demonstrating that the power to defend the nation that the Constitution grants him is justified by circumstances that are not and cannot be delineated in any precise manner before they arise. The president's power, to be exercised in an unknown and unknowable future moment, anchors itself in the past by originating from the Constitution. This power, in order to accommodate specific and unpredictable occurrences, must remain flexible. Díaz Ordaz's appeal to the Constitution legitimized his authority and post-Revolutionary Mexico's founding document at the same time, for the actions he would take in Tlatelolco did not simply stem from the authority granted him by the Constitution as if this latter were a static source of power. His actions also interpreted the Constitution, adding meaning to it by stating that it authorized him to act in a specific way in a specific moment.

By referring to the Constitution, Díaz Ordaz appealed to the source of the law in order to preserve the law. But this originary gesture failed to justify the violence of Tlatelolco, and in fact it contributed to the decline of the national-popular state's hegemony. In the terms laid out by Walter Benjamin in his essay

"Critique of Violence" (1920), Díaz Ordaz's words and the repression they authorized speak to the impossibility of absolutely separating "lawmaking" and "law-preserving" violence. Benjamin proposes that the codeterminacy of these two kinds of violence produces the law's decadence: "all law-preserving violence, in its duration, indirectly weakens the lawmaking violence represented by it" (300).[19] The force Díaz Ordaz authorized by referring to the Constitution did not delegitimize the Constitution as much as it undermined the power of the Revolutionary government's appeal to the past. It eroded the government's authority as a custodian of the past whose hegemony depended upon interpreting its own origins as emerging from the Revolution and defining the Revolution as an ongoing struggle for a more united and inclusive nation.

By approving the massacre at Tlatelolco,[20] Díaz Ordaz played out his role as a judge whose decision was guided, but not determined, by the Mexican Constitution. In "Force of Law," like Benjamin before him, Derrida explains how interpreting the law necessarily reconstitutes the law's legitimacy. Derrida focuses on justice and justification, two concepts the Mexican government struggled to monopolize in the wake of Tlatelolco. But the effects of Díaz Ordaz's decision could not be contained. Derrida writes that "To be just, the decision of a judge [...] must not only follow a rule of law or a general law but must also assume it, approve it, confirm its value, by a reinstituting act of interpretation, as if ultimately nothing previously existed of the law, as if the judge himself invented the law in every case" (961). The decision to enforce the law justly requires bridging the necessary separation of the law as it is written from the specific context to which it is applied. This gap appears in Díaz Ordaz's *cuarto informe* when he alludes to a future set of circumstances that will oblige him to exercise his constitutionally sanctioned authority. The challenge for the government becomes suturing that gap in a way that maintains the integrity of the poles that constitute it: the government's decision to use force and the law. The Mexican government in 1968 failed to meet this challenge.

One day after the massacre, the Mexican Senate defended the president's decision, arguing that: "El Senado de la República considera que la actuación del Ejecutivo Federal se ha apegado a la Constitución Política del país y a las leyes vigentes, que le señalan como deber, el mantenimiento de la seguridad interior" (Ramírez 2: 401). On the same day, the Senate also made an effort to place Tlatelolco firmly in the past by appealing to an opportunity for renewal that would restore national integrity. Referring to Díaz Ordaz's famous "mano tendida" speech of August 1, 1968, in which the president extended, although rather cynically, an olive branch to student demonstrators, the Senate proclaimed: "Renovamos el llamamiento que el propio funcionario [el Presidente] hizo a los demás grupos estudiantiles para restablecer la unidad y la armonía nacional, colaborando en el fortalecimiento de nuestras instituciones democráticas" (Ramírez 2: 401).

Since Tlatelolco was explained as necessary for restoring national security and renewing national integrity, the government's failure to justify its use of force—the impossibility of justifying such force—exposed another gap: the disarticulation between the Mexican nation and the Revolutionary state. The national unity and harmony the Senate hoped to restore after Tlatelolco did not exist before the massacre except as the illusory promise of communitarian fullness that grounded the state's hegemony. After Tlatelolco, the viability of this promise became harder, if not impossible to sustain.

III

The official story attempted to define Tlatelolco's violence as tragic yet unavoidable. In addition, it presented the end of the Student Movement as providing the opportunity for Mexico's rebirth. A number of Mexican writers saw things differently, and they tended to be more concerned with what Tlatelolco dismantled than they were sure of what it established. Enunciating a preoccupation with subjectivity that also structures Mendoza's novel, Carlos Monsiváis contends that 1968 transformed his generation by destroying its sense of identity, producing "Un yo devastado por la duda, por la revisión exhaustiva y nerviosa del pasado inmediato" (*Días* 66). Elena Poniatowska defines Tlatelolco as an event of incomprehensible grief, the loss of Mexico's children: "ese grito distorsionado que todo lo rompe, el ay de la herida definitiva, la que no podrá cicatrizar jamás, la de la muerte del hijo" (*Noche* 164). Writing twenty years after Monsiváis and Poniatowska, Paco Ignacio Taibo II dwells on the corrosive doubt that Tlatelolco still engenders: "¿Cómo se guardan volantes en las bolsas de pan? ¿Qué significaba el CNH? ¿Por qué cayó Romeo a causa de una minifalda? ¿Dónde arrojaron a nuestros muertos? [...] ¿Dónde mierdas arrojaron a nuestros muertos?" (13). Taibo angrily communicates the affective and ethical intensity of questions that will probably never be answered. The pain and frustration that his and Poniatowska's words express give credence to Monsiváis's conclusion that "Después de una ingracia injusta, irreperable, impune como la matanza de Tlatelolco, las cosas no vuelven a su lugar. La certidumbre desaparece, las seguridades se eliminan" (*Días* 75).

Not surprisingly, the Mexican government tried to put everything back in its place after Tlatelolco. The official rhetoric that preceded and followed October 2 argued that saving the nation required destroying the Student Movement. From this perspective, Tlatelolco was not ultimately about exclusion. Instead it was meant to maintain the state's inclusionary promise. Yet Mendoza and many others could only see exclusion.[21] This fissure between state ideology and critical narrative, fictional or otherwise, simply could not have existed with such intensity before 1968. For example, *La región más transparente* and *José Trigo* represented the nation and its historical trajectory, to significantly varying degrees, as operating under a principle of inclusion. As I have argued, this principle exposed its limitations, implicitly in *La región* and explicitly in *José Trigo*. In Mendoza's text, by contrast, exclusion dominates the national imaginary.

Though *José Trigo* already exposed the exclusive foundations of a national historical teleology sustained by the capture and hegemonic incorporation of popular experience, *Con Él* responds to the fact that Tlatelolco introduced a new element to state violence, namely, an unprecedented assault on Mexico's burgeoning middle class. The vast majority of those who were imprisoned, killed, and disappeared between late July and early October 1968 were students. In contrast to the popular classes portrayed in Fuentes's and del Paso's novels—prostitutes, street performers, *braceros*, railroad workers—many of those persecuted in 1968 were generally more able to air their grievances publicly by publishing poems, essays, novels, testimonials, and chronicles in books and magazines, and by making documentary and fiction films.[22] In addition to Mendoza's novel, many other fictional or partly fictional texts written by people affected by the events of 1968 attracted varying degrees of popular and critical attention, including José Revueltas's allegorical novella *El apando* (1969), Luis González de Alba's documentary novel *Los días y los años* (1971), and Jorge Aguilar Mora's sprawling totalizing novel *Si muero lejos de ti* (1979).[23] *Con Él, conmigo, con nosotros tres* is a particularly fascinating yet understudied voice in this chorus of responses to Tlatelolco that resoundingly declared that the emperor had no clothes.

IV

Mendoza's novel asks what can be written in the gap between nation and state that became so starkly visible to so many after 1968, and its challenge is to wrest Mexican history from its violent appropriation by the state. Written in the wake of the state's attempt to justify the events of October 2, Mendoza's novel not only condemns official efforts to conceal what happened, but it also exhibits a relationship to totality defined by Tlatelolco. *Con Él* speaks to the crisis of an entire hegemonic structure for imagining the nation, and the history it in turn constructs fails to function as an organizing force that endows the national community with meaning. The Mexican government's decision to repress the Student Movement produced a naked display of power that could not be disguised by the ideological trappings of hegemony. Yet it was precisely the government's excessive violence, which includes its excessive rhetoric, that exposed the state's limits and revealed how the hegemonic connection between state and national history was contingent, and thus not necessary. Teleology relies on origins and destinations that encompass a series of events defined as following a necessary logic. Mendoza's novel undermines the purported necessity of Mexico's historical logic by exposing and destabilizing notions of individual and collective subjectivity that legitimize exclusion. Its ironic use of language and its insistent questioning of what words are necessary and what words are not serve to loosen the rhetorical foundations of national identity. *Con Él* does not provide an alternative to these foundations, but it does expose their contingency as it affects all Mexicans.

Like her protagonist Delfina, Mendoza lived in an apartment that looked out on Tlatelolco Plaza and from which she witnessed the October 2 massacre.[24] Her own world shocked by state violence, Mendoza constructs a narrator who filters her perception of collective experience through her individual experience. Lanin Gyurko describes Mendoza's novel as an adroit fusion of "several historical periods in Mexican history: the tragic events of 1968; the Decena Trágica [...]; and the reform period of Benito Juárez" (270). In a statement that symptomatically restricts "daily life" to middle- or upper-class experience—and that also attests to the effects that the social composition of the Student Movement had on literary criticism—Sara Sefchovich proposes that *Con Él* represents a moment in the history of Mexican fiction when politics descends from the heights of institutional power and spreads out into people's daily lives (221). Gyurko's and Sefchovich's observations both describe how Mendoza's text represents history: through a series of anecdotes that portray the narrator's ancestors and contemporary family members as participating in or being directly affected by significant political events.

The totalizing effects of the trauma produced by the violent separation of state hegemony from national historical teleology appear in the following early passage of Mendoza's novel, which describes Mexico and the world on October 2 as frozen in time. This paralyzed totality awaits those who will produce meaning, those who can explain what has happened. Mendoza's text casts doubt on the ability to produce anything meaningful after Tlatelolco, let alone to contain the meaning of what has happened:

> A la espera estaba todo el mundo esa noche-sangre. Los ministrazos sin sombrero y dando vueltas en sus despachos con murales cerca del techo que cuentan en art nouveau la abundancia, el progreso, la fe, la libertad. Deteniéndose nada más para contestar los teléfonos, ellos mismos, sin saber qué hacer ni a dónde iba a conducir lo que sabían que se había hecho. Listos para correr a donde los llamaran. Esperaban los directores de periódicos en todos los idiomas escritos, con las

> mangas de las camisas arriadas y el titipuchal de cables en el escritorio, cables marcados uno dos, enrevesados tres cuatro, por traducir cinco seis, por mandar siete ocho a la primera plana, a las ocho columnas: ¡México, qué país, Pancho Villa sigue al trote! ¡México! pues, ¿no que ya no había sacrificados piramidales?, ¡qué país! ¡México, Olimpiada, qué país! ¡México, todo es posible en la paz! ¡Qué país! (21–22)

Incorporating official slogans about peace and the Olympics, referring to stereotypical notions of Mexico's "barbarism" like Villa and human sacrifice, enumerating the efforts of journalists across the world to keep track of what is going on, portraying panicked officials unable to control Tlatelolco's consequences as they pace beneath allegorical murals, this passage exemplifies how Mendoza's novel critiques the official story and its composition, casting the trappings of the hegemonic totalizing narrative in objective and scathingly ironic terms. It demonstrates how the totality of Mexican experience as a teleological construct no longer bears upon individual experience as an explanatory code, even among middle- and upper-class intellectuals who had been traditionally invested in reproducing such a code. The state showed all of its cards in 1968, and it played its hand so strongly that critical writers like Mendoza could no longer construct collective identity around the so-called justification for what turned out to be the state's pyrrhic victory: the violent imposition of national-popular teleology.

With her focus on language—the passage cited above is remarkable for its irony—and her critique of how history is employed to justify violence, Mendoza has produced a text whose concern with what can be said after Tlatelolco engages with the supplementary character of language. The official justification of Tlatelolco exemplifies the concept of supplement as presented by Derrida because it is a sign that so transparently functions as "a substitute" meant to "make one forget the vicariousness of its own function and make itself pass for the plenitude of a speech whose deficiency and infirmity it nevertheless only *supplements*" (*Grammatology* 144; original emphasis). Derrida continues, "If [the supplement] represents and makes an image, it is by the anterior default of a presence" (145). In the context of Tlatelolco and the government's justification for violence, this insufficient presence is the national community *and* the government's purportedly necessary relationship to this community as a defining and guiding force. Tlatelolco exposed the contingency of this relationship by reenacting the foundational violence of the post-Revolutionary Mexican nation (which is indeed intrinsic to any nation) that repeated itself throughout the twentieth century in characteristic conflicts like the Cristero Rebellion and the STFRM strike. It is not that Tlatelolco caused the government's representative power to be insufficient. Instead, it exposed the always already insufficient character of that representative relationship, in a word its supplementarity. For Derrida, the supplement, "as substitute, [...] is not simply added to the positivity of a presence, it produces no relief, its place is assigned in the structure by the mark of an emptiness. Somewhere, something can be filled up *of itself*, can accomplish itself, only by allowing itself to be filled through sign and proxy" (145; original emphasis). The imposition of state authority in the Mexican government's excessively violent response to the Student Movement was simultaneously too much and not enough. The state's excess revealed its insufficiency.

V

In his previously cited poem, "Intermitencias," Octavio Paz explicitly associates the violent excess of the massacre to the insufficiency of the state's representative authority. Furthermore, "Intermitencias" critiques the concept of origin by denying the state the ability to define the Plaza de Tlatelolco as the surface from which Mexico would experience its rebirth. Both Paz's poem and *Con Él* elaborate theories of writing through their critiques of Tlatelolco and the state's efforts to whitewash what happened there. Like *Con Él* and its focus on pleonasm, Paz's poem poses the problem of distinguishing between necessary and redundant words after the massacre, particularly in the way that it juxtaposes the central image of municipal workers cleaning blood from the Plaza—"(Los empleados / municipales lavan la sangre / en la Plaza de los Sacrificios.)" (*Ladera* 68)—to another stained surface, the paper Paz is writing on. Condemning the government's cover-up, the poem opens with a declarative phrase, which reads, "La limpidez [...] No es límpida" (68). This phrase contains another phrase that appears in parentheses:

"(Quizá valga la pena / Escribirlo sobre la limpieza / De esta hoja)" (68). At the poem's conclusion, just after the verses that describe the municipal workers, another reference to the poet's efforts appears: "Mira ahora, / Manchada / Antes de haber dicho algo / Que valga la pena, / La limpidez" (68–69).

"Intermitencias" plays on the concept of cleanliness, which it mobilizes around the use of three very similar words: *limpidez*, *limpieza*, and *límpida*. Both *limpieza* and *límpida* are relatively common to Spanish. *Limpieza*, a noun, denotes cleanliness as well as the act of cleansing. *Límpida* is similar to the English adjective "limpid," whose Latin root noun, *lympha*, translates as "clear liquid," and that denotes both "clarity" and "purity." The noun that appears in the poem's first verse, *limpidez*, is a less common word, used most frequently in the vocabulary of connoisseurs to refer to a given wine's color and clarity. *Limpidez* emerges in the first few verses of the poem as a word able to combine the different suffixes of *limp-* (*lympha*): *-ieza* and *-ida*. Just after stating that *La limpidez* is not *límpida*, the poem goes on to explain that *La limpidez* is, in fact, "una rabia / [...] Extendida sobre la página" (68). Repeating the pattern of the poem's first phrase, this last phrase also includes a parenthetical phrase, which reads, "(Amarilla y negra / Acumulación de bilis en español)" (68). The phrase "*La limpidez*" opens and closes the poem. Its polysemic richness, based upon the phonetic combination of words that also appear in the poem, owes itself to the chain of associations it highlights around the related concepts of cleaning and staining: clarity (*limpidez*), cleansing (*limpieza*), pure and clear (*límpida*), bile (*bilis*), blood (*sangre*), and stained (*manchada*).

Another liquid, in addition to blood and bile, that is implied by the poem but not mentioned is, of course, ink. It emerges as the clearest liquid of all, though not completely clear, and not only because it does not appear as explicitly associated with the violence of Tlatelolco as the other liquids do. Paz turns the tables right from the start by declaring that *La limpidez* is not *límpida*. Not only is this a contradiction of sense, for *limpidez* is defined as possessing the characteristic of being *límpida*; it is also a contradiction of form since the two terms are so similar phonetically. What follows is a wholesale assault on the concept of cleanliness, not only its relationship to government hypocrisy, but also its deceptive character, its role as an impediment to discovering the truth.

Undermining the value of cleanliness allows Paz's poem to introduce the positive valence of the stain in its final verses: "Look now, / Stained / Before having said something / That is worth it, / Clarity." The efficient economy of Paz's poem is revealed in the feminine adjective ending of the word *manchada*. Grammatically, at the level of the sentence, *stained* refers to "clarity," thus repeating the poem's opening declaration of clarity's unclean nature. The adjective's feminine ending also allows associations with the two surfaces enumerated in the text, the plaza and the page. If "stained" is taken to refer to the plaza, then it is obvious that the surface has been stained before the poet could say anything that was worth it, that, in the Spanish expression, was literally "worth the pain." If, on the other hand, "stained" is taken to refer to the page, then the last sentence adopts an ironic tone that suggests that the poem itself is not worth it. But even though Paz's words could never be worth the murders of Tlatelolco, they are indeed worth something. And that something is their condemnation of the concept of cleanliness, which returns the final sentence to its grammatical meaning, that clarity is unclean, stained. But ink appears implicitly as a productive kind of stain on a page that is as always already stained as the Plaza of Tlatelolco. In "Intermitencias," writing rejects originary clarity by recognizing its own stains as its necessary starting point. Furthermore, writing, unable to start from a blank page, must be an incursion into a history that has always already begun. In turn, elucidating this history requires the supplement of writing.

VI

Paz's poem critiques the originary thinking the Mexican government employed when the latter attempted to conceal its foundational violence through rhetorical justification. By refusing to sustain an illusory notion of purity, "Intermitencias" speaks to the question of pleonasm, that term that appears so often in Mendoza's novel. And, as I will discuss shortly, Mendoza's novel adds to the concept of pleonasm a sexual connotation that structures the text's discussion of patriarchal violence, female sexuality, and self-expression. Though Paz's poem states that its words are worthless, it actually communicates their necessity. When it justified Tlatelolco, the government tried to close the book on the massacre in an effort to render any additional words about it superfluous. "Intermitencias" stains the page with ink in order to return the bloodstains to the Plaza.

Con Él opens with a similar gesture:

> Sangre. La sangre. Embarrada en la pared provocaba náusea. Había quedado allí en cinco rayas de la mano que se agarró un instante para sostener el cuerpo acribillado; el instante de la esperanza. No era grande esta sangre, era angosta, vertical y larga. Luego bajó y dibujó en la pared por última vez su nombre de mancha, de estorbo, de ira, de rebeldía. (11)

Mendoza's novel begins by displaying the signs of death that will forever interrupt the government's efforts to present the origins of its power as unstained and self-sufficient. The limit of death reveals the limit of the state, and Mendoza's text operates on that limit by asking what it can do with the necessary contingency of meaning.

One of the first things *Con Él* does is pose the limits of the novel as a genre by calling itself a "cronovela." An additional strategy it employs to reveal the novel's limits is to portray its protagonist Delfina's struggles to write about Tlatelolco, which mirror Mendoza's struggles. For example, when Mendoza remembers the column she published in *El Día* just before Tlatelolco, she condemns it for being, "tan frívola, tan esperanzada, tan totalmente estúpida la mañana en que apareció" (*La O* 112). Delfina tries to compensate for the emptiness she feels in the months following the massacre, during which, she writes, "No ha pasado nada" (*Con Él* 48). The paralysis that she and her friends suffer after October 2 bears directly on the text Delfina writes: "Gimoteamos pues, esperamos, sin nada que contar para que la crónica se novele o al revés volteado" (48). When Delfina worries that the present provides no basis for the chronicle to novelize, or vice versa, she alludes to the way in which Mendoza, the author, classifies *Con Él*. In addition to appearing on the text's title page, the term *cronovela* also appears in the statement of acknowledgments after the novel's conclusion: "Esta cronovela fue escrita en el periodo becario 1968–1969 del Centro Mexicano de Escritores" (186).

These parallel classifications, on title page and final page, construct a *parergon* that, at the level of the novel's structure, replicates the novel's thematic critique of the originary thinking that presupposes presence. In Derrida's terms, a *parergon* is a supplementary framing device that does not complete or delimit the work it contains as much as it attempts to overcome a lack within the work. In his example of the columns that frame an entrance, Derrida writes, "What constitutes them as *parerga* is not simply their exteriority as a surplus, it is the internal structural link which rivets them to the lack in the interior of the *ergon*. And this lack would be constitutive of the very unity of the *ergon*. Without this lack, the *ergon* would have no need of a *parergon*" (*Truth in Painting* 59–60). By attaching the label of *cronovela* to either side of her work, Mendoza attempts to overcome the lack expressed within the narrative, which her protagonist describes as occurring during a time when nothing can be chronicled or described novelistically. The term *cronovela* implies the limit of two genres, chronicle and novel, and its appearance "outside" and "inside" the principal narrative highlights the text's recognition of these limits, which in turn advances the text's position that a critique of substance—that which can or cannot be described after 1968, for example—must also be a critique of form. The generic structure that frames *Con Él* calls attention to the text's own limitations. Indeed, the use of the term *cronovela* within the novel's pages explicitly turns the text into its own intertext. The novel's acknowledgment of its own limitations strengthens its critique of the limitations of the state's narrative because by doing so *Con Él* avoids replicating the totalizing, originary epistemology the state resorts to in order to legitimize its narrative of domination.

The novel's most specific critique of the official story appears in an intertextual manner when it alludes to the tablet in the Plaza of Tlatelolco dedicated by López Mateos in 1964. The tablet never appears in its entirety in Mendoza's novel, and the narrator never explicitly names it as the source of the words she cites. On two occasions portions of its text appear in quotation marks, and a third time they do not. The different references to the tablet reflect different ways of integrating it into the novel, tracing a trajectory from citation to incorporation. The first allusion to the tablet appears in the novel's opening description of blood on the Plaza, "a secas, seca, negra, oxidada, rechupada por la piedra, vorazmente tragada [...] hacia adentro, deglutida en la panza de la Plaza de las Tres Culturas de Tlatelolco—'no fue ni triunfo ni derrota'—" (12). The reference to the plaque that concludes this passage is repeated less than twenty pages later in the description of twelve students who are murdered by soldiers on October 2. The narrator calls the students "los mismos actores de siempre, en el mismo papel desde que los españoles trajeron el trueno de la pólvora a Tenochtitlan, a Tlatelolco [...] 'no fue triunfo ni derrota fue el doloroso nacimiento del pueblo mestizo que es el México de hoy'" (30). The exhaustion and frustration Delfina conveys in her description of the students' murders emerges from her sense that she is witnessing something that has happened before, a grotesque pleonasm of death that stems back to 1521, to the Decena Trágica of 1913, and that leads up to October 2, 1968. Her allusions to the tablet undermine its official message by revealing that the only thing born of the "painful birth of the mestizo nation" is more death.

These first two allusions to the plaque evoke the sentiment expressed by Paz in "Intermitencias," by Delfina in *Con Él*, and by Mendoza in her newspaper column when all three lament the futility of their writing in the wake of Tlatelolco. After the massacre, they seem to ask, is all writing doomed to be a pleonasm, little more than the worthless repetition of what everyone already knows? The clear answer they provide to this question is no. The very act of writing undermines the question's validity. Simply put, if writing were indeed worthless, why would Paz, Mendoza, and a whole host of Mexican intellectuals continue to put pen to paper following the events of 1968? Paz and Mendoza respond negatively to this question by demonstrating the need to undermine the government voices that perpetuate their tireless monologue. Both Paz and Mendoza specifically attack an important narrative thread that sustains this monologue, which portrays sacrifice and violence as necessary for rebirth. This narrative was advanced explicitly in the proclamations by Díaz Ordaz and the Mexican Senate before and after Tlatelolco. Notably, violence and birth are two themes that structure Mendoza's novel. Adding a dimension to writing that is absent from Paz's poem, these themes coincide most explicitly in the character of Altagracia, Delfina's grandmother, who, as I mentioned above, committed suicide when giving birth to her twelfth child.

VII

Altagracia experiences her pregnancies and childbirths as something terrible, a never-ending series of rapes perpetrated by her despised husband: "El terror...la fecha en que falta la sangre, a saber que todo va a empezar otra vez, una vez más enferma día a día, con la saliva endemoniada a mares fluyendo aún cuando duermo, la saliva de los tiempos que se repiten" (62). Like the pleonasm of history that doomed the twelve students, Altagracia's twelve births are described as an inevitable repetition that will cease only when she can tolerate no more. Yet it is precisely in the passage describing Altagracia's death that the sexual—and sometimes positive—connotations of the term *pleonasm* begin to emerge for the reader. The first appearance of the word *pleonasm* occurs in a description of Delfina's lover, whom she calls at one point, "mi pleonasmo" (34). It appears again in the passage that describes Altagracia's exhaustion and final desire to die, which refers to her as "la que tuvo el pleonasmo del sexo una desolada, sanguínea vez en la vida [...] la de la trabazón de las piernas para morirse dos años después en el último parto" (114). The "pleonasm of her sex" pertains to the moment when, just after giving birth to her tenth child, Manuel (Delfina's father), Altagracia bled so much that nothing seemed capable of stopping the hemorrhage except for her husband's fist. Adding another layer of inaugural meaning to the image of blood, whose stains structure Paz's poem and open Mendoza's novel, the passage that describes Manuel's birth is tied explicitly to national history and the "birth of a nation." Manuel is described, after all, as completing Altagracia's "decena trágica" (111). This tenth birth also coincides with the only time in her life that Altagracia experiences orgasm, which is not described as anything pleasurable, but instead as yet another violation. Delfina writes,

> Solamente el puño cerrado de mi abuelo que entró, como siempre entraba él [...]: brutal, arrojado, duro y venoso, consiguió ponerle un hasta aquí a tal cascada. [...] Dicen que cuando nació mi padre mi abuela Altagracia sintió por prime-

> ra vez, y única, el estrangulamiento del deseo con aquel puño formidable [...] la asombrosa contracción involuntaria por la que se pierden las mujeres y se ganan los hombres. (112)

In addition to describing female orgasm as a phenomenon utterly structured by patriarchy, this passage supports the idea that the word *pleonasm* in Mendoza's novel operates as an index of orgasm.

Another violent association between pleonasm and orgasm, and which also alludes to masturbation, appears in the story of Delfina's cousin Juan, who was masturbated by his friend Socorro the night before he moved from Guanajuato to Mexico City, where he dies in the Plaza de Tlatelolco. The passage that describes the gunshot that kills Juan combines erotic memories, including his final night with Socorro, with the realization that he is dying:

> ¡Dios mío! exclamó Juan al sentir la venida en el vientre, la venida temblorosa que estalla y entibia el pantalón y que nace ¡como una flor en la bragueta! entre el ombligo y el erecto falo poderoso. Como un pleonasmo se dijo [...] un verde seno de Lucía, los ojos inteligentes de Socorro [...] agarró el chorro de sangre que franqueó su vientre como si lo que se le hubiera roto fuera nomás la pretina del pantalón y lo que bajaba fuese el pantalón y no la cascada rojísima [...]. (105–06)

Though his final moments recall moments of sexual pleasure, as a student deemed unworthy of living by the Mexican state, Juan is symbolically raped by the patriarchal, dominant discourse mobilized in the Tlatelolco massacre.

A later reference to pleonasm in the text—like the first that defines Delfina's lover metonymically as her pleonasm, her orgasm—alludes to orgasm in more wholly positive terms. Hinting at a troubled relationship with her mother, Delfina enumerates the two pleasures she provided her mother: "el regalo más grande, el único placer que le he dado a mi madre —aparte del instante en que conoció el pleonasmo del embarazo de mí— es la bolsa de confites de violetas cristalizadas que le traje de Nueva York" (131). The final reference to the term occurs in the context of memories from Delfina's childhood, and it also alludes to masturbation. Describing how urine travels out of the sewer pipes of her aunts' old Mexico City house, Delfina writes, "¿A dónde vas?, para arriba. ¿De dónde vienes?, de abajo. ¿Subes para arriba? ¿Bajas para abajo? Pleonasmo, pleonasmo, tú piensas" (145). With a degree of ambiguity typical of Mendoza's style, it first appears that the "you" in the opening questions refers to what she has just previously described as "orines bajando desde arriba hasta abajo" (145). But by the end of the passage it becomes clear that this "you" is also Delfina. The up-and-down motion she describes works with the fifth use of the term *pleonasm* to suggest masturbation.

Unlike Juan and Altagracia, whose pleonasms/orgasms are produced by violations and emerge in moments of horror, Delfina is the only character who masturbates herself. Furthermore, orgasm is predominantly pleasurable for her. A key second-person passage associates masturbation with writing, linking auto-eroticism to self-expression. Death, birth, orgasm, taboo, and self-determination appear together, as they also do in Altagracia's story, in Delfina's reflections on writing and the massacre:

> ¡Ah, qué poco de ti tienes que decir! Hay que llenar de palabras el silencio, hay que manchar con letras la blancura, hay que ensangrentar la plaza para que los mexicanos aprendamos a portarnos bien. Tú tienes que portarte bien, en el NO aprendido con sangre, como entran las buenas letras. Ves las montañas acasito de ti desde el banco de la escuela de la azotea, escondida de los ateos, aprendes a escribir en el abecedario de San Miguel, eme a, ma… Nomás estás pensando en los tejocotes de piel que se pega en el paladar, en los pecados de la carne que ya sabes cuáles son: debajo de la cama el calor y el deleite del toque dulcísimo, no importa nada del peligro y del miedo, simplemente es estar acostada en lo oscuro, tibia, como en la tina de agua, o en los balcones altos, o debajo del foro del Teatro Juárez, o en la trastienda de la botica que huele a picosas medicinas de polvos y semillas. Pecar con las manos, felicidad de la infancia, pecar con el vientre es otro idioma. (141–42)

This passage's second-person perspective attests to Delfina's divided sense of self, which is similar to the alienation that Altagracia identifies when she laments her endless string of pregnancies. Speaking in an earlier passage in the first-person,

Altagracia wishes again to die: "con la panza por delante y yo allí detrás [...] a ver si se me desaparece y nos morimos las dos, los tres, ella el hijo y yo" (67). This observation alludes to Mendoza's novel's title in its evocation of split subjectivity—"her" and "myself"—and its identification of a third person, in this case the child. Further evidence of Delfina's divided sense of self is the observation that opens the longer passage cited above, "What little you have to say about yourself!" What follows that opening is a series of associations that interrelate writing, authority, punishment, sexual fantasy, masturbation, pregnancy, and sin.

Altagracia's torment, the novel's title, and Delfina's reflections express the desire for a dialectical shift from division to unity. Altagracia desires that unity in death, whereas Delfina finds it, though it remains ultimately elusive, in writing and the sexual pleasure that, to repeat Kristeva's observation I cited earlier, rejects "all that is finite" but assures "the life of the concept" of the self. Delfina's thoughts to herself reveal that her self-expression requires struggling against the structures of authority implicit in learning to write and learning to masturbate. Learning the first is a function of the state and the Church. Delfina is taught to write in a Catholic school, and like the terrible machine in Kafka's "The Penal Colony," the state appears in this passage as inscribing an irrefutable NO in the flesh of citizens who do not "behave," like the students whom Díaz Ordaz would like to force along the "correct" path. Learning to masturbate is a transgression, a "sin" committed in dark, secret places.

The allusions to medicinal powders, seeds, and the curative herb *tejocote* help explain the passage's final sentence, which contrasts sinning with the hands to sinning with the womb, and which quite intentionally distinguishes the sins as different languages. The medical allusions refer to the fact that Delfina is unable to bear children, a fact first made clear to the reader when, in another second-person passage, her aunt Natividad is described as lamenting her niece's sterility (82). Delfina's inability to bear children is never fully explained. But it becomes significantly associated with writing in the novel's final chapter. Once again frustrated by what she cannot put into words, Delfina expresses dismay that writing does not produce pleasure.

On a hot night in her apartment, she imagines a tropical beach where she could "desnudar [...] y a zancadas meterse entera ahí en lo tibio, en la pulpa suavísima de las olas vencidas y encarceladas en minúsculas crestas como anchoas, [pero] nada de eso estaba en su instante de escribir la novela que había planeado, y que evidentemente no iba a continuar" (159). The surreal image of anchovy crests imprisoning waves in the pulsating sea suggests a freedom of expression that does not coincide for Delfina with writing her novel, which must reckon with Tlatelolco, her family, and her own infertility, her "vientre [...] devastada" (159), which she recalls on the night she decided to write her novel: "esa noche de la negruridad en que se sentó a pasar en limpio su vida y a escribir la novela que debería terminar por el amor de Dios ya que no empezó el hijo que tanto se hubo prometido" (160).

The use of the Spanish expression *pasar en limpio*, which I translate as "starting from scratch," recalls once again Paz's poem about writing and stains, an association that Mendoza's novel also makes explicitly in the passage about writing and masturbation. For Delfina, it is impossible to start from scratch since history weighs so heavily upon her, not only national history, as embodied by Tlatelolco, but her family history, which the novel associates with watershed moments of Mexico's formation as a modern nation. Adding a layer of meaning to the critique of origins in Paz's poem, Delfina's thoughts on writing also recall her inability to fulfill the role of mother that patriarchal society asks of her, and which drove her grandmother Altagracia to kill herself. Unable to bear children, Delfina must reckon with not only her own infertility, but "la esterilidad de su apellido" (159). Finally, she did not choose infertility. By obliging her to replace a child with a novel, her inability to have her own children establishes a condition for writing that makes it impossible for writing to start from its own origins, to start from scratch. Like Paz in "Intermitencias," Delfina wrestles with limits established by history, specifically the inability to start anew, regardless, for example, of what the Mexican Senate proclaims. Furthermore, writing is explicitly associated in *Con Él* with authority. It is not easy to wrest its power away from those able to justify the cruelest acts through their words.

Though Delfina struggles with writing and the taboos associated with masturbation, both activities gradually provide her with at least limited degrees of self-expression and self-determination. As mentioned above, Delfina is the only character described as masturbating herself. Unlike her grandmother, she experiences orgasm as pleasure. Furthermore, "sinning with the hands," though not something she is limited to by choice, serves as a kind of proxy for "sinning with the womb," which would cause Delfina to comply with the social pressure to reproduce the patriarchal order. In the novel, this order represses Altagracia and exercises paternalistic violence on Mexico's unruly youth in a brutal assertion of the national community's immutable presence and the state's purported ability to define and reproduce that presence. The association between writing and masturbation, so tightly connected in Mendoza's novel, recalls Derrida's discussion of masturbation in Rousseau's *Confessions*, wherein Rousseau worries over "this dangerous habit" (qtd. in Derrida, *Grammatology* 150). Rousseau's ultimate justification, Derrida explains, has to do with his idea that he is only harming himself: "Egotism is redeemed by a culpability, which determines auto-eroticism as a fatal waste and a wounding of the self by the self" (156). Derrida's conclusion to his discussion of Rousseau's preference for masturbatory fantasy over actual sexual intercourse returns to his central idea that the supplement is always already operating in signification, that presence is always already mediated. The "perversion [that] consists in preferring the sign" (156) is revealed to be a preference for the sign that is already a sign of something else, which is also a sign of something else, and so on, "an infinite chain, ineluctably multiplying the supplementary mediations that produce the sense of the very thing they defer: the mirage of the thing itself, of immediate presence, of originary perception. Immediacy is derived" (157). The self in Mendoza's novel is always already split. Not only does the title suggest this, but the novel's narrative structure, which describes Delfina alternately in the first-, second-, and third-person, reinforces the idea of subjective division. Masturbation is described by Delfina to herself in the second person, as is writing. Alienation desires unity, but Mendoza's novel ultimately acknowledges the inaccessibility of presence. This recognition fuels *Con Él*'s critique of paternalistic state discourse and oppressive national historical teleology.

VIII

The text closes with a fantastical return to the portrait of Delfina's ancestors taken in 1901. Delfina contemplates this photograph throughout the novel. Gazing at pictures of her family anchors her story of herself, as Delfina struggles to include herself within an identifiable historical continuum, a struggle that reflects her desire for presence, for a personal origin story capable of fulfilling the strong lack she feels, that which she calls "la historia de la nada que me fue heredada" (53). Marianne Hirsch analyzes the connections between the act of looking at family photographs and autobiography, contending that the means by which a subject structures herself in relation to family helps reinforce an illusion of subjective coherence: "Difference or otherness, in this conception, is not an external difference, but an otherness within—within a circumscribed cultural group, such as a family, and, also, within the self, reflecting the subject's own plurality over a lifetime, the intersubjectivity that is subjectivity" (83). Hirsch further emphasizes the contradictions intrinsic to this effort to sustain the notion of coherent subjectivity, explaining that:

> The illusion of the self's wholeness and plenitude is perpetuated by the photographic medium as well as by the autobiographical act: both forms of misrecognition rest on a profound misprision of the processes of representation. Autobiography and photography share, as well, a fragmentary structure and an incompleteness that can only partially be concealed by narrative and conventional connections. (84)

Mendoza's text is an elaborate meditation on the tension between the illusion of presence and the reality of incompleteness, as played out in the novel's alternating narrative perspective and its title, in the themes of masturbation and writing, in the repetitive use of the term *pleonasm*, and in the critique of the official national narrative in its reading of the tablet in the Plaza.

Delfina's meditations on her family portrait perform an ekphrasis, or textual commentary on an image. Ekphrasis tends to reproduce the notion that the image is self-sufficient, an observation that Alberto Moreiras makes in his analysis of the images that appear in Salvador Elizondo's novel *Farabeuf* (1965):

> La contradicción ekfrástica es la siguiente: en el procedimiento ekfrástico hay a la vez una postergación del sentido, puesto que la literatura refiere a la mediación de sentido dada en otra representación estética, y un adelantamiento del sentido, dado que la ekfrasis refiere, no ya al mundo en general, sino al mundo interpretado en otra representación, y por lo tanto a un sentido ya manifiesto. (*Tercer espacio* 324)

Moreiras continues by describing how a common effect of this contradiction is to endow the analyzed object with a certain opacity, positing an image as merely an object of interpretation and not a subject of the interpretation of a prior event, and thus casting that object as something whose origin of production is ignored or mystified (324). The fiction of coherence (re)produced by this process is similar to the plenitude Hirsch identifies in her analysis of photography and autobiography. A novel that undermines coherence at every turn, *Con Él* ends up doing something different with its ekphrasis, namely, recontextualizing the production of the photograph she analyzes for her present moment. Martha Robles alludes to this type of ekphrasis when she identifies Mendoza's style as presenting "Lugares comunes en palabras nuevas imágenes fotográficas que rompen su inmovilidad [...] por la memoria sensorial" (1: 328).

In the conclusion of *Con Él*, Mendoza literally breaks Delfina's photograph's immobility when the latter's ancestors, dressed just as they were in the photograph from 1901, and her cousin Juan, who died in Tlatelolco Plaza, knock on the door of her apartment and enter. Referring to an earlier moment in the novel when Delfina looks at herself and the photograph in her mirror, the third-person narrator writes, "Como cuando se veía en el espejo buscando la cara de su sangre [...] un montón de gente idéntica a ella en la boca trompuda, en los ojos tristísimos, en la nariz aguileña, en la frente cóncava [...] estaba allí tocando a su puerta" (177). Delfina recognizes herself in the host of people that enters her apartment, making detailed connections between their and her physiognomy. Shocked upon seeing the people who once inhabited photographs coming to life in her doorway, Delfina slowly recovers: "Pero alueguito se adueñó de nuevo de sí misma porque tuvo conciencia de volver a estar, ineludible, definitiva" (177). Encountering the photograph in a markedly material fashion contributes to Delfina's definitive sense of coherent subjectivity. Incorporating herself into her family, penetrating the photograph, she fills a space that was left open for her but that also halts the self-definition she exercises through writing: "Vinieron los suyos por ella, nada más la estuvieron esperando, cascándola a que creyera que ya había terminado de escribir sus tinieblas" (181). Thus the comfort she feels at her newfound coherence is also described as a false hope that impedes Delfina's self-analysis. Definition is death.

The description of how her dead family members enter Delfina's apartment ends with the words of her cousin Juan, who, unlike the others, "todavía conservaba la costumbre de la voz" (182). Delfina never met Juan when he was alive, and he reproaches her for not having responded to his screams when he died in the Plaza underneath her apartment because she was, according to Juan, "muy entretenida con los mis tíos retratados" (182). He piques even further Delfina's sense of guilt by resignedly proclaiming, "Después de todo qué soy yo, uno de los muertitos de allá abajo [...]. Por eso no me conoces, Delfina, por eso, y por otras cosas que no estoy para contarlas ni tú para saberlas, cosas de sangre... pero aquí te quiero ver..." (183). Like Paz in "Intermitencias," and like Taibo who doesn't know where his friends' bodies are, Mendoza expresses through her semi-autobiographical character Delfina the frustration of the living at experiencing the absolute limit of death, in Monsiváis's paraphrase of Malraux, the difficulty of the need to navigate "la eternidad de los vivos y no la eternidad de los muertos" (*Días* 77). The fact that Delfina did not hear Juan because she was looking at photographs from the past suggests that history—personal and national—not only does not hold the answer for explaining Tlatelolco, but it is, furthermore, an obstacle to comprehending what happened on October 2.

Yet the novel's emphasis on national history, and this history's influence on Delfina's family, also suggests that there is little else but that history. One cannot simply start anew. Furthermore, Delfina's family appears to have no future, since Delfina is unable to have children. She has ancestors but no progeny. Caught in the tension between historical determinism and the desire for self-determination, Delfina ultimately finds a way out, but only in death. A break in the text after Juan expresses to Delfina his desire to "see you here," signals a moment of change. After the strange nighttime encounter with Delfina's dead relatives, dawn breaks over Tlatelolco when the sun shines into her apartment and "irrumpe el día por las ventanas" (183). The passage that follows resembles most closely *Con Él*'s efforts to accede to a sublime totality. Like the stream of consciousness passages that appeared in the final pages of *La región* and *José Trigo* (and with what seem to be clear references to del Paso's novel), the passage that constitutes the penultimate page of Mendoza's text accelerates. It moves as swiftly as the time it traces:

> Y a tal amanecer tal mediodía y tal atardecer, la vida le hace a Tlatelolco lo que el aire a Juárez: transcurre en golpes luminosos del día a la noche, al través de la historia. Es a su tiempo imperio de palacios, mercado noble y esclavizante, lugar de conversión, isla y meseta, refugio, territorio libre y cárcel de criminales, río sanguíneo, puerta de escape, plaza de ferrocarril, paraíso de los trenes perdidos [...]. Ayer chirrido locomotriz, tránsito de campanas, humaredas, faro horizontal, [...]; hoy recuerdos de ayer, pasado de un romance que fue, cuna de sangre, sangre de buena cuna, muerte sin buena cama [...]. Fríos los mis pies e las mis manos. [...] ¡mama! ¡papa!, ¡agua! porque ya me voy a morir ¿verdad? batallón Olimpia, olímpica ilusión, mira el cohete verde cómo reverdece, porque ya me voy a morir. Así es Tlatelolco, guerras para qué os quiero. No ha sido una derrota. (184)

This final reference to the tablet in the Plaza—"It has not been a defeat"—for the first time appearing in the text without quotation marks, has integrated the official doctrine of the birth of the mestizo nation into Delfina's personal story. Yet like the government's transformation of the Plaza, so imbued with historical significance, into a space of death and only a horribly cynical space of rebirth, the integration of the official story into Delfina's personal story requires her death. This passage traces, as in passages from *José Trigo*, Tlatelolco's trajectory from Aztec market to modern times. In Mendoza's novel, though, this trajectory ends in 1968, first with the *batallón Olimpia*, the secret police regiment that helped carry out the massacre on

October 2 and which was responsible for detaining the leaders of the Student Movement, and second with the shattered illusion of Mexico's hoped for entrance into modernity symbolized by hosting the Olympic games.

IX

The site of the mestizo nation's birth has been transformed into the site of its death, a "crib of blood." The sublime totality of Uranga's vault, with its capacity to absorb and imbue meaning into everyday experience is constructed in Mendoza's novel as crude materiality, as a space where the everyday experience in the mestizo nation leads only to death, and where it can only be understood from death. This final irony, the living testimony of someone who died, Delfina, appears on the novel's last page, when the narrative shifts from the national-historical surface of Tlatelolco Plaza to the personal-historical surface of the photograph, constructed as a fantasmatic *tableau vivant*, and recorded on the surface of the page. Delfina and her family's ghosts arrange themselves in the room that overlooks Tlatelolco, posing one more time:

> Ven para adelante como si los fueran a retratar. Manuel Zebadúa Albarrán con su vestido blanco y negro sigue recargando su brazo derecho en la rodilla de la su abuela. Sentado en el banco se ha hecho un poco para allá dejando campito a un personaje que no va, que no hace juego, que no concuerda, anacrónico, asustado, con los ojos de plato congelados en el puro ver para afuera. Está. Está sentada junto al padre de seis años. [...] Mira, mira, mira espantada como si. En la plaza los empleados municipales lavan con cepillos la sangre seca, los lamparones de la sangre, los cascarones de los gritos que no pudieron subir. Delfina Zebadúa Latino empieza a madurar en mitad de la sala. Verdad que ya se murió. La pura verdad. (185)

The novel ends with one last reference to Paz's poem and one last pleonasm. The repetition of the phrase that attests to Delfina's having died becomes the text's ultimate irony, its last demonstration of the pleonastic framing device and the characteristic tension it produces by trying to contain experience, to reduce it to something understandable and justifiable while at the same time communicating it to the future, to resist the connection between definition and death. The state's narrative could never coincide exactly with history even though its oppressive desire was to exhibit this coincidence thoroughly. In attempting to explain Tlatelolco and its space in the national-historical trajectory, Mendoza's novel radically rejects the notion that narrative and history could ever coincide completely; that speech, writing, photography, and sexual pleasure could ever accede to presence. By striking at the roots of historical narrative's powerful claim to presence, to authorized representability, *Con Él*, like Paz's poem, advances a critique of written expression that necessarily critiques its own representative ability. Unlike *La región*, *Con Él* does not attempt to appropriate the past. Nor does it appropriate daily experience by referring to an overarching conception of national meaning, as mid-century Mexicanist thinkers tended to do. Like *José Trigo*, Mendoza's novel relies upon animation more than appropriation. Unlike *José Trigo*, it does not question the novel's ability to animate the popular; it questions the novel's ability to animate the middle class, the intelligentsia itself. Responding to Tlatelolco, as it must, Mendoza's novel shakes the very foundations of the notion that a response could be authorized by allusions to history. The state poisoned the ground that allegedly birthed the mestizo nation. *Con Él*, like Paz's poem, starts with the assumption that national foundations are always already poisoned, but that ignoring them, trying to find a blank surface upon which to inscribe that assumption, is just as dangerous as pretending those foundations are pure.

Though profoundly pessimistic, Mendoza's novel asserts a minor victory of sorts in its final paragraph. When Delfina appears awkwardly in her family's portrait, she takes the place of Altagracia, who did not appear in the photograph because she was already dead by 1901. Having invented familial coherence through writing, Delfina then invents a place for herself. That she doesn't quite fit there coincides with the novel's demonstration of writing's necessarily supplementary character in relation to presence. Delfina parallels Altagracia by mothering her narrative, for which she also dies. Yet in this textual progeny, both Altagracia and Delfina live on. Starting where Altagracia ended, Delfina defies social expectations while she exposes the deadly deceit that underlies the patriarchal assertion of access to presence.

Chapter Four

Totality in Post-Tlatelolco Mexico

Subjectivity and Interpellation in Jorge Aguilar Mora's *Si muero lejos de ti*

Jorge Aguilar Mora's second novel, *Si muero lejos de ti* (1979), tells a remarkable and strange story about violence and paintings set in Mexico City during the Student Movement of 1968 and the years following the Tlatelolco massacre. Its protagonist, Yoris, is a young artist who struggles to maintain relationships with his friends and lovers, and to understand the meaning of his life during a period of Mexico's history defined by trauma and repression, both physical and psychological. A nomadic figure, Yoris traverses a dangerous cityscape populated by brutal police, paramilitary thugs, and intimidated or apathetic citizens doing their best to ignore the violence that surrounds them.

Yoris, who collects matchbox reproductions of European paintings, encounters another more serious art collector named José Dziadeck, a Polish immigrant to Mexico who is also an expert falsifier of medieval and Renaissance paintings. In his basement, Dziadeck displays five works he has stolen from various museums, which now house his forgeries. They are Uccello's *Portrait of a Young Man* (c. 1450), Messina's *Condottiere* (1475), Titian's *Man with a Glove* (c. 1520), Bronzino's *Portrait of a Young Man with a Book* (c. 1550), and Caravaggio's *Boy with a Basket of Fruit* (c. 1593). In search of Martini's *Annunciation* (1333), a sixth painting that will complete his collection, Dziadeck sends Yoris to Europe to steal the original and replace it with a fake. In Europe, Yoris meets Nicole, who is charged with giving him Dziadeck's forgery. Notably, Yoris and Nicole fail to complete Dziadeck's request and instead spend their time passing through various train stations and inventing games intended to help them break out of the oppressive narratives that define their lives.

Dziadeck's relationship to the paintings he possesses is a symbolic manifestation of the oppressive power he wields over six orphans, whom he has adopted and christened with names that correspond to the five works he owns and the sixth he desires: Uchelo, Mesina, Tisiano, Bronsino, Caravayo, and Martina. In return for his care, the orphans perform a number of tasks for Dziadeck. He even contracts them out as *halcones*, or shock troops informally associated with the state and hired to repress and sabotage the Student Movement.[1] When Yoris does not return as planned with the stolen painting, Dziadeck sends the orphans on another mission, to find and bring Yoris back to Mexico. In one of the novel's particularly perverse reflections on subjectivity, Dziadeck takes advantage of the orphans' travels and arranges for them to undergo plastic surgery in Italy. Following their operations, each orphan's face matches the portrait painted centuries earlier by his or her eponymous artist. The orphans do not capture Yoris, and after Uchelo dies in France the remaining five return to Mexico. The identities that Dziadeck has imposed upon them compel the orphans to question who they are and where they came from. What becomes an obsession with origins divides the once tight-knit group of friends, who gradually lose touch with one another and suffer lonely, separate fates. The despair that besets them also awaits Yoris upon his return to Mexico City, where he meets a fate at least as horrific as the surgeries that transformed the orphans' faces. When Yoris arrives, Mexico City is sinking in its own sewage, and the apocalyptic scene of the capital's destruction closes the novel.

By making a series of late medieval and Renaissance paintings into characters who represent disenfranchised young Mexicans, Aguilar Mora's novel establishes a critique of subjectivity that is at first glance absurd but ultimately poignant and thorough. The particular paintings Dziadeck wants to bring to Mexico trace a continuum of representations of the human figure that begins with the almost two-dimensional, seemingly distorted figures, especially for modern eyes, of Martini's fourteenth-century work to the lifelike, three-dimensional body idealized in the sixteenth-century Caravaggio. Dziadeck's violent transformation of the orphans suggests that he wishes to impose upon them a teleology of human form that corresponds to traditional European standards. The orphans' distorted names are only the first clue that Dziadeck's vision does not quite correspond to reality. Their conversations about their own identity and the crises they suffer by trying to understand themselves are much more serious reflections on the fissure between who they are and who a dominant power, in this case Dziadeck the adopted father, wants them to be.

In this chapter, I propose that the orphans appear as an allegory in Aguilar Mora's novel for the consequences of dominant ideology and how it interpellates individuals and groups. Ideological violence is associated most directly in the novel with three phenomena. First, for Yoris, is the irresistible feeling that he has forgotten something, that he must complete his understanding of the past, Mexican society, and himself. Second, for the orphans, is the imposition of identities imposed upon them by Dziadeck. Third, for both Yoris and the orphans, is the Tlatelolco massacre, which incarnated national-popular ideology in an act of mass murder.

Through its analysis of Yoris's and the orphans' trajectories, this chapter makes the following conclusion: while *Si muero* reveals the violence of dominant ideology, it does not sustain the illusion of distinguishing itself completely from that which it critiques. It both challenges totality and desires continuity and coherence. Such ambivalence characterizes the historical period from which *Si muero* emerged. By the late 1970s, Mexico's promising, national-developmentalist trajectory has clearly lost its course. But their doubts about Mexico's progress do not lead intellectuals of this time to reject wholesale a teleological conception of national identity. Concerns about Tlatelolco's consequences and about increasingly visible signs of Mexico's political and economic dependency provoke scholars and writers to ask which elements of the Revolutionary promise can be salvaged and what can be learned from 1968. Though some thinkers, most notably Roger Bartra, critique strongly the concept of nation, most others reflect upon Mexico's predicaments from within a predominantly nation-centered framework.

What *Si muero* contributes to a greater understanding of post-Tlatelolco Mexico is its near-visceral portrayal of the tenacity with which the concepts of totality and teleology inform any discussion of community, especially national community.

Through the stories it tells about the orphans and Yoris, *Si muero* associates the persistent strength of totality and teleology most consistently with the equally seductive appeal of autonomous subjectivity.

The novel's reflections on totality, teleology, and autonomy are germane to the period, as Mexico in the 1970s was a nation forced to reckon with its lack of autonomy vis-à-vis global political and economic forces. After all, Tlatelolco was in no small way a symptom of a political and economic crisis that was shaped by Mexico's dependency. In turn, the traumatic events of 1968 were also the source of an ideological crisis that the state, as primarily an ideological construct itself, was obliged to negotiate. This chapter presents a brief historical summary of the factors that exacerbated Mexico's dependency and its domestic crisis during the post-Tlatelolco years in order to provide a clearer understanding of the reasons for the state's ideological dilemma. As a cultural construct that reflects upon the nation's destiny, Aguilar Mora's novel corresponds more directly to this ideological crisis, especially through its depiction of the impacts of Tlatelolco, than to the political and economic factors that contributed to it. Nevertheless, understanding those factors is important for comprehending the relationship between the novel and its context, especially in regard to the 1970s, when Mexico's crisis became patently visible to all social sectors.

I

Appropriately for a novel that contemplates the cultural consequences of crisis, ideology appears in *Si muero* in a sense similar to the way Louis Althusser famously defined it when he proposed that "Ideology represents the imaginary relationship of individuals to their real conditions of existence" (162). Sustaining the national imaginary as a means of concealing both domination and the impossibility of fulfilling the Revolutionary project became almost impossible for the national-popular state after Tlatelolco. Aguilar Mora's novel suggests, however, that Mexicans still found themselves forced to negotiate the dominant ideologies of collective identity. *Si muero* portrays Yoris and the orphans as distorted by ideological interpellation and their responses to it in a remarkably material fashion, recalling Althusser's emphasis on ideology as a force that affects behaviors, attitudes, and practices (167). Ideology literally shapes subjects, influencing the way people move, how they interact with others, how they talk, etc. Althusser identifies an important dialectical relationship between ideology and subject formation, wherein subjectivity constitutes ideology, and ideology, in turn, constitutes subjects. An important result of this dialectic is that the formation of subjectivity is essential for the reproduction of ideology:

> [T]he category of the subject is constitutive of all ideology, but at the same time and immediately I add that *the category of the subject is only constitutive of all ideology insofar as all ideology has the function (which defines it) of "constituting" concrete individuals as subjects.* In the interaction of this double constitution exists the functioning of all ideology, ideology being nothing but its functioning in the material forms of existence of that functioning. (171; original emphasis)

Similar to the way in which Althusser argues against a simply linear relationship between subject and ideology, Bartra rejects the notion that political power emanates unidirectionally from the state to civil society (*Jaula* 187). Instead it permeates all aspects of Mexican society, including cultural production, and it is a force that ideologically interpellates, and thus constitutes, subjects. Bartra's critique of Mexicanist ideology exposes the restrictive consequences of the latter's dreams of autonomous self-definition and national subject formation: "En el espacio de la unidad nacional ha quedado prisionero y maniatado el ser del mexicano, como un manojo de rasgos psicoculturales que sólo tiene sentido en el interior del sistema de dominación" (*Jaula* 188–89).

Aguilar Mora's text similarly demonstrates that a unifying, defining concept of the nation functions and reproduces itself through the violent constitution of individual and collective subjectivities. For example, the materiality of history and collective identity traumatizes Yoris from the novel's opening pages. Already in its first scene, *Si muero* portrays historical memory as a force that supersedes the perceptive powers of Mexico's citizens, exposing to what extent they do not control what they remember and what they forget as much as they are instead *controlled by* memory and its lacunae. The novel's characters are not subjects who perceive, but instead subjects who are perceived by the history that surrounds them.

The novel begins by describing Yoris on a crowded bus traveling south through Mexico City. The realization that he has forgotten something hits him with visible force and provokes an immediate reaction from his fellow passengers: "Yoris sintió el dolor de haber olvidado algo y movió la cabeza con tanta violencia que todos los pasajeros del camión voltearon a verlo con un aullido de animal pateado a traición" (11). In spite of his embarrassment, Yoris is unable to control his movements. The physical symptoms of his oversight begin to extend beyond his self, and they cause everything around him to thicken and swell, just like his blood, which is now pulsating "a flujo perezoso" (11). Everything surrounding Yoris is transformed into "un sopor que deseaba dominar forzando la memoria de todos: como si el aire fuera un músculo para recordar y retener todos los dolores" (11). The dense, elastic air on the bus is weighed down with collective pain and endowed with a memory that obliges people to remember they have forgotten something without revealing to them precisely what it is, as in the case of Yoris: "Lo que le hacía mover violentamente la cabeza era la localización imprecisa y ubicua del olvido que se apoderaba de él" (11). The reader's introduction to Yoris thus describes him as subject to—literally constituted as a subject of—a ubiquitous and unidentifiable force associated with memory and its lapses. Precisely what it is that Yoris has forgotten only becomes clear to the reader in the novel's final pages, which I analyze below. But the novel's opening episode is significant for portraying Yoris as the victim of the incommensurability between the desire for a complete, coherent community, on one hand, and the violence emerging at the limits of integrative, totalizing ideology on the other.

While Yoris represents the male, middle-class individual, the orphans stand in for Mexico's popular classes in the novel. The most developed depiction of the violent consequences of ideology that the novel establishes in relation to the orphans centers around the only female in the group, Martina. Like Gladys García and the other female characters in *La región* and Altagracia and, to a lesser degree, Delfina in *Con Él*, Martina finds herself in a radically liminal space in relation to dominant discourse.

The painting that corresponds to her is the earliest in the series, suggesting a stunted subjectivity that is reinforced by the fact that Martina is also aphasic. By constructing the particularly distorted character of Martina, Aguilar Mora's novel at once portrays the violence of integrative ideology and its limits.

The *Annunciation* painted by the Sienese artist Simone Martini (c.1290–1344) is the only one of the six paintings that is not a portrait.[2] Instead, it represents a number of figures in a scene that, when read in the context of Aguilar Mora's novel, convincingly portrays an ideological interpellation. Inspired by the novel to examine the painting itself, the reader will find that the central panel of Martini's triptych portrays the Virgin Mary just as she receives the word of God from the archangel Gabriel. The angelic salutation is written on the surface of the painting and forms a physical link between Gabriel and Mary. Taken from the Gospel of Luke, it reads, "Ave gratia plena Dominus tecum" (Hail, full of grace, the Lord is with thee; Luke 1.28). In her detailed history of this salutation, Ann van Dijk refers to the subsequent verse from Luke, which describes Mary's reaction to the angel's words. "Who having heard, was troubled at this saying, and thought with herself what manner of salutation this should be" (Luke 1.29) (Van Dijk 420). Further evidence of Mary's perturbation in Martini's painting is the fact that her right hand touches her chin, a "classical convention for expressing perplexity" (Van Dijk 424). The position of her body and the expression on her face also communicate bewilderment or even unpleasant surprise: "Mary [...] seems to recoil from the angel's greeting as though from a physical object. Indeed [...] the angel's words float mysteriously [...] with an actual physicality appropriate to the weightiness of their import" (Van Dijk 420). Van Dijk continues her analysis and concludes convincingly that Martini's work fits into a rich, centuries-old tradition of devotion to the Virgin.

Aguilar Mora draws his inspiration primarily from Mary's apparent unease. At one point in his novel, the character Martina experiences a kind of divine summons similar to the encounter in Martini's *Annunciation*. Lifted mysteriously off the ground by the daylight she absorbs with her eyes, Martina expands and eventually explodes into "cúmulos de luz" (210). Her violent transformation scars the sky and leaves behind "una bóveda de girones como si se hubiera descascarado y detrás sólo se viera la solidez del vacío en un negro inexpresable" (210). Whole once more, she returns to earth, "sudaba, al alcance de las manos de Mesina y de la piedad de todos los demás" (210). In the *Annunciation*, the Virgin becomes the mediating force between God and humankind (Van Dijk 429). Likewise, Martina is now a conduit between the state, particularly its foundational violence, and her fellow orphans, who feel the effects of the massacre of Tlatelolco through her voice: "sus cuerpos ya entendían aunque ellos no entendían, sus cuerpos [...] comenzaban a contorsionarse de dolor por esa voz de la vida que les hablaba directamente en la sangre, en los huesos, en los nervios, en los músculos" (211).

Aguilar Mora's adaptation of Martini's *Annunciation* typifies his novel's portrayal of ideology as well as its critique of transcendent, totalizing reason. Like Yoris on the bus, Martina is violently and physically affected by a force beyond her control. But Martina reveals the limits of dominant ideology by scarring the firmament and revealing that behind that shattered vault lies only a solid abyss, and not, as Uranga's imagery suggests, a space upon which daily, individual actions could be inscribed and comprehended as part of a historical, national experience. Like the forgotten that besieges Yoris, and as Martina's friends are compelled to acknowledge, Tlatelolco exceeds comprehension. Its violent force precedes reason and cannot be explained by the national-developmentalist ideology the Mexican state mobilized to justify the massacre. Like *Con Él, conmigo, con nosotros tres* and "Intermitencias del Oeste (3)," *Si muero lejos de ti* rejects the idea that an unstained surface of inscription either stands at the foundations of national history or provides a space for renewal. Furthermore, *Si muero* exposes as wholly destructive the totalizing vision that Fuentes's novel constructs and del Paso's critically negotiates.

II

In one of the few critical analyses of *Si muero*, a sorely understudied text, Rebecca Biron argues that the novel attempts to establish masculine authorial control over the chaotic chronotope defined by Mexico City's demographic explosion and the trauma of Tlatelolco (68–69, 77–78).[3] The text's focus on Yoris as the male artist certainly reinforces Biron's position. Regarding the disorder that besets the novel's characters, Biron writes that they "suffer from an inability to locate the lines of demarcation that make identity and subjectivity possible" (69). While I certainly agree with Biron that the novel exhibits a masculine focus and that it emphasizes the disorientation that defines Mexican experience in the 1970s, I am less persuaded that *Si muero* tries to assert representational mastery and overcome "the single-author complex" (82). Instead, I read *Si muero* as a text whose critique of subjectivity applies as well to its author and itself. Consider, for example, the novel's introductory note, which expresses a fascinating desire for totality:

> Noticia: Durante los años de su escritura, la primera ambición de esta novela fue siempre el ser escrita por todos. Todos prometieron escribirla; pero el transcurso azaroso de las estaciones hizo imposible llevar a cabo esa ilusión. De todos quedaron dos: Rosario Ferré y Severo Sarduy. Una parte de su cuerpo, una parte de su escritura, entregaron a ellos a esta novela: cada uno contribuyó con un capítulo. Qué capítulos son, no es necesario indicarlo; ellos lo saben, lo sabe el texto, y lo sabrán todos, mientras este cuerpo siga creciendo. (7)

By explaining that Ferré and Sarduy wrote two of the novel's chapters, this passage rejects the notion of sole authorship, a position reinforced by the personification of the novel, and not the author, as the entity whose ambition it was to be written by everyone. This preface also presents the novel as an ever-expanding body, whose growth will ultimately enable everyone to identify the origins of its parts and understand how they work together. Thus the novel ostensibly aspires to embody an inclusive collective vision, an ambition that establishes strong points of comparison with the promises of national-historical integration and realization that defined the conclusion of Fuentes's *La región*, the appeal to a process of unfolding authenticity in Mexicanism, and the construction of the Revolution as the origin and destiny of national-popular state ideology. To varying degrees of explicitness, the novels I have analyzed thus far have demonstrated the ultimate impossibility of constructing the social totality. Gladys García, the railroad workers, the Cristeros, the students, all emerge at and as the limits of the integrative project. *Si muero* explores those limits with special emphasis on the viability of the concepts that ground integration: totality, teleology, and subjective autonomy. As with *Con Él*, Tlatelolco is an especially important historical point of reference for *Si muero*. Although the Student Movement and Tlatelolco only impinge tangentially on the novel's plot, they have significant thematic importance, especially in the case of the massacre.

Si muero's description of the Tlatelolco massacre, whose imagery recalls Martina's terrible epiphany and Yoris's experience on the bus, provides an important example of why the promise of integration is not sustainable as a rational force of transcendent collective subjectivity. On October 2, 1968, Revolutionary state ideology collided head-on with the critical vision that over the course of the Student Movement had been assembled by tens of thousands of Mexicans, and, by extension, an entire generation. Citing the student leaders who try to maintain order as the army moves in, the novel describes the massacre as an irrational force that subjects bodies to its inscrutable designs:

> Porque en ese momento una inquietud sorda corrió por todos los cuerpos, como si el aire se hubiera hecho de polvo y corriera entre todos los cuerpos alarmándolos: como si todos los huesos se estuvieran hablando en un lenguaje secreto que nadie entendía excepto los cuerpos, nuestros cuerpos. Y el pánico nos agarró a todos, uno por uno y todos vimos en los cuerpos de los otros las garras del pánico ya impresas y alguien gritó por el micrófono: ¡Calma, calma, es una provocación, es una provocación! Pero los cuerpos habían encendido ya lo que nadie entendía, los cuerpos habían escuchado ya el futuro de la muerte entrando por todos los costados de la explanada. ¡Calma, es una provocación! (416)

When Manuel Gamio wrote in 1916 about incorporating Mexico's indigenous populations into the national community he used language eerily similar to Aguilar Mora's. According to *Forjando patria*, the integration of ethnic minorities would transform the "fuerzas [...] en estado latente y pasivo" hidden within indigenous cultures "en energías dinámicas inmediatamente productivas," and "comenzar[ía] a fortalecerse el verdadero sentimiento de nacionalidad" (28). Like Gamio, Aguilar Mora traces animating forces that shape a collective. Yet the "secret language" that the massacre victims' bodies understand produces a disturbing flip-side to Gamio's vision of integration: it is separate from reason and only announces destruction. Furthermore, the incorporative logic of Gamio's thought also informed the state's justification for the violence it perpetrated in 1968 against those who failed to conform to its vision of the nation. *Si muero*'s description of the massacre thus reveals the inevitably exclusive ground of an ostensibly inclusive teleology. Its emphasis on a historical force that precedes and exceeds reason places the novel and its production within a context defined more by irrational subjection than ordered mastery.

The national-popular state's ideological crisis, which emerged patently after Tlatelolco, was also the consequence of a loss of authority. No longer able to transpose a narrative of domination into a narrative of incorporation—a key component of any state's ideological purpose according to Philip Abrams—the post-Tlatelolco Mexican state struggled to sustain its hegemony. The coherence of the state's ideology was not only threatened by the impact of Tlatelolco on many different sectors of Mexican society, but also by the long-developing processes of political and economic dependency that constrained Mexico's autonomy and, in part, led the government to impose solutions as rash as the Tlatelolco massacre, the Jueves de Corpus massacre of June 10, 1971, and the counterinsurgency campaigns of the late 1960s and early 1970s.

III

Of course Aguilar Mora did not work alone in his efforts to make sense of Tlatelolco. Since 1968, numerous historians, sociologists, chroniclers, novelists, poets, literary critics, and other writers have wrestled with the meaning of the massacre. A general conclusion to be gleaned from those who have studied the political and social impacts of 1968 is that Tlatelolco exposed and exacerbated the Revolutionary state's weakening ability to sustain consensus regarding the definition and trajectory of the Mexican national community. Like the subjects in Aguilar Mora's novel, and the novel itself, the Mexican nation-state was forced to reckon with its lack of autonomy and self-determination in the decade following the massacre.

The government's response to the pervasive uncertainty that followed Tlatelolco adopted its most concrete form in President Luis Echeverría Álvarez's broad program of "*apertura democrática*," which, according to Alejandro Álvarez, combined self-criticism and the search for solutions to social conflicts that combined politics and repression (18). As Claire Brewster details in her more recent assessment of Echeverría's presidency, the leader "worked to improve relationships with campesino and indigenous groups" (69). Brewster explains further: "Roads and schools would be built, and electricity supplied to rural communities. In an attempt to appease the students, he pledged to include young people in his government, and the voting age was lowered to eighteen" (69). The *apertura*'s achievements, though limited, included opening up spaces for critical cultural production. For example, under Echeverría, the mass media, especially television and cinema, became the primary stage upon which the opening was to be performed (Aguilar Camín, "Cenizas" 117–22).[4]

Echeverría's *apertura* ultimately failed to arrest the decline of the Revolutionary state's hegemony. Writing with some hindsight in 1989, historians Héctor Aguilar Camín and Lorenzo Meyer emphasize that the 1970s and early 1980s witnessed the dissolution of the state's capacity to construct an authorized vision of the nation and its destiny. They define the period from 1968 to 1984 as a transition "de orden histórico que reabre la pregunta sobre la duración y el destino del sistema político e institucional derivado del pacto social que conocemos como Revolución Mexicana" (239). While doubts about the Revolution's ideological and political viability as sustainable and promising social pact circulated long before 1968,[5] Aguilar Camín and Meyer insist that the events of that year lead to a significant rupture of the state's capacity to portray itself as the principal guarantor of order and progress. Highlighting the series of post-Tlatelolco developments that challenged centralized political power in the early 1970s—the Tendencia Democrática of the labor movement, the increasing independence of the entrepreneurial and banking sectors, and insurgency in the countryside and the cities—Aguilar Camín and Meyer conclude regarding the Mexican political system that its "concierto institucional no incluía ya todas las notas, ni siquiera algunas de las más importantes" (295). The Student Movement's middle-class character exacerbated the system's crisis. The impacts of state violence in 1968 fell squarely on the generation that was set to "culminar el tránsito y a asumir las riendas del México industrial y cosmopolita del que era el embrión" (Aguilar Camín and Meyer 241).

However, the gap between the political past and future was hardly absolute. In his 1978 analysis, sociologist Sergio Zermeño cautions that during the 1970s the Revolutionary state was still able to corrupt even the most democratically minded of those who had participated in the Student Movement:

> Una de las derivaciones lógicas es entonces el aspirar al Estado, incluso como éste aparece hoy, porque en él se descubre poco a poco al único agente unificador, en el que la potencialidad dirigente se vuelve capaz de abarcar e impulsar las dos grandes lógicas [national populism and developmentalism]. Sin embargo, también poco a poco se descubre que esto es una ficción, que esas fuerzas democráticas de donde surgieron muchos de los cuadros que ahora miran al país desde lo alto, representan, en verdad, los destructores de las expectativas unificadoras y dirigentes que se suponían atributo del Estado, y el demócrata de ayer deviene el represor de hoy. (*México* 326)

But while Zermeño argues that the state is still the strongest political actor in the late 1970s, he also pinpoints its significant faults, the gravest of which is its inability to lead and unify a democratic nation.

The Revolutionary state's crisis emerged gradually over the mid-twentieth-century decades that made up the height of the national-popular period. Its ability to maintain consensus declined alongside its ability to sustain political and economic autonomy. According to Zermeño, the state's developmentalist logic demanded increasing dependence on foreign investment,[6] which in turn strengthened an elite economic class that began to compete with the traditionally nationalist sectors of the government for political power. Still, developmentalism continued to reinforce state power. As Zermeño observes, "el impulso desarrollista que el Estado promueve es, en primer lugar, un acto movilizador, dirigente y, en tanto tal, un acto que refuerza la legitimidad del esquema populista, del papel fuerte y hegemónico de su promotor indiscutido" (*México* 321). Yet Zermeño also notes that the same developmentalist logic produces a bourgeoisie with even stronger ties to foreign capital and a middle class that eventually challenges the strong populist state's hegemony (321). The developmentalist crisis illustrated how the struggle for economic and political power within Mexico corresponded to the economic and political interests of other nations, especially the United States. The economist José Alfredo Castellanos Suárez concludes that the national-popular government emphasized fiscal stability at the expense of national sovereignty.[7] In his analysis of the way President Díaz Ordaz secured foreign investment, Castellanos Suárez, like Zermeño, highlights the relationships between domestic and foreign corporate interests: "La estabilidad monetaria pudo continuar a cambio de socavar la soberanía nacional; fomentando la inversión extranjera de empresas transnacionales y endeudando más y más al país. Promovió y protegió [...] la producción empresarial, lo cual redundó en beneficio tanto de monopolios mexicanos como de transnacionales (ante todo de E.U.)" (223–24).

Another factor that was both a symptom and a cause of the Revolutionary state's weakening autonomy was the government's increasing reliance on repression as a response to social conflict. Aguilar Camín and Meyer contrast the generally more violent 1960s and 1970s to previous decades, when, on the whole, the state was able to conceal its repressive measures more effectively, absorb dissent, and appease political demands with a more balanced combination of consensus and coercion (241). Castellanos Suárez attributes ill social effects to economic dependence; and this process tended to intensify political opposition (225). Not surprisingly, the repression of the Student Movement further radicalized dissent.[8]

The connection between the Mexican government's waning autonomy and its increasing reliance on repression also becomes clearer upon considering the global context. Particularly significant was the containment doctrine of the Cold War–era United States, which demanded the "incorporation of regional allies into the global struggle against communism," and established a hemispheric framework wherein "Mexico was viewed as an important linchpin and compliant ally in the anti-communist struggle" (Bagley and Aguayo 4).[9] US-sponsored counterinsurgencies in El Salvador, Nicaragua, and Guatemala during the 1970s and 1980s typified a period of heightened US intervention that coincided with and helped shape the Mexican government's crackdown on domestic resistance. Though US involvement in Central America was more extensive and visible, Mexico was certainly not ignored. As Sergio Aguayo explains:

> As a matter of record, Mexican stability and its effects on U.S. security started being discussed by the end of the 1970s. In 1977, the CIA recognized, in passing, that Mexico had "entered a period of internal transition." Two years later [...] [sociologist] Richard Fagen concluded that, according to the establishment, the "primary Mexican security threat...is a Mexico torn by civil and political strife." [...] Over the years, the number of references to security has increased. ("The Uses" 100)

Aguayo's analysis of how US hemispheric security concerns affected Mexico further clarifies the extent to which national autonomy became more tenuous in the 1970s.

For Zermeño, the national-popular state's dependence upon foreign investment helps explain how the Revolutionary state was never truly national or popular (*México* 91). But this disjunction worsened by the late 1960s, which witnessed the increasing "pérdida de distancia entre el Estado fuerte y la burguesía, principalmente en su fracción asociada al capital extranjero" (91). The increasing ties between the state and the bourgeoisie signaled Mexico's transformation from an "Estado populista" to an "Estado de clase" (90), a process that also undermined the government's nationalism, since it was fueled predominantly by foreign investment (92).

IV

Tracing nationalism's decline into the late 1980s, Roger Bartra argues that it eventually became a reactionary ideology that exacerbated Mexico's dependency, "the symbol of an authoritarian political regime that has not yet been able to establish either a solid economy or avoid its transnationalization" ("Revolutionary Nationalism" 168). Bartra's work on ideology and Mexican national identity stands out for its insistence upon studying political power and cultural production as interrelated phenomena, neither separate nor separable. *Si muero lejos de ti* is a dramatic case in point. Its critique of political power is not independent of the seductive nature of political power's epistemology, which rests upon coherent, self-sustaining notions of identity and teleology.

As I argued in the first chapter, *La región más transparente* both criticizes the Revolutionary government and upholds dominant ways of imagining the national totality. Fuentes's first novel thus exemplifies how critical cultural production tends to struggle with itself as it vacillates between reinforcing and resisting power. *Si muero* does not escape this dilemma. On the contrary, it exposes and contemplates the parameters of this struggle without rising completely above them. The novel's pages are charged with contradictory impulses of exclusion and inclusion, autonomy and dependency, and the desire for and the rejection of dominant ideology. Like Martini's Virgin, *Si muero* is troubled by the forces that interpellate it. Its distorted structure and tortured plot mimic the fear and unease that Martini's *Annunciation* suggests, and which *Si muero*'s portrayal of Martina heightens to abject, devastating proportions.

Bartra's description of the Revolutionary state's ideological crisis casts it in corporeal terms that help clarify my understanding of how *Si muero* corresponds to its context. Like the sky Martina scars, the coherent, authorized conception of national culture is damaged in 1968 when, as Bartra puts it, "personajes imprevistos rompieron la continuidad cultural de la comedia en la que los destinos nacionales se enlazaban amorosamente con la historia olímpica universal" ("Cultura" 82). He continues, "desde entonces el sistema político ha quedado malherido; los personajes del drama con frecuencia tartamudean y cojean en las tablas de la identidad nacional" (82). Not only do Aguilar Mora's characters stutter and stumble—Martina is aphasic and Yoris cannot always control his body—but his novel does as well. Its Frankenstein's monster-clumsiness is a necessary result of its direct and frank engagement with totality during a moment of Mexico's history when appeals to totality created aberrations like Tlatelolco.

V

Given the mid-century Mexican novel's contradictory relationship to totality, it is not surprising that other genres and media have more often been praised for contributing to the relatively progressive culture of social and political critique that has gradually emerged in Mexico since the 1970s. Claire Brewster's recent analysis of the nonfiction writings of Octavio Paz, Carlos Fuentes, Carlos Monsiváis, and Elena Poniatowska is thus paradigmatic.[10] It focuses on how the chronicle and the testimonial, especially as practiced by Poniatowska and Monsiváis, have helped bring about the "hesitant growth of civil society" (203) in post-Tlatelolco Mexico. Brewster is correct in arguing that Poniatowska and Monsiváis have produced texts that have been consistently critical of dominant political power. Indeed, their work has strengthened a general trend of challenging established cultural and political norms over the past few decades. This tendency is visible in a number of disciplines and media. The works of Lorenzo Meyer, Héctor Aguilar Camín, and Sergio Zermeño, cited above, exemplify critical historical and sociological analysis. The emergence of the weekly *Proceso* in 1976 and the daily *La Jornada* in 1984 represent important developments in print media. In literature, chronicles, testimonials, and narrative works have focused on a number of previously taboo subjects, including Tlatelolco, counterinsurgency, political corruption, the protection of human rights, and struggles to recognize and help alleviate the oppression of women, indigenous populations, and sexual minorities.[11] The release of politically charged films like *Canoa* (1975), *Rojo amanecer* (1989), and *La ley de Herodes* (1999) testify to significant changes in cinema. Finally, it is important to note a growing culture of political and social movements, such as the citizens' relief organizations that formed after the earthquake of 1985, the Zapatista insurgency's dramatic appearance in 1994, and the tentative efforts to uncover and prosecute political crimes of the past, especially Ignacio Carrillo Prieto's Fiscalía Especial para Movimientos Sociales y Políticos del Pasado (FEMOSPP).[12]

This cursory list does not do justice to the rich spectrum of phenomena that characterize the more openly critical Mexican cultural production of the past three decades, but it does give credence to the portentous description of the positive impact of 1968 that Poniatowska made in 1978:

> Aparentemente todo ha quedado igual y sin embargo el aire a veces trae el rumor de las manifestaciones, el júbilo que se oía en las calles, el ímpetu que a todos nos deslumbró y entonces uno siente que todavía subsiste en los jóvenes el arrojo del 68 pero ahora con una mayor reflexión, un sentido más profundo y una proyección en la que quisiéramos adivinar el rumbo terco y decidido que nos salvará históricamente. (*Fuerte* 77)

Also writing in 1978, Monsiváis makes a similar observation about the social and cultural influences of 1968. His prologue to Zermeño's study of the Student Movement concludes that, "Con sus fallas, carencias, contradicciones, limitaciones ideológicas y actitudes irresolubles, el Movimiento Estudiantil de 1968 es una hazaña del México contemporáneo, recapitulación y nuevo punto de partida de las grandes luchas de las mayorías, y de los derechos, conjuntos y separados, de mayorías y minorías" ("Dramatis" xxiv). These statements are significant for their use of teleological language and they attest to the difficulty of avoiding appeals to notions of new beginnings and salvation when placing events as weighty as the Student Movement and Tlatelolco into context.

VI

Si muero contributes to an understanding of post-Tlatelolco Mexico by examining the destructive potential of teleology, renewal, and redemption. Yet its critique of the historiographical concepts that grounded the Revolutionary state's ideology leaves Aguilar Mora's novel struggling to find alternative points of reference. In a text that is less commemorative than his prologue to Zermeño's book, and which is titled "La pasión de la historia" (1980), Monsiváis addresses this struggle. He argues that the writing of history must develop a critical collective identity, and that it must "fortalecer y ampliar la conciencia colectiva; para hacer de la recuperación y el olvido selectivo del pasado un instrumento de identidad crítica" (171). Notably, Monsiváis rejects a totalizing conception of history when he argues for a recovery of the past that incorporates selective forgetting. At first glance, and for good reason, selective forgetting recalls the oppressive power of the state to control history; the most obvious example of which is the Mexican government's efforts to whitewash Tlatelolco. On the other hand, *Si muero*'s reflections on forgetting complement Monsiváis's observation because they demonstrate, by negative example, the repressive consequences of mobilizing a totalizing vision of history in order to define national community. It is precisely Yoris's efforts to remember what he has forgotten and the orphans' attempts to identify their origins that define their subjectivity. The national-allegorical message communicated through these characters' stories is that the more one seeks totality the harder it is to maintain one's autonomy.

When Ixca Cienfuegos approaches Gladys García at the conclusion of *La región más transparente*, he has already lost his physical form, his ethereal presence having become the sublime totality of the Mexican nation and its history. Yet his challenge must always remain the incorporation of García, whose subjectivity Ixca shapes by casting her as the final piece to the puzzle of totalizing national identity. In *José Trigo*, the explanatory totality—the organizing force of the sublime—emerges for an instant during the railroad workers' final demonstration. This transcendent moment of all-seeing unity follows their reconstruction of Luciano's body. The workers' self-definition and autonomous subject creation is violently interrupted by government repression. The brutal, subject-forming foundations of patriarchal state authority appear starkly in *Con Él, conmigo, con nosotros tres*, a novel that refuses to ignore the violence that grounds a totalizing conception of history, and which rejects the idea that purity must be a precondition for renewal or critique. Still, Mendoza's novel ironically establishes death as a space from which Delfina critiques patriarchy and state-sponsored violence. Though *Si muero* does not offer death as a potentially critical space outside history, it does try to imagine subjectivity as separate from understandings of time and space that are informed by the desire for continuity and coherence. But the forces that do succeed in shaping history and national identity in Aguilar Mora's novel relentlessly assault the novel's characters, leaving them without even imagined alternatives.

Such a force emerges suddenly in an encounter between Yoris and two men who assail him, and whose identity remains undetermined (they are either *halcones* or members of the secret police). The depiction of Yoris's beating connects his individual pain to the collective trauma Mexico experienced during the weeks and months of the Student Movement and the government's repressive response. It appears to be July 30, 1968, about two months before Tlatelolco.[13] The brutality Yoris suffers in the assault devastates his sense of identity: "se había convertido en puro dolor, no tenía nombre, ni pasado, ni memoria, ni futuro, ni manos, ni deseo, ni imágenes, todo era dolor" (111). After huddling in a doorway for some time, Yoris begins to recover. And his eyes fixate upon something lying in the gutter:

> fue poco a poco reconociendo el objeto que atraía su mirada. Ahí, en la orilla de la banqueta estaba tirada una caja de cerillos de la Central y desde la puerta distinguía al joven con canasta de frutas de Caravaggio, número 12 de la colección. Eran las once pasadas en su reloj, pero se lo acercó al oído para saber si con la caída no se había parado. Al tratar de oír el ruido de la cuerda lo que oyó fue un ruido sordo, una explosión seca, mortal, definitiva, como una cuchillada en el tímpano. Y la noche se desmoronó entonces en astillas, gritos, quejidos, lamentos, disparos. (111)

Before the air around him rends itself apart, Yoris finds the matchbox he needed to complete his collection. He does not voluntarily see it. Instead, it is an object that attracts his gaze. Reproduced upon the matchbox is the Caravaggio portrait whose face the art-collector Dziadeck surgically implants onto the orphan Caravayo. The matchbox-painting missing from Yoris's collection is, notably, the culmination of a European artistic teleology tracing the completeness and perfection of the human form.

His sense of self destroyed by his assailants, Yoris does not see the picture as much as the picture sees him and draws his gaze toward it. This episode and the description of the traumatic bus ride attest to the way in which *Si muero* portrays subjectivity as a force beyond the control of the individual. In his rejection of the notion of an individual consciousness capable of apprehending others and thus a representation of itself, Jacques Lacan emphasizes the fundamental importance of lacunae in the visual field, arguing that "Psycho-analysis regards the consciousness as irremediably limited, and institutes as a principle, not only of idealization, but of *méconnaissance*, as [...] *scotoma*" (82–83; original emphasis). *Scotoma* is defined as "a stain or a gap in the visual field," related to subjectivity as the gap or split the subject is unable to control, and that, in turn, determines the subject. The desire to overcome this split is an essential aspect of the gaze: "the object on which depends the phantasy from which the subject is suspended in an essential vacillation" (83). Thus the gaze does not emerge from the subject, but is instead an irrecoverable, external force to which the subject is repeatedly and tenaciously compelled, in Lacan's words, "an unnamed substance from which I, the seer, extract myself" (82). Instead of producing and controlling an idealized notion of its own identity, the subject is produced by that fantasy, controlled by it, suspended from it in an effort to wrest itself from its grip.

The perfect form of Caravaggio's painting is the external fantasy upon which Yoris is suspended. It represents the ideal of his individual subjectivity. Yet Yoris has no time to palliate the split in his identity exacerbated by the assault he suffered. Just as he finds the matchbox, the vault of the city's night explodes, leaving him with nothing but a forgotten past that can never be fully recovered. He is left with no clear space upon which to inscribe his life and make meaning of it. Instead, he is forced to confront a space that emerges as the force *that inscribes him* with the irresistible compulsion to remember what can only remain forgotten.

Yoris's failed attempts to remember what he has forgotten and his fixation on the miniature Caravaggio exemplify the novel's simultaneous critique of and appeal to subjective coherence and temporal continuity. The destinies of Dziadeck's orphans help explain the novel's critique of identity by showing how the search for identity and its origins is precisely that which impedes its fulfillment. The compulsion to remember begins to afflict the six orphans after their faces have been altered upon Dziadeck's orders. By subjecting them to plastic surgery, Dziadeck violently projects his desire for order and perfection onto the orphans. Shortly after their surgeries, this formerly tight-knit group of friends struggles to recognize the ties that bind them: "No podíamos intercambiar nuestras perspectivas por un destino común aunque al vernos con nuestros nuevos rostros todos presentíamos que algo común e inevitable ya estaba injertado en nuestro nombre, en nuestra imagen, en nuestro tiempo, en nuestra muerte quizás" (321). Though aware that something controls them, the orphans cannot identify it. This unease causes them to worry about their origins for the first time:

> no habían podido recuperar íntegramente el poder de sus miradas [...] nunca pudieron, tampoco, recuperar la beligerancia en la competencia o en el interés político de una decisión: pero si nunca se recuperaron, sin embargo aquello se pudrió en tal forma sobre el recuerdo de su unidad que muy pronto nutrió la inquietud por un origen o por una justificación. Sin decírselo, todos se preguntaban por qué estaban juntos y por qué todos parecían conducidos hacia el mismo destino. (321)

The orphans' dilemma seems comically absurd. Yet it is also a horrifying allegory that helps explain how subaltern subjectivities are produced at the limit of an allegedly universal desire for a perfected collective identity. Like the molding of citizens that early- to mid-twentieth-century Mexicanist thinkers advocated in their efforts to understand the national psyche, Dziadeck distorts the orphans according to an ideal of physical beauty and a progression of aesthetic advancement. The comparison between Mexicanism and Dziadeck's bizarre project becomes explicit in the novel when the orphans ask themselves why they have been chosen to suffer this transformation:

> —¿Por qué nos ha escogido a nosotros y no a otros? ¿Por qué a nosotros? —preguntó Bronsino.
>
> —¿Cómo saberlo? Él nunca nos lo va a decir.
>
> —Algo en común, debemos tener algo en común que nosotros no sabemos. (322)

When Caravayo then supposes that Dziadeck chose them out of "azar, puro azar" (323), Martina—who in addition to being aphasic often speaks backwards—says, "raza, raza" (323).

Caravayo's response elucidates the novel's critique of identity: "si no fue por azar entonces fue por la raza. En el fondo es lo mismo" (323). Caravayo thus exposes the arbitrary nature of not only the teleological progression of identity that Dziadeck imposes upon them but also the appeal to authenticity that motivated the Mexicanist project.

Even if they recognize that Dziadeck's project is not essential, the orphans have clearly internalized its validity and goals. Their search for origins comes after they have been violently interpellated by Dziadeck, and the novel describes this search as something rotten that conceals the memory of their previous unity. This desired unity may be described, in Lacan's terms, as the "where it was" of the subject, or the absolutely inaccessible unified fantasy home of "the real" (45). Portrayed earlier as a coherent group, the orphans once enjoyed a collective identity that was always already inaccessible to Yoris, as his experience on the bus illustrates. This contrast helps explain the orphans' allegorical presence in the novel by emphasizing how the question of national culture fully permeated the Mexican social context that helped produce *Si muero*, a novel that here proposes that national culture had become a preoccupation as destructive as it was unavoidable.

Yet *Si muero* cannot merely reject the idea of a coherent, definitive, and defining national culture. On the whole, the novel takes very seriously the concepts of continuity, totality, and community that ground the strong collective desire for a stable, knowable social identity. The following passage typifies the novel's contradictory totalizing impulse. While its language and technique betray the desire for totality, its content critiques the arbitrary dominance that defines Mexican society:

> y el campesino de Guerrero que se vuelve soldado raso y los oficinistas y los burócratas y los obreros y las amas de casa y las secretarias y las empleadas y los gerentes y los médicos y los ingenieros y los estudiantes y los pasajeros de camiones que se cruzan y se vuelven a cruzar, que se miran, se tocan, se juntan, se separan, se huelen, se ignoran, y todos tejen ese rostro de rejas y figuras que la sociedad dispone para llamarse sociedad [...] conserva lo que eres para que otros sigan siendo lo que son para los ojos de este cuerpo entero, de este cuerpo total que se resuelve por zonas, por valles, por costas y montañas, que es una patria, nuestra patria [...] mírate en

> la sociedad y te reconocerás [...] y más allá no encontrarás nada, más allá del espejo total de la sociedad no hay nada. (86–88)

Yoris, like every Mexican, must recognize himself in the society that surrounds and shapes him. Like his relationship to the matchbox painting that appears to be his salvation, he is unable to separate himself from the total mirror that is society. Society's organizing power is reinforced by the compulsive, logical desire for community that the novel, often through Yoris, consistently expresses.[14]

By constantly abutting them, *Si muero* elaborately portrays the limits that stand just this side of the Lacanian real, which Slavoj Zizek has described as "*simultaneously* the Thing to which direct access is not possible and the obstacle that prevents this direct access; the Thing that eludes our grasp and the distorting screen that makes us miss the Thing" (77; original emphasis). In *Si muero*, something like the Lacanian real emerges as both the explanatory totality that is inaccessible *and* the supposition that such a totality exists, a supposition that further impedes access to totality. The novel traces the shift that Zizek identifies from that which "eludes our grasp," to the "distorting screen" that keeps it forever at arm's length. By naming its lack, the orphans will never recover their unity; by identifying coherence as his goal, Yoris will never be a coherent subject. *Si muero* does not take the easy way out and proclaim ideology as merely a veil. In fact, the novel's complex approach to the critique of ideology keeps it from positing access to that which Zizek defines as the Lacanian real, namely, the fantasy of unity. The novel's ingenious reflections on ideology recognize that positing such access as possible would simply produce yet another ideology.

VII

The tension between exposing and reproducing ideology that *Si muero* enacts appears again and again as the novel constantly worries over a guiding, inaccessible force that controls individuals and their relationship to community. Yoris's experience on the bus is exemplary. In an interview published the same year the novel came out, Aguilar Mora expresses an interest in portraying reality as an illusion when he states that "En la novela [...] está esa obsesión de que la realidad es un cristal, una pantalla que es necesario rasgar" (de Luna and Patiño 23). Note that Aguilar Mora says "scratch," and not, for example, "penetrate" or "remove." Like that which Yoris has forgotten, the forces behind the screens are never fully accessible to those who seek them. Furthermore, as Zizek's analysis of the Lacanian real suggests, the harder one looks, the less one finds. Instead of being rewarded upon identifying a transcendent notion of Mexicanness that unfolds and eventually reveals the totality of the national community, those who seek totalizing meaning in *Si muero* suffer the caprices of an unpredictable, destructive, determinant force whose strength is fueled by their investigations.

Yoris's investigations explore the temporal and spatial manifestations of totality. He hopes to glimpse the totalizing machine that organizes all change, which he describes as that "máquina inmensamente transformada, inmensamente dueña de todas las metamorfosis" (141). But he fails to make sense of change when he interrogates temporal logic and asks about the purpose of what he calls "momentos transitorios" (141–42). Such moments, Yoris contends, "No tienen otro fin que servir y desaparecer, no tienen otro fin que dejarnos pasar a la otra orilla y desaparecer, no tienen otro fin que dejarnos pasar y desaparecer, y ése es el secreto que nos irrita" (142). Associating time and subjectivity, he then asks himself, "¿Y si yo fuera un momento así?" (142). His answer expresses a desire for collective understanding of time as a logically developing process, but, significantly, it does not discover the secret of the transitory moments, the lacunae that sustain teleology:

> Nada tendría que preguntarme entonces, sólo me bastaría con pensarme tendido horizontalmente en el filo de mi vida y desapareciendo en ese filo a la llegada del otro momento, del momento que será algo, del momento en que algo será declarado para memoria de todos ustedes; pero el momento anterior, el que le dio paso, se habrá confundido con el filo mismo de su tiempo y ahí habrá quedado, línea pura del secreto de no servirle de soporte al tiempo, ni a la memoria, línea recta del secreto por donde pasa el tiempo y la memoria para encontrarse con la historia mientras los puentes desaparecen. (142)

These transitory moments vanish once the teleology they help construct has been consummated. And this teleology casts a shadow back onto the transitory moments, concealing and distorting their individual natures by defining them only as functions of a process whose ultimate aim could not be wholly foreseen from the perspective of the transitory moment. Thus through its portrayal of Yoris's meditations on totality, *Si muero* mobilizes a critique of teleology that exposes the violent potential of the national promise, of, for example, Gamio's indigenous populations, whose true natures would only reveal themselves once they had helped complete a national project of which they would only serve as component parts and definitely not as designers.

Yoris's thoughts on totality impinge upon Mexican national community by considering the crucial year of 1968 and trying to imagine the total trajectories of others, including Tosca, Yoris's erstwhile lover. In a passage similar to the novel's introductory note, the text reads:

> Algún día me dedicaré a preguntarle a todos los que conozco: ¿qué hacías tú la mañana del 3 de agosto de 1968? [...] Esa es la única manera en que la historia, mi historia, sería verosímil; cuando todos ustedes, y tú, Tosca, digan qué hacían el 3 de agosto de 1968 [...] que todos lo escriban en una hoja tamaño carta, lo coloquen en un sobre y lo manden a la misma dirección y yo no haré sino leer las narraciones de todos hasta que la vida se me agote: sólo así podré reconstituir este fragmento de la máquina y sólo así podré decir que en algún momento te conocí, máquina universal llena de alas. (146)

Yoris's reflections on time, space, and total knowledge attest to the frustration that inevitably arises from the desire for transcendence. But they also reveal the compulsory nature of that desire, of the effort to glimpse at least a fragment of the forces that order time and space.

When Yoris describes the totalizing machine as composed of wings, he alludes to its sinister nature, because these wings constantly threaten to destroy him. Similar to the force that interpellates him on the bus, the wings of the machine assault Yoris, as in the following scene, when "Movió la cabeza violentamente para desprenderse de esos aletazos de murciélago que le rompían la mirada y le cortaban con una navaja el aire que respiraba y le dejaban su cuerpo hecho arena perfumada e insípida" (282–83).[15] The totalizing machine not only assaults Yoris but also the orphans, who frequently feel an immense skin descending upon them. It first appears as a howl they hear when they are following Yoris and Tosca through Mexico City:

> una voz que parecía arrastrarse, en pánico, por las fachadas de los edificios y de las casas como un animal herido [...]. Y guardaron silencio, y se dieron cuenta que [...] no la oían sino que la veían; veían la voz de un animal, un animal al que sólo le quedaba la piel, una piel purulenta que se untaba a las fachadas de los edificios y de las casas. (84)

Descending, the howl changes from an intangible voice into a visible, material presence that comes into grotesque contact with the cityscape.

The novel associates this howling, descending force with the constitution of subjectivity when it describes how the orphans respond to Dziadeck's announcement that he is going to order the surgical alteration of their faces: "Teníamos miedo [...] y todos pensamos en aquella piel que habíamos visto gritar en las calles de Polanco" (220). The image of the suffocating skin provokes fear, which in turn leads the orphans to preoccupy themselves with their origins and a common destiny, trajectories pointing to the past and the future whose meanings can never become entirely clear. After they return from Europe, and plastic surgery, the orphans encounter the howling skin once more, and this time it conceals the city from them. Then they begin to suffer acutely from an affliction similar to Yoris's inability to locate himself in the present:

> cada vez eran más confusas, más difusas las líneas, más huecas las paredes, más deleznable el aire, más diáfana la oscuridad de la noche [...] los días no eran una trampa, pero tampoco eran una salida [...] no eran ni siquiera una fecha ya con un término, con alguna referencia temporal [...] o alguna referencia geográfica. (456)[16]

This confusion prompts Bronsino to ask questions similar to those Yoris ponders: "¿desde dónde se puede ver la totalidad de estas piezas? Yo sólo soy un hilo pero ¿dónde puedo ver el tejido completo?" (455). Perceiving totality becomes

Bronsino's obsession, which ultimately leads him to climb to the top of Mexico City's tallest building, La Torre Latinoamericana, "para tratar de ver la totalidad, al menos de esta ciudad" (460). Bronsino's descent recalls Ixca Cienfuegos's transformation and flight over Mexico City, but it fails to communicate the explanatory transcendence embodied by Ixca's epiphany. Bronsino falls from the tower and becomes "una hemorragia de deseo, una hemorragia de contacto que salía de su cuerpo, y que al desprenderse caía vertiginosamente desde esa altura para desparramarse lenta pero seguramente por toda la ciudad" (460). Even though Bronsino begins to form part of the suffocating surface that covers the city, his radical transformation does not allow him to see everything: "Era un espejismo esa altura; esa propiedad, ese poder, era un espejismo, seguía siendo una pieza y su deseo seguía esperando y no vencía" (461).

Faced with the limits of their perceptions, Yoris and Bronsino are not assuaged by a reassuring level of understanding that produces the pleasure of an encounter with the sublime. The totality they cannot perceive instead perceives them, in no small part because their desire for totality endows totality with its palpable, distorting, and in the case of Bronsino, deadly, strength. The following passage appears as the novel comes to a close, when Yoris has returned to Mexico City to find that it is sinking into its own sewage. Struggling to make sense of the apocalypse that greets him once he steps off the plane from France, he returns obsessively to the totalizing machine. The narrator describes this machine as a cinema, in which images are projected onto a screen from behind in what amounts to a perverse retelling of Plato's allegory of the cave. Not only is it impossible to distinguish between reality, screen, and projector, but also the search for such distinctions makes them that much harder to identify:

> La realidad se ha convertido en una membrana, en una pantalla donde todo se proyecta; pero la luz no surge de este lado [...] sino del otro lado [...] de aquel lado inalcanzable donde se producen las imágenes que aparecen ante nosotros como ámbito mismo de nuestros cuerpos, hasta hacernos aceptar que nosotros también somos parte de esa proyección. [...] de vez en cuando queremos romper esa membrana, queremos rasgarla con nuestro cuerpo sin brillo [...] y descubrimos

> que detrás no hay nada [...] está la tramoya de cables, poleas, cicloramas, bambalinas, telones de fondo [...] nos quedamos entonces con las imágenes, con la membrana cicatrizada y sabemos y preferimos, contra todas las ironías, esa realidad llena de imágenes que son la realidad aunque no la hagan ellas [...] y nos damos cuenta también que entre más cicatrices tenga esa pantalla más relieve tendrá [...] más fácil será confundirse con ella [...] allá detrás, en las bambalinas, en la tramoya, no hay nada, están sólo los instrumentos del poder que entregados a nuestro arbitrio no sabemos qué hacer con ellos. (519–20)

Reality is a screen upon whose surface are projected images that originate in the totalizing machine that infects and constitutes subjects, especially those who wish to expose it. Each time people are able to scratch the surface of the screen and catch a glimpse of the pulleys, ropes, and props that belong to the projecting theater, they become more integrated into the screen.

VIII

The pessimism evinced in the novel's description of how resistance to the oppressive totalizing machine only strengthens it permeates the text and its discussion of ideology's distorting force. Yet *Si muero* also alludes to potential liberatory trajectories, or "lines of flight," to use the term Gilles Deleuze and Felix Guatarri theorize in *A Thousand Plateaus* (1987). These lines always run parallel to one another in Yoris's experience. They resist incorporation into a convergent conception of history, and they reject teleology. In reflections similar to the meditations on time and space cited above, when Yoris remembers his recent travels through Europe, he fails to capture their reality and narrate his experience simultaneously. The third-person narrator writes, describing Yoris, "¿Dónde estaba Amberes veinte años antes, cuando oyó por primera vez ese nombre [...]? Amberes se había quedado allá [...] y había recorrido toda su vida, pero nunca como un recuerdo, sino como una pasión paralela, como una esperanza siempre paralela, siempre presente, siempre presente, compañera constante" (359).

Earlier in the novel, Yoris and Nicole, who is in charge of providing Yoris with Dziadeck's Martini, devise a plan to capture the infinity of the parallel present and thus resist the reductive order of teleological narration. In an effort to experience the separate meaning of the transitory moment, they visit a new train station every afternoon and study its different elements: departing trains, arriving trains, the waiting room, the restaurant, the ticket counters. The identities that pass through the station constantly change because the station does nothing but mark change: "Cuando Yoris y Nicole ponen el primer pie en la estación, no hay pasado; cuando retiran el primero para poner el otro, no hay pasado. No queda paso, ni pasado dentro de las estaciones; la eternidad reina aquí para los que vivimos dentro de las estaciones" (200).

Repetition characterizes the novel's descriptions of the constantly changing space of the train station; and *Si muero* attributes emancipatory value to repetition in a refrain that describes the relationship between trains and hope. Appearing four times in the text, the refrain reads, "El tren sigue su ritmo, rimando velocidad con rieles, rimando el incesante transcurso de la vida de los otros con la dirección infinita de la esperanza, de la praxis" (290, 299, 331, 387).[17] Different from the trains and stations that anchor the present to the past in *José Trigo*, Yoris and Nicole's visits to stations and this refrain about the train suggest spaces and trajectories outside of the logical sequence of meaning that the characters who populate *Si muero* simultaneously resist and desire. The rhythm of the train, a non-linguistic sound, makes another sonorous association, a rhyme, between speed and parallel rails. This association is followed by another that is more abstract, but that is still described as a rhyme: the comparison of the never-ending trajectories of the lives of others with the infinite direction of hope. The final allusion to praxis turns the text back on itself, revealing how the repetitions that the novel includes represent a means of embodying the hope that lies dormant in the expression of a totality that is not ordered chronologically or directionally.

IX

Ultimately, however, totalizing order overtakes Yoris. When he returns to Mexico City to discover that it is drowning in its own sewage, everything Yoris has forgotten comes back with a vengeance. In a scene parallel to the opening scene on the bus, Yoris realizes he has forgotten something. This time, though, he gets to see what it is. The novel's final passage reads:

> la presencia olvidada comienza a aparecer, como si lo hubiera estado esperando [...] Por el agua estancada [...] se oye un chapoteo masivamente minúsculo, como el latido de miles de manecillas de reloj que no quieren ahogarse; y por reflejos azorosos Yoris empieza a distinguir pequeños resplandores, pequeñas heridas de marfil en la noche estancada del lago [...] chillidos minúsculos pero filosos, agudos, ensordecedores, continuos, profundamente continuos, y Yoris en ese momento recobra la imagen de lo que ha olvidado, pero ya es demasiado tarde. Su cuerpo se contrae de terror, abandonado por su deseo, por su ilusión, por su esperanza, y en ese instante ya no le queda nada [...] mientras aquel olvido sigue acercándose, [...] el grito bárbaro y afirmativo de la destrucción, el rostro verdadero de nuestra noche. (522)

Finally, the novel identifies the forgotten that plagues Yoris, but like the forces that interpellate Martina and enter the bodies of the victims of Tlatelolco, the monstrous forgotten presence can only be identified after it is too late to prevent its destructive effects. The arrival of the forgotten in the novel's final scene is announced by the mechanical sound of the totalizing machine, and the final product of totality is oblivion. This passage's juxtaposition of totality and the forgotten reveals the novel's central warning against totalizing thought: the effort to remember and the consequences of forgetting necessarily become stronger in direct proportion to the strength of the desire for totality.

When *Si muero* finally ends, its apocalyptic vision of the appeal to totality seals off the escape routes of hope that it identified earlier, just as the forgotten chases hope from Yoris's body. The impact that the conclusion creates by explaining how the force of the forgotten defines the identity of Mexico's night depends upon a totalizing, determinant identification between forgetting and national community. The aesthetic charge of this final passage rests on the appeal to a glimpse of the unitary fantasy of the Lacanian real, which is precisely the appeal that plagues the novel's characters' attempts to order their lives and communal identities. In this sense, *Si muero* hints at the continuing power of the sublime that informs efforts to define

Mexican national identity, and which appears to offer a true vision of everything, if only for a brief moment. But the determinant force in Aguilar Mora's novel is at best a degraded version of the sublime because it proposes no identifiable order to be realized in the future. Not only is totalizing force in *Si muero* consubstantial with the people and places it shapes, but it always precedes their comprehension, never allowing its subjects to understand their relationship to a future horizon that may help them define themselves.

Aguilar Mora's text struggles to defy the destructive consequences of successive logic. It incorporates "unwritten" chapters; chapters written by others; the repetition of entire passages, which destabilizes specific meaning; and unclear boundaries between realist and highly symbolic portrayals of its characters. *Si muero* constantly refers to the repressive effects of totalizing thought. Nevertheless, the novel's framing and guiding image, the structuring power of absences, specifically the forgotten, exists in an irresistible tension with the appeal to totality. Perhaps there is no way to escape the relationship between forgetting and remembering, described by the six orphans as that which "rotted in such a way over the memory of their unity that very quickly it fed the anxiety about an origin or a justification." Opening and closing with the forgotten that besets Yoris, the novel leaves no space for a unity that precedes the divided subjectivity that yearns for a completeness that it can never achieve. *Si muero* thus embodies the terrible paradox that nothing threatens the autonomy of the subject, either individual or collective, more than the desire for autonomy itself.

Two long-term historical factors that shaped the context within which the Tlatelolco massacre took place speak to the validity of this paradox that Aguilar Mora's novel so painstakingly explores. First, the desire for economic autonomy led to Mexico's increasing reliance on foreign investment, which in turn aggravated the problem of foreign debt. Unsustainable economic development triggered and exacerbated the uneasiness of Mexico's urban, middle-class youth, the population most active in the Student Movement and most persecuted by the state's violent response to it. Second, the desire to be considered a modern nation provided a strong impulse not only to host the Olympic Games in Mexico City in 1968 but also to ensure that they would go on no matter what. The decision to plan and carry out the massacre at the Plaza of the Three Cultures was ultimately made by the Mexican government. But, it must also be understood within the global economic and political context as a symptom of the lack of national autonomy that, in turn, exposed the lack at the heart of the national-popular narrative that became more and more visible during the years between the publication of *La región más transparente* and *Morir en el golfo*, the text I analyze in the concluding chapter.

Chapter Five

The "Machine of Savage Stories"

State, Fiction, and Totality in Héctor Aguilar Camín's *Morir en el golfo*

The unnamed narrator of Héctor Aguilar Camín's first novel, *Morir en el golfo* (1986), is a journalist who finds himself wrapped up in the investigation of a series of what appear to be politically motivated murders. In March 1976 his erstwhile friend Francisco Rojano Gutiérrez shows the narrator a number of grisly photographs of the victims and explains that he (Rojano) could be next in line. Persuaded as much by Rojano's fear as by his interest in Rojano's wife Anabela Guillamín, another old friend, the narrator agrees to write about the murders in his newspaper column, operating under the assumption that publicly exposing the truth will prevent the murderer from striking again. Rojano suspects Lázaro Pizarro, a powerful leader in Mexico's petroleum workers' union. The narrator quickly learns that his investigation of Pizarro could disturb the sensitive balance of order and chaos that defines Mexican politics during the latter half of the 1970s. It takes him longer to understand that seeking the truth is a fool's errand.

Another unnamed character in *Morir* is the narrator's informant in the Secretaría de Gobernación. The national director of security, he is defined both by his cool demeanor and predilection for Dunhill cigarettes and by his extraordinary ability to control and manipulate knowledge. The narrator was initially introduced to his informant through his journalist friend René Arteaga. He met Arteaga in 1969, a year when, as the narrator describes it in the hardboiled style his speech often adopts, "calientes [eran] todavía las heridas de Tlatelolco y más caliente yo en mis inicios como reportero de policía" (44). When they met, René explained to the narrator how educational his new job could be: "la historia de las revoluciones está llena de cuerpos policiacos que sobreviven a ellas y son los sótanos del nuevo régimen. [...] si quieres conocer los fundamentos de una sociedad, lo que menos cambia en ella, debes ser reportero de la fuente policiaca" (45). About eight months after he met Arteaga, the narrator met his government informant and eventually established a strong working relationship with him, a collaboration based partly on the fact that both are from Veracruz. Years later, the informant seconds Arteaga's lessons about social surfaces and the forces that operate beneath them. He tells the narrator, who began a daily column called "Vida Pública" in 1974, that "Los periódicos son el sismógrafo del estado [...]. Y los columnistas, los sismólogos" (46–47). In November 1976, just before José López Portillo is to take the presidential sash from Luis Echeverría, the narrator visits his informant in the latter's office and causes a minor earthquake when he asks about Pizarro. Describing what happened after he left his informant's office, where he learned very little about Pizarro, the narrator writes, "Al cruzar por el escritorio de su ayudante en el pasillo, esuché el timbre insistente, casi histérico ahora, que venía del escritorio de mi paisano" (49).

In his analysis of Raymond Chandler's *The Big Sleep* (1939), Fredric Jameson emphasizes the disruptive nature of the detective's search: "The appearance of the detective breaks the balance, sets the various mechanisms of suspicion ringing, as he triggers the electric eyes, snooping and preparing to make trouble in a way which isn't yet clear" ("On Raymond Chandler" 143–44). When Aguilar Camín's narrator tells Rojano that he has decided to investigate the murders, the latter responds, "No sabes lo que vas a encontrar" (44). Trouble is what he has found by the end of the novel, when Rojano and Pizarro are dead and Anabela is a widow. What remains unclear is the truth, as nothing surrounding these deaths is ever fully explained. But as Jameson also explains in his analysis of Chandler, "the underlying crime is always old, lying half forgotten" (147). What really matters is less the murder than "descriptions of searches" (143), a judgment that holds true for Aguilar Camín's novel as much as for Chandler's.

A compelling thriller, *Morir* organizes its plot around a search for the truth that reveals the rotten underbelly of Mexican power politics. This chapter proposes that through dark humor and a scathing critique of figures and events that are either slightly fictionalized or identified by their actual names, Aguilar Camín's novel objectifies and dismisses the validity of integrative totality in a merciless parody of bankrupt, national-popular ideological pieties. Significant to my analysis is the fact that *Morir* shares certain important characteristics of the detective genre as it has been analyzed by numerous critics, namely, the search motif and a tendency toward social criticism. Because *Morir* takes important formal cues from a genre borrowed from Europe and the United States, this chapter also emphasizes how critics have identified parody as one of the Latin American crime novel's central elements.

The most important parodic figure in the novel is Pizarro, the oil industry's union leader. The second half of the 1970s in Mexico witnessed unprecedented growth in oil extraction and export. The characters in *Morir* are more than willing to kill each other in their efforts to control even a piece of the incredible wealth generated by Mexico's oil boom. Since oil is also a symbolically important industry for Mexico, the novel's critique of the corruption that drives this economic sector is also a critique of national-popular ideology. Understanding the importance of the ideological renewal that the oil boom appeared to afford the dying national-popular state demands a summary understanding of the oil industry in the late 1970s and early 1980s, which rapidly went from boom to bust.

Pizarro appears in the novel as the incarnation of national-popular ideology, and it is in descriptions of his philosophy and economic activity that the novel reflects most explicitly on an integrative totality. Pizarro's dream is to construct an autonomous, coherent society under his rule. *Morir* exposes the limits of Pizarro's ambitions by comparing the area under his control to the vast remainder of Mexican society, which continues to suffer considerable misery and injustice. By identifying inclusive totality with Pizarro, the novel inserts it into a sphere that is separated from actual Mexican history. Another kind of totality emerges in the novel in the form of the remarkable quantity of information that is at the fingertips of the narrator's informant in Gobernación. But this totality, which reaches much farther than Pizarro's does, is a sinister instrument of repression, with no aspiration toward inclusion. Furthermore, the informant's totality does not even pretend to connect itself to some kind of historically rooted authenticity. The priority of appearance and a tactical regard for the truth fuel the informant's worldview and the totalizing narratives he constructs.

Near its conclusion, *Morir* evokes the sublime in terms very similar to what Kant calls "the mathematically sublime." Yet for the novel, the sublime is also a parody of itself, contained within the pages of the text as a force susceptible to the novel's narrative manipulations, and not as a force exterior to it toward which the novel strives to accede. The chapter concludes by emphasizing that Aguilar Camín's novel can be understood as a text that helps explain why appeals to the national totality could no longer support an inclusive ideology that concealed political domination once the national-popular state's hegemony was irreparably damaged by the oil bust and the devastating debt crisis it produced.

I

The narrator's search in *Morir* becomes a search for totality as he learns more about Pizarro, Rojano, Anabela, and the Mexican state. Jameson's article on Chandler, originally published in 1970, develops his preoccupation with representing the social totality, which corresponds to his Marxist perspective and which has helped define his career as a cultural critic.[1] Regarding *The Big Sleep*, he reasons, "Since there is no longer any privileged experience in which the whole of the social structure can be grasped, a figure must be invented [...] through [the detective] we are able to see, to know, the society as a whole" (127–28). In an earlier discussion of the detective genre, Richard Alewyn also focuses on the way mystery stories reveal hidden truths about a given society. Identifying the origins of the detective story in the writings of E.T.A. Hoffmann, Alewyn connects the genre to German Romanticism. He explains, "For romanticism, mystery is the condition of the world and all external appearance is merely the hieroglyph of a concealed meaning" (74). While *Morir* organizes its plot around the gradual revealing of previously hidden or unknown information, much of which involves a high degree of political intrigue, its narrator's search for totality ultimately asks whether there really is any meaning behind the surfaces he disrupts.

The fact that neither the narrator nor his informant has a name not only calls the reader's attention to their other similarities—after all, both are investigators who tell stories—but it also suggests a fundamental ambiguity surrounding the specificity of meaning. The doubling of the narrator and his informant highlights the parodic character of Aguilar Camín's text in particular, and attests to the importance of parody, in the Bakhtinian sense of linguistic hybridity, to detective fiction in general.[2] At one point in *Morir* a dialogue between the narrator and Rojano, in which the former comments on the latter's speech, typifies the novel's parodic style by highlighting the distance that the narrator adopts in regard to his friend's plight.[3] Rojano tells the narrator, "Empezó la guerra, hermano." The narrator's response echoes the reader's reaction to Rojano's melodramatic proclamation. First he describes Rojano to himself and the reader: "Sin rasurar, despeinado, con los labios resecos y los ojos inyectados, era un poco ridículo, sobreactuado." The narrator continues aloud: "La guerra de las putas," to which Rojano responds, "Es en serio, cabrón" (119).

To return once again to Jameson's article on *The Big Sleep*, it is worth noting that in terms of Chandler's style Jameson is most interested in his dialogue, particularly his use of American slang, which, written by an author schooled in England, comes across as distant and detached: "even those clichés and commonplaces which for the native speaker are not really words at all [...] take on outlandish resonance in his mouth, are used between quotation marks" (123). The "stylistic experimentation" enabled by Chandler's detachment corresponds to his novel's modernism, according to Jameson; but it is a specific kind of modernism: "in the earlier works [of the first decades of the twentieth century], modernism was a reaction against narration, against plot: here the empty, decorative event of the murder serves as a way of organizing essentially plotless material into an illusion of movement, into the formally satisfying arabesques of a puzzle unfolding" (124). Similar to the way in which his article on Chandler prefigures Jameson's later writings on postmodernism, Michael Holquist's discussion of Robbe-Grillet and Borges, in an article published in 1971, identifies a shift between what he calls the "classical" and the "Post-Modern" detective story, an unsettling of the belief that human experience can be ordered and understood through reason: "Post-Modernists use as a foil the assumption of detective fiction that the mind can solve all: by twisting the details just the opposite becomes the case" (155). Holquist contrasts Borges and Robbe-Grillet to Modernists around a similar shift, arguing that the former have "fought against the Modernist attempt to fill the void of the world with rediscovered mythical symbols. Rather, they dramatize the void" (155).

Jameson's "satisfying arabesques" and Holquist's dramatized void seem to me particularly apt metaphors for totality as it appears in Aguilar Camín's novel. *La región más transparente* aspires to embody the Mexican national totality. So does *José Trigo*, but at the same time it explicitly acknowledges the exclusive foundations upon which totality grounds itself. *Con Él, conmigo, con nosotros tres* mourns the destructive effects of totalizing thought. *Si muero lejos de ti* mounts an attack against totality whose exhaustive character attests to the difficulties involved in any serious effort to reject totalizing thought completely. *Morir en el golfo* does something different. It *contains* totality more than it tries to embody it, express it, or contest it. And by containing totality Aguilar Camín's novel is able to manipulate it and portray it explicitly as a socio-political construct divorced from any notion of essential meaning. In *Morir*, totality becomes an objectified concept whose parameters are defined; and this approach to totality enables parody.

II

In his study of detective fiction, Ilan Stavans explains how this genre must be parodic in Mexico and Latin America, since it is so clearly borrowed from its original US and European contexts. Stavans argues, "the idea of parody is well entrenched in [Ibero-American] culture, not always via humor but through variation, stylization, appropriation, and, above all, by way of [...] generic memory" (35). Proposing that Borges is the "master of parody in Western culture" (36), Stavans concludes that his story "Pierre Menard, Author of the *Quixote*" develops a heightened sense of parody that undermines originality and authenticity (37).

Morir adapts the detective genre to a specific Mexican context, and it also adapts totality to a specific national-historical context: the oil boom and bust of the late 1970s and early 1980s. Totality is parodied in at least two ways in Aguilar Camín's novel: first, in the representation of Lázaro Pizarro's activities as an important leader in the oil workers' union; second, in the representation of the narrator's government informant and what this character reveals about the Mexican state. In both cases, the novel challenges the idea that a totalizing representation of the nation has anything to do with originality or authenticity.

Taking a view on the detective story that highlights its testament to disorder, Alewyn writes that the genre exposes social order as little more than a fragile surface: "the apparently so prosaic and secure everyday life of the modern metropolis [has] turned out to be nothing but a thin and brittle cover, undermined by a labyrinth of criminal conspiracies" (75). In their discussions of Mexican detective fiction, Stavans and Jorge Hernández Martín emphasize that such a sense of security, even if only a flimsy veneer, is particularly precarious in Latin America. For Stavans, the Mexican and Latin American detective novel must be understood as emerging from a "chronic climate of agitation and fragile civil equilibrium" (58); and Hernández Martín paraphrases Paco Ignacio Taibo II—Mexico's, and arguably Latin America's, most famous practitioner of the detective genre—who argues, "Given the social conditions of Latin America, to expect the kind of stability that would allow for a detective to arrive at a solution through methodology [is] [...] unrealistic, even ludicrous" (160). Yet while Taibo's detective, the Basque-Irish Hector Belascoarán Shayne, fights corruption and other crimes with a distinct "humanist moral sense" (169), Aguilar Camín's narrator ultimately finds it impossible to do the right thing when his ethics become inextricably mired in politics.[4]

Ethics, politics, and economics intersected in an especially fascinating way in Mexico during the latter half of the 1970s, when most of the action in *Morir* takes place. This intersection took place around oil, a natural resource whose promise of future wealth lay just beneath the surface of the land, and whose historical legacy of national independence—embodied by President Lázaro Cárdenas's expropriation of US and British oil companies in 1938—lay just beneath the surface of the present. Ostensibly, the oil boom of the late 1970s would enable the Revolutionary state to do right by the Mexican people because the wealth it could generate would sustain populist social and economic development programs. In *Morir*, this ethical conception of the state is embodied in the figure of Pizarro, an ideological descendant of his *tocayo* Cárdenas.[5] Politically and economically the oil boom represented, at first glance paradoxically, both a motor for and a threat to Mexico's independence. When the bottom fell out of the global oil market in the early 1980s, it became clear that all that was left of the Mexican oil boom was an unmitigated disaster. The illusions of wealth and national independence that it once promised had vanished. The political challenge then was to hold the country together. This priority is similar to how the government informant in *Morir* understands his contribution to politics: "Mi tarea es la tranquilidad pública" (199).

III

In 1976, on the verge of the boom and a half-decade before the bust, Antonio J. Bermúdez, who was the Director General of Petróleos Mexicanos (PEMEX) from 1946 to 1958, published a memoir-cum-prescriptive analysis of the Mexican oil industry titled *La política petrolera mexicana*. In 1973, Mexico was a net importer of oil. So when the price of oil jumped by a factor of four that year (Beltrán Mata 35), Mexico found itself struggling to meet its energy demands. This predicament provoked Bermúdez to examine what had gone wrong with the oil company he used to run. His book tackles a number of relatively mundane problems, including an unfavorable debt-to-income balance, corruption, lack of sufficient reserves, and the insidious incursion into PEMEX's management of what Bermúdez considers bad politics, "aquella actividad dedicada directamente a la conquista del poder" (97). But Bermúdez is more concerned about something less tangible and more ideological. For him the "época de oro" of Mexican oil, 1938 to 1952, was sustained by "un alto espíritu interno —la mística petrolera" (38), which drove Mexico's oil workers to fulfill Cárdenas's vision of transforming nationalized oil into the "instrumento clave del desarrollo económico independiente de México" (35).[6] By the 1970s, according to Bermúdez, the petroleum mystique has all but vanished, its absence the gravest crisis that PEMEX faces

(111). Bermúdez is particularly adamant on the importance of restoring the mystique as a strong, guiding moral force: "Ésta no es vana fantasía ni verbalismo patriotero sino que consiste en la vigencia de los ideales de realización social y, por consiguiente, personal, que se hacen vida y orientan la conducta de todos los petroleros. Permite, como se demostró tantas veces en la historia petrolera mexicana, grandes realizaciones" (117).

Like oil under Mexican soil—or the true meaning of Mexicanness waiting to be discovered by mid-century philosophers—the petroleum mystique lies dormant, waiting to be tapped. Bermúdez could not make this message any clearer than he does when he describes the moment he stepped down as Director General. He writes in the preface to his book that President Adolfo López Mateos said to him, "'Don Antonio, le voy a hacer un vaticinio: mientras usted viva y hasta que exhale el último suspiro, por sus venas correrán sangre y petróleo'" (7). Then Bermúdez asks his readers, "Si esto ocurrió conmigo, que sólo fui un transitorio de doce años, ¿qué no pasará con los petroleros que han dedicado la totalidad de su vida al servicio de la industria?" (7). Implicit in Bermúdez's assessment of Mexico's waning petroleum mystique is the argument that these workers, who bleed oil, require a leader capable of guiding their intrinsic power, which is wasted when they and oil, Mexico's prime natural resource, are mismanaged. Thus for Bermúdez, who was 83 when he wrote his book, the national-popular dream is still attainable as long as the forces that lie below the surface of Mexico's land and its workers can be properly harnessed and guided.

Indeed there was a great deal of oil waiting to be harnessed in Mexico as Bermúdez wrote his book. The statistics are astounding. In the first half of the 1970s, significant oilfields were discovered in the states of Chiapas, Tabasco, Veracruz, and Tamaulipas (Bermúdez 16), and Mexico's oil production reached an all-time high of 1.15 million barrels per day in 1975 (15). By this same year, Mexico was no longer obliged to import oil. In fact, it had become a net exporter of crude (Beltrán Mata 41). Between the late 1970s and early 1980s, Mexico's reserves and production levels increased dramatically. Confirmed reserves rose from 20 billion barrels in 1978 to 72 billion in 1982; daily production from 1.6 million barrels a day in 1979 to 2.35

million in 1981. By 1982, it had become evident that Mexico possessed the fourth largest amount of oil reserves in the world (Beltrán Mata 43–44). Money earned by selling oil grew alongside another source of income, loans from foreign banks. Due to the success of its petroleum industry, Mexico was considered a safe bet by global lending agencies. Consequently, its foreign debt rose dramatically during the period of the oil boom, from 21 billion in 1977 to 76 billion in 1982 (Beltrán Mata 44). But at the same time the Mexican economy grew at an average of 9% between 1978 and 1981 (Beltrán Mata 45). Government spending increased roughly 30% per year during the same time period (Beltrán Mata 44), and the public benefited from the oil wealth, at least in the short term. Electricity was available to twice as many people in 1982 as it was in 1977; 1.8 million jobs were created between 1977 and 1981; salaries grew 39% in 1980, and so did buying power (44–45).

In fact, oil became explicitly significant in López Portillo's rhetoric as the fuel for the government's social programs, and by extension, the re-legitimization of the state as central actor in Mexico's economic and social development. In a speech to the oil workers' union delivered in 1978, for example, López Portillo states, "debemos de tener el talento y la voluntad para resolver de una vez por todas, a través de nuestro arduo trabajo, el problema de la miseria. Para dicho propósito, el petróleo es y debe ser el factor de apoyo más importante" (qtd. in Székely, *Economía* 71). López Portillo, whose term coincided almost exactly with the oil boom and bust, planned to take advantage of Mexico's newly discovered oil wealth by emphasizing exportation. At the beginning of his presidency he "released a six-year program which called for production to climb" with the goal that "half of the output would be exported" by 1982 (Grayson 62). When more oil was discovered than had originally been expected, the six-year plan was modified accordingly (Grayson 63). Oil exportation and foreign loans enabled López Portillo to legitimize the state's role as a driving force in Mexico's economy. For instance, in his third address to the nation in 1979, he proclaimed, "And to the extent that the resources that will shore up the finances of the state are now available, the state can assume its full position of manager of our mixed economy" (qtd. in Gentleman 124). State-centered rhetoric also characterized his administration's Plan Global de Desarrollo 1980–1982, which contains the following national-populist sentiment: "it is the state that puts forth a national project: the state creates the unity, creates the necessary conditions for the formation of the social classes in the country and acts as the motor of development" (qtd. in Gentleman 124). The Mexican state suffered a serious crisis of hegemony following Tlatelolco. But newfound wealth in the sector of Mexico's economy most clearly associated with one of the nation's most revered presidents, Lázaro Cárdenas, seemed to be exactly what was required to resurrect and sustain national-popular ideology.

But the dream was not to last. While the price of oil grew steadily from $11.60 per barrel in 1975 to $33.18 per barrel in 1981, in 1982 the price dropped to $28.64, beginning a steady decline that reached a low point of $11.84 in 1986 (Székely, "Oil Industry" 263). With 76 billion dollars worth of debt and an obligation to pay 27% of it by 1983 (Beltrán Mata 51), the Mexican government found itself in a serious crisis. The oil bust and debt crisis of the early 1980s proved to be the economic death knell of the national-populist Revolutionary state. Ideologically and politically wounded by the events of 1968, after the economic crisis surrounding the oil industry—whose production as a portion of GDP grew from 3.8% in 1977 to 7% in 1980, and, significantly, as a portion of Mexico's total exports grew from 15.2% in 1976 to 74.4% in 1981 (Álvarez 83–84)—the Mexican government was forced to adopt dramatic economic reforms that helped define the so-called neoliberal model of economic development in Latin America (Lustig 86). Economic statistics from 1982 do not paint a rosy picture: the inflation rate had reached 100%; public spending was 66% over budget; unemployment was at 8% and underemployment 22% (Beltrán Mata 50). A remarkable indicator of the crisis that Mexico suffered in the 1980s—shared by other Latin American countries as well (Mota 27)—was the unfavorable ratio of export prices to import prices, which caused developing countries to bleed wealth. As one economist observed in 1998, "América Latina transfirió al exterior el 4% de su PIB en forma anual. Este nivel no tiene ningún precedente, por lo menos desde los años cincuenta" (Mota 24).[7]

Thus the beginning of what is often called the "age of globalization," whose parameters in developing countries Mexican political theorist Pablo González Casanova outlined as early as 1968 in his extraordinary essay "Aritmética contrarrevolucionaria." Bolstering Sergio Zermeño's analysis of Mexican economic crisis over the long term, González Casanova writes, "Los grupos de presión más poderosos de empresarios nacionales y extranjeros a lo largo de un periodo relativamente largo, [...] logran medidas político-económicas que les permiten quedarse con una proporción cada vez mayor del producto nacional" (8). He continues, "En lo económico la crisis se manifiesta con un desequilibrio acentuado de la balanza de pagos que disminuye el producto monetario nacional y los ingresos del Estado, derivando en un incremento de los préstamos extranjeros [...], que hace más dependientes las decisiones de los adminstradores-políticos" (15). González Casanova's words provide a useful summary for precisely what Mexico began to experience intensely in the 1980s.

IV

But before the fall, exuberance and state-centered rhetoric characterized the short-lived optimistic years of the López Portillo administration. Published after the oil bust, such rhetoric is parodied in Aguilar Camín's novel through its portrayal of Lázaro Pizarro. When his friend Rojano explains to the narrator why he seeks his help he expresses his fear that Pizarro is behind the string of murders that have claimed the lives of a number of people who share one important trait: they all own, or used to own, land around the small Veracruz town of Chicontepec, an area that, the narrator learns, "en cuatro años [...] habría de volverse el más ambicioso complejo de explotación petrolera y petroquímica de América, y uno de los mayores del mundo" (94). Since Anabela's family owns land there, Rojano not only wants to benefit personally from the coming flood of oil wealth, but he is also afraid, for the same reason, that he and his wife are on Pizarro's hit list. After agreeing to help Rojano, the narrator arranges through his informant a trip to Poza Rica so that he can see for himself what motivates the suspicious and ambitious union leader of northern Veracruz.

From the moment he enters Pizarro's compound, the Quinta Bermúdez, in March 1977, the narrator is struck by the labor leader's impressive economic, social, and political power. In one of the novel's comic moments, for example, the narrator describes what it was like to join Pizarro for breakfast. The latter only consumes one portion of *natas* and a glass of carrot juice. But he serves the narrator a veritable feast. Overwhelmed as much by Pizarro's discourse as by the servants who constantly bring him more food, the narrator fails to get a sense of how much he has been served until his dining companion has retired to his office: "Se paró y se fue. Me quedé solo en la mesa y caí entonces en la cuenta de que estaba totalmente rodeado de bandejas de frutas, huevos ahogados, atoles, frijoles, picadas, tortillas y jarras de diversos líquidos" (57). At the breakfast table, Pizarro performs in miniature the spectacle he has planned for the afternoon, when he guides the narrator through the agro-industrial complex he has constructed just outside Poza Rica.

But before his guided tour through "La Mesopotamia," as the complex is named, the narrator witnesses Pizarro's social and political power. A lot like Vito Corleone in the first *Godfather*, Pizarro sets himself up at his desk, which is "inmenso, hasta faraónico," and awaits the clients who seek his help (57).[8] The first is an alcoholic who has practically destroyed his family trying to pay for his habit, even going so far as to prostitute his daughter, which caused his wife to attempt suicide. Pizarro agrees to help reconcile the family on one condition: "No vas a tomar otra copa jamás en tu vida" (60). The fact that Pizarro's command has already become a description of the way things are becomes clear in the following explanation and display of his totalitarian power:

> Porque a ti nadie te va a servir otra copa en Poza Rica y si alguien te la sirve, en alguna parte, ahí junto va a haber otro que impida que te la tomes. Y por cada copa que sepamos que pediste e impedimos que te tomaras, te vas a llevar una madriza igual, por lo menos, a las que le has puesto a tu mujer Antonia [...]. Y si te acabas de tomar la copa porque no pudimos impedírtelo, una sola copa que alcances a tomarte, será la última que te tomes, porque nosotros nos vamos a encargar de que así sea. (60–61)

Pizarro backs up his brutal tactics with an equally totalitarian philosophy, which distinguishes between useless and fertile deaths. He describes to the narrator a series of deaths that have recently occurred, most associated with alcoholism. Pizarro abhors them especially because "No dieron frutos, no brotaron, no abonaron el bienestar de otros." He continues, "Esas son las muertes que hay que combatir, las muertes estériles, las del mezcal y la ignorancia. Muertes violentas ha de haber siempre, porque esa es la ley de la historia. Volverlas muertes fértiles, muertes creadoras, es lo que nos toca a nosotros. Nada más" (87).

Pizarro, whom the narrator's informant describes as practicing "maoísmo petrolero" (48), explains his ideas to the narrator under a photograph of Lázaro Cárdenas, the Mexican president whom historian Alan Knight compares to the Chinese leader: "Less intellectual than Mao Zedong, he nevertheless shared with Mao (his almost exact contemporary, also of petit-bourgeois provincial origins), a fierce patriotism, a hankering after military glory, and a voluntarist faith in the efficacy of action and will and in the essential goodness of the people, whose interests he embodied" ("Politics" 99). Though Pizarro's collective vision may be more brutal than Cárdenas's was, it is no less inspired, and its achievements range from keeping order in Poza Rica to the construction of the agro-industrial complex called La Mesopotamia.

Pizarro gained enough power to build and manage La Mesopotamia—the name prompts him to ask the narrator, "Dicen que en Mesopotamia empezó la civilización, ¿no?" (83)—through sheer force of will and hard work, the latter determined by Pizarro to be "lo único verdaderamente chingón y respetable que hay sobre esta Tierra. Lo único" (66). Clearly, Pizarro is moved by the petroleum mystique, and his complex stands as proof of what it can accomplish. The first thing that impresses the narrator about La Mesopotamia is its size, which suggests infinity because the strip of pasture that borders it disappears "a oriente y poniente en el horizonte" (75). Its productive capacity is equally overwhelming. Its machinery repair shop, Lázaro boasts, is the biggest between São Paulo and Brownsville. It also represents a model of import-substitution-industrialization that appears to be more successful than when the same plan was implemented by the Revolutionary state as a means of achieving economic independence.[9] As Pizarro explains, "Arreglamos y vendemos piezas más barato que nadie. Hacemos piezas también. Compramos una vez fuera, pero pieza que cae aquí, pieza que empezamos a ver cómo producimos directamente" (80). He continues by demonstrating how his workshop is also a model of successful technical innovation and exportation: "Trabajamos también aquí cosas para PEMEX. Diseñamos una polea para la perforación de pozos que ahorró millones de dólares. Las tenemos patentadas y las están usando ya los árabes y los venezolanos. Y le cobramos a PEMEX muy caro, pero ni la tercera parte de lo que les hubiera costado comprar eso fuera" (80). While the repair shop exemplifies successful national economic development that promotes autonomy, the production plant at La Mesopotamia reminds the reader of the narrator's prodigious breakfast and suggests that Pizarro's plan, if implemented nationwide, would take care of the Mexican population's nutritional needs. The plant is described by Pizarro in the totalizing, enumerative style the novel often adopts when recounting the narrator's visit to La Mesopotamia. It includes "una empacadora de huevo, una descascaradora y empacadora de arroz, una pasteurizadora de leche, un rastro frigorífico y banda de transporte automatizada, una carpintería [...] una planta eléctrica, un laboratorio agrícola con huerto experimental de media hectárea, un pequeño troncal de ferrocarril" (79).

Further examples of the way Pizarro's efforts represent a parallel political, economic, and social system to the national one are his other "huertos sindicales," or union-based agricultural production sites, named, appropriately enough, Egipto and Tenochtitlan. The narrator's years-long investigation into Pizarro's allegedly murderous tactics includes the following descriptions of these other complexes, their origins in Pizarro's tremendous will, and their ability to conceal or at least distract from their more-than-likely violent foundations. After all, for Pizarro, "dos vidas valen más que una y tres vidas valen más que dos. Es la aritmética de la historia y de la verdadera igualdad" (86). Commenting on Pizarro's complexes, the narrator explains how they contain an "extraño e increíble circuito económico, ajeno al mercado." He continues,

> eran la traducción precisa, en su solidez interna y su autonomía alucinante, de la voluntad de Pizarro. No había en todo ese mundo fértil y abundante una sola cosa que recordara la zona oscura de Pizarro [...]. Este era el espacio del orden y la armonía, una comunidad sustraída al abuso, la especulación

> y el desastre productivo que afligían al resto de los consumidores y productores del país. [Era] una verdadera *utopía realizada*, que bastaba para explicar y justificar la adhesión de los beneficiarios, su apoyo ferviente y hasta su veneración al liderato de Pizarro. (150; original emphasis)

At times the narrator seems to fall under Pizarro's spell. But in addition to his familiarity with Pizarro's rigid philosophy and his well-grounded suspicions of Pizarro's brutality, other aspects of the novel delimit the world the union leader has constructed, setting it up as an object of parody.

For example, during their tour of La Mesopotamia, Pizarro describes his workers as volunteers. Even though the narrator explains the loyalty of some, one must wonder how optional Pizarro's workers' employment is in light of the union leader's power over the inhabitants of Poza Rica, as exhibited by the scene with the alcoholic. Further evidence of rather sinister working conditions are the slogans posted all around the complex, which include, "El trabajo te hará libre" (78), one of the clearest signs of the novel's efforts to communicate to the reader that all is not well in the kingdom of Pizarro. The parody of Pizarro's power over his work force achieves grotesque heights when he and the narrator are welcomed at the gates of La Mesopotamia by cheerleaders who shout in call-and-response: "¿Cuál es el líder más chingón del sindicato petrolero? —gritó la güera sin perder el ritmo. —Lázaro Pizarro —corearon desafinadas las otras" (76). The grandiose, populist leader is thus welcomed at the factory by a gang of enthusiastic supporters who bring to mind the voters by the truckload paid to vote for the PRI presidential candidates in so many national elections.

V

In his well-known 1986 discussion of "third-world literature" and national allegory, which though flawed by generalizations is still insightful and instructive, Jameson argues that preoccupations with national integrity in the "third world" are the result of uneven development (68–69), or the seemingly paradoxical coexistence of economic forms, like feudalism and capitalism, that in an ideal developmentalist teleology would pertain to different historical eras.[10] In one of its most hyperbolic moments,

Morir portrays Pizarro as having integrated the past and the present in La Mesopotamia by building his complex around the ruins of an ancient pyramid, which the narrator describes as "una ruina de quince metros de alto [...] como una revelación, el efectivo paso a un tiempo ajeno a la cuadrícula tecnificada que había alrededor de este islote de selva" (82). Yet it is not a foreign time but still the present from which Pizarro witnesses the inexorable march of history and economic development that he has helped guide. He explains to the narrator, "De tiempo atrás estas tierras estaban hechas para la mano del hombre. Ya le llamaban La Mesopotamia. [...] Y así es la historia [...]. Lo que está para suceder, no hay poder humano que lo impida" (83). From the top of his pyramid, Pizarro imagines himself at the pinnacle of history, the present-day culmination of an age-old process defined by gradual and unstoppable progress.

In one of its few extensive totalizing passages the novel clearly traces the boundary of La Mesopotamia—and by extension all of Pizarro's holdings—by describing the town of Poza Rica, which lies just a short distance away from the complex the narrator visits. Poza Rica not only stands in the novel as a reminder of how much work Pizarro has left to do in order to extend his already accomplished political and economic vision, but more importantly it also serves to debunk the stately discourse of progress that La Mesopotamia and the other *huertos sindicales* embody. The narrator recounts his drive with Pizarro through Poza Rica on the way to La Mesopotamia, thereby anchoring the reader's perspective on the exaggerated descriptions to follow in the present-day misery and inequality that defines the Mexican society that persists beyond the walls of Pizarro's domain.

Poza Rica, Veracruz, is Pizarro's home base and, historically, the headquarters of PEMEX's Central Zone (Grayson 60). The narrator describes how it has been transformed by the oil boom, beginning with the following impressionistic, fragmentary description of the sky:

> A lo lejos, por entre los edificios chaparros y contrahechos en su espantosa mezcla de dinero y mal gusto, el límpido cielo azul, claramente interrumpido aquí y allá por el humo como dibujado de los mecheros de gas encendidos que rodeaban la ciudad, haciendo borrosas y trémulas distintas franjas del

> horizonte. Circulamos entre tractocamiones y grúas y picops importadas, símbolos activos de la civilización petrolera, sus máquinas y sus desechos. Una abultada riqueza sin tradición ni cultura propias, que iba acumulando en la ciudad cementerios de tornos, poleas y cascarones oxidados, carísimas vulgaridades en los hoteles de lujo con sus vidrios negros y sus molduras doradas, grandes camellones ocupados por manchas de aceite y cascajo, restoranes de primera con puestos de fritangas en la puerta, y tragafuegos que ejercían su oficio en medio de los transeuntes. (74)

This totalizing view of Poza Rica enumerates chaotically the myriad effects of rapid growth due to oil wealth. It is clear that, outside of Pizarro's complexes, Mexico's petroleum civilization is hardly a model society. Furthermore, this passage associates oil development, pollution, and inequality by implicitly comparing burning gas jets to fire eaters, who may very well be former farm workers displaced by industrialization and urbanization.[11] The stark contrast between La Mesopotamia and Poza Rica enhances the sense of parody that underlies the narrator's description of Pizarro and his complexes. This parody takes the form of irony when, having learned of another murder around Chicontepec, the narrator muses, "Lázaro Pizarro, guía de pueblos, fundador de civilizaciones" (126).

VI

The violence that provides the ironic distance for the narrator's mocking assessment of Pizarro's guiding and founding powers is the strongest indictment of the oil workers' union as it is portrayed in the novel. The description of Pizarro's accomplishments establishes a parody of the national-popular state and its national-developmentalist economic model. In a less parodic vein, the descriptions of Pizarro's violent acts—which ultimately include Rojano's brutal murder at the hands of a mob apparently incited by Pizarro—mount a critique of the Mexican state. They condemn what the state actually has done, commit violent acts against its own citizens or turn a blind eye while others do so. And these descriptions highlight what the state has failed to do, promote truly independent and sustainable economic development. When the narrator perturbs his government informant by suggesting that Pizarro has something to do with the murders Rojano describes to him, it is clear that the informant knows more about Pizarro than he is willing to share, including, most likely, knowledge of his violent, land-grabbing tactics. In the novel Pizarro not only appears as a symbol of general corruption, but he also embodies a more historically specific form of corruption of Mexico's Revolutionary ideals. His expansionary goals represent an extreme version of a particularly controversial reform that in late 1977 the López Portillo administration and the Mexican Congress enacted in order to facilitate petroleum development: an amendment to Article 27 of the Mexican Constitution (the article that enshrined land reform even if it did not often guarantee its implementation) that "permitted PEMEX's temporary or permanent occupation or expropriation of land deemed necessary for investigation, exploration, or exploitation" (Grayson 190). Pizarro's designs on Chicontepec, apparently known to the narrator's informant and likewise ignored, thus figure in the novel as the logical consequences of the motivations behind the constitutional reform and the corruption that enabled certain forms of violence to remain uninvestigated, not to mention unpunished.

The state's complicity with Pizarro's violence is not the only type of corruption that Aguilar Camín's novel critiques. The oil boom of the late 1970s and early 1980s produced corruption within the oil workers' union that "flourished as never before because of the volume of oil produced, the higher prices which it command[ed], and the rush to accelerate output" (Grayson 97). The most notorious figure associated with this corruption was undoubtedly La Quina, an incredibly influential leader in the Sindicato de Trabajadores Petroleros de la República Mexicana, or STPRM, the oil workers' union founded in 1935.[12] Writing in 1980 Grayson calls the STPRM "one of the most powerful unions in Mexico if not in all of Latin America" (88), and he continues by noting that "This position is enhanced by the leaders' skill in portraying their organization, which kept oil flowing in the difficult postexpropriation period, as a major contributor to the fulfillment of the Mexican Revolution" (89). Pizarro's power, influence, and self-styled emulation of Lázaro Cárdenas in Aguilar Camín's novel thus has its counterpart in the history of the oil boom. Consider also, for example, the narrator's description of his trip with Pizarro from the union leader's ranch to his STPRM local in Poza Rica, when, after getting into Pizarro's car, he notices, "Arrancó adelante una vagoneta con hombres armados y dos galaxies atrás" (69). Describing his own interview with La Quina, Grayson writes, "[Enjoying] close ties with elected officials [...] [,] La Quina and his supporters regularly influence the appointment of government officials, especially in oil-producing regions [...]. He did arrive that evening [...] in a three-vehicle caravan, apparently for protection" (90). Though Aguilar Camín's novel makes it clear that La Quina and Pizarro are not the same person when it describes the latter speaking of the former on a number of occasions, it is equally clear to the novel's readers that its author was indeed incorporating the more colorful and notorious aspects of La Quina's reputation to shape his character Pizarro. Pizarro's caravan, his role as Poza Rica's Godfather, and his ability to make Rojano mayor of Chicontepec—and then apparently kill him off when he failed to cooperate—are all traits that coincide with Grayson's description of La Quina.[13]

During the oil boom, PEMEX, the STPRM, and the national government functioned together in a balance whose disruption would threaten to strike at an important source of power and wealth for workers, managers, and government officials. For example, Grayson describes how Jorge Díaz Serrano, the general director of PEMEX between 1977 and 1981, "apparently struck a bargain" with the STPRM: "Petróleos Mexicanos will not contest the STPRM's many social, political, and economic prerogatives, there will be no full-scale attack on corruption [...]. In return, the union has backed the new director general to the hilt" (101). Furthermore, the union "defended the government" against criticism of policies that threatened to undermine Mexico's economic independence, such as the notoriously fraught, and ultimately aborted, attempt to connect a natural gas line to the United States (101).[14] Thus when Aguilar Camín's narrator begins investigating Pizarro and publishes articles that condemn him, he is treading on dangerous ground.

Morir frames the rise and fall of oil and its illusory promise by alluding often to historical figures with their actual names. In addition to La Quina, López Portillo, and others, the novel refers specifically to Díaz Serrano, providing an opportunity to parody the PEMEX director's exuberant optimism about the oil industry. On June 17, 1977, the narrator attends a speech delivered by Díaz Serrano. He sets up the director's discourse by referring to the atmosphere of apprehension and anxiety that shaped the perspective of journalists and leading politicians during the first years of López Portillo's presidency. All they could talk about, writes the narrator, was "austeridad y crisis, del desastre financiero del país, su quiebra productiva, la baja inversión, el deterioro de la confianza, etcétera" (97). By contrast, Díaz Serrano "hablaba justamente de lo contrario: del fin de la pobreza mexicana, la llegada de una nueva oportunidad histórica." The narrator continues citing, "La potencialidad petrolera, decía Díaz Serrano, borraba de un plumazo la escasa capitalización interna, condicionante número uno de nuestro subdesarrollo" (97). In light of the terrible economic crisis that was to follow the oil boom, the narrator's introduction to Díaz Serrano's speech is also a prophecy.

Another technique the narrative adopts in its description of Díaz Serrano's ultimately unfounded optimism is to introduce a foil who is equally as historical, Manuel Buendía. Buendía was a noted journalist who was as famous for his unflinching critique of power as for the mysterious circumstances of his death, which appears to have been a politically motivated murder meant to silence him.[15] When Buendía asks Díaz Serrano about the topic of union corruption it unsettles him. Furthermore, the narrator introduces his fellow journalist's question by noting that he was "el primer columnista de México, a quien luego mataron, por la espalda, un 30 de mayo de 1984" (99). This particular detail serves three purposes. It gives the lie to Díaz Serrano by casting a renowned and respected journalist as his critic. It also highlights the danger involved in the narrator's investigation, suggesting that he too could be killed for digging too deeply. Finally, it adds depth to the parodic effect established by the narrator's introduction to Díaz Serrano's speech because it provides the only date within the novel that goes beyond the narrative, whose principal plot ends in 1980 and thus before the oil bust. The reader understands only here how far into the future the narrator's perspective is based, and that it is rooted squarely in post-oil-boom Mexico. This temporal reference reinforces the message that Díaz Serrano's optimism was, to say the least, premature.

The allusion to Buendía's murder in 1984 provides a reference to the oil bust that is external to the narrative but familiar to the novel's readers. Within the narrative, the bust has not happened yet, and the Mexican government is working hard to develop the oil industry and protect those whose interests depend upon it. No character in the novel better represents the government, especially as protector of oil interests, than the narrator's informant. When the narrator visits him in his office on the day he begins asking about Pizarro, he catches a glimpse of a totality different from the one he is later to perceive when he visits La Mesopotamia.

VII

Pizarro's compound is rooted in the ideals of the national-popular state and import-substitution industrialization. As a sign of this legacy, in Pizarro's office at the union local there is a photograph of him and Lázaro Cárdenas signed by the famous expropriator, whose dedication reads: "Para Lázaro Pizarro, última / camada de la Revolución mexicana / L. Cárdenas / noviembre, 1958" (72). The expression on Cárdenas's face is significant, as he is described by the narrator as "mirando hacia el infinito" (72), a gaze that also characterizes Cárdenas in the photo of him that hangs in the office at Pizarro's ranch: "los ojos perdidos en una contemplación melancólica y dulce como si acabara de venirse" (58). The photographs of Cárdenas identify Pizarro as the direct and sole heir to the former president's oil-nationalizing Revolutionary promise. They also portray an encounter with the sublime, or the ecstatic apprehension of infinity as an ordering horizon toward which destiny leads the nation. Clearly, the connection between Cárdenas and Pizarro within the context of the novel provides the ground for a parodic critique of the Revolutionary dream that is perhaps best encapsulated by the narrator's appraisal of the former president's ejaculatory melancholy.

Even though both instances of totality are ultimately parodied by the narrator, the historical totality that converges in Pizarro's kingdom is substantially different from the totality the narrator encounters in his informant's office. The latter is not rooted in history or some form of Revolutionary promise.

In fact, it must lack roots, since its primary purpose is to preserve the ephemeral order of the present by storing, organizing, and utilizing information. The narrator's informant has greater access to information than any character in the novel, which is why the narrator seeks him out, observing, "en esos días finales de noviembre de 1976, en medio de la especulación política producida por el cambio presidencial, mi informante [...] pareció el único foco capaz de ofrecer una aproximación segura al caso de Pizarro" (47). After the narrator recounts the story Rojano told him, the informant proceeds to rattle off a number of specific facts about Rojano, leaving the narrator astonished. As with his description of Cárdenas's face in Pizarro's photographs, the narrator focuses on his informant's eyes: "Abrumaba la memoria que había tras esos ojitos de galán de cine de los cuarenta" (48). The informant's memory is aided by a sophisticated system of index cards, including one that makes it clear to the narrator that he may be getting in over his head: "Regresó el subordinado con dos juegos de tarjetas que puso sobre el escritorio, bajo la mirada de su jefe. El jefe empezó a mirarlas una por una, concentradamente, las de Rojano primero. —Aquí aparece usted —dijo extendiéndome una tarjeta" (49).

The informant's filing system is somewhat rudimentary by contemporary standards, but it still produces the magical effect that Jameson attributes to communications technologies in his analysis of cinematic suspense thrillers, technologies that "become magical only when grasped as the allegories of something else, of the whole unimaginable decentered global network itself" (*Geopolitical* 13). The network in *Morir* may be national, but its importance, especially in the case of Pizarro and the oil industry, is a function of Mexico's rapidly increasing insertion into the global economy, represented not only by the oil market but also by transnational financial markets. After all, the novel's narrator notes, in 1977, "Sólo para el sector energético se había contratado más del total de los 3 mil millones de dólares de deuda aprobados por el FMI. [...] PEMEX [había] contratado sola, en los últimos dos meses, más créditos que todo el gobierno mexicano durante el año anterior" (109).[16]

The security network the narrator's informant controls is charged with keeping the peace and guaranteeing the stability necessary for securing oil development and foreign loans. This network remains inscrutable to the narrator and for that reason tantalizing. It inspires in narrator and reader alike the desire to know more and thus embodies "that promise of a deeper inside view [that] is the hermeneutic content of the conspiracy thriller in general" (Jameson, *Geopolitical* 15). The foundational distinction in *La región más transparente* between Ixca Cienfuegos and Gladys García that is grounded in the former's ability to access the sublime and the latter's inability to do so is reproduced, in a parodic fashion, in Aguilar Camín's novel when the narrator recognizes the limits of his perception in comparison to his informant's. Again focusing on the eyes, the narrator writes, "Empezó [el informante] a ver el otro juego de tarjetas, las de Lázaro Pizarro. Una por una también, y detalladamente, hasta quedar sumergido en ellas, el ceño fruncido, los ojos incendiados en la inspección minuciosa" (49). Even though the informant denies having learned anything of interest from the cards, the narrator is sure there is something there, especially when, in the passage I cited at the beginning of the chapter, the informant frantically rings for his assistant once the narrator has left his office.

In the end, neither the narrator nor the reader finds out for certain what the informant knows. The crucial explanation for this failure in the novel is the realization that the truth is less important than narrative. *Morir en el golfo* does not refer to an external, national totality that pre-exists a fictional representation of or allusion to it. Instead, it presents totality within its pages explicitly as artifice. What the informant knows is less important than how it seems. If appearance and substance coincide, all the better, but if not, it does not matter as long as that disparity can be concealed or sufficiently mystified.

After Rojano is lynched by the townspeople of Chicontepec, Anabela plots revenge against Pizarro by tacitly approving that one of his enemies kill him. The would-be assassin wounds but does not kill Pizarro, and shortly thereafter he dies in a mysterious car accident. Fearing for Anabela's life and his own, the narrator turns once again to his informant, who is now preoccupied with cleaning up what is to him a potential public-relations nightmare involving a very important leader of the oil workers' union. Describing him metonymically as "Gobernación," and thus associating him even more explicitly with the state as a whole, the narrator recounts his informant's version of what happened to Pizarro, which implicates both himself and Anabela. When Anabela challenges him by asking if his version describes what really happened, the informant replies, "Les he ofrecido la versión política de esos hechos, la versión objetiva. No es la verdad, pero es la realidad que ustedes tienen que encarar como si lo fuera: objetivamente, sin hacerse ilusiones" (199).

For the informant, truth is tactical. Regardless of what has actually happened, Anabela must leave Mexico because her life is in danger. Protecting her is another metonym, this time for protecting public tranquility, the informant's prime directive. Appearance is paramount for the informant, who believes that if society appears tranquil, even if it is not, then it can become tranquil. He understands that a wisely placed narrative, true or false, can have actual political effects. Observing his informant in this context, the narrator writes, "Era diáfano e impersonal, una máquina de historias salvajes regulada por un sistema de pesas y medidas ajeno a la lógica de los eslabones débiles; una moral de la eficacia al servicio de la estabilidad y la superficie pulida de las instituciones" (200). This "machine of savage stories" is the mouthpiece of the state, manufacturing tactically useful narratives and adjusting them when necessary. The totality of knowledge to which the informant has access is not anchored in the truth or history, not even the immediate past, but instead it is defined by its own ever-shifting utility and reliable malleability.

VIII

The chasm between truth and story becomes even clearer to the narrator after his final visit to Pizarro, who is dying; whether from cancer or complications due to the gunshot wounds of Anabela's trigger man is a fact that remains unknown. In their earlier encounter, the informant told the narrator that Pizarro had been wounded. Now the story is different. Driving away together from their meeting with Pizarro, the narrator and his informant stop and talk. It is March 18, 1980, the 42nd anniversary of Cárdenas's expropriation of US and British oil concerns. The two men get out of the informant's car in a small plaza populated by teenaged couples, elderly men, and sidewalk vendors, an idyllic scene typical of "la santa paz mexicana del aniversario petrolero" (213). This veneer of tranquility frames the conversation, whose entire focus is the difference between truth and appearance. The informant explains why he told Anabela earlier that Pizarro had been wounded, though whether this explanation is true remains open to doubt. Again, the emphasis is on public order:

> Ya era bastante complicado el caso de ustedes, políticamente quiero decir. Demasiado escándolo y jaloneo, y extraordinariamente peligroso, entiéndame. Era peligroso para ustedes y para las relacions del gobierno con el sindicato petrolero. [...] Si le hubiera dicho a la viuda de Rojano que Pizarro tenía cáncer, hubiera creído simplemente que quería sacarla de la jugada. Le dije entonces que su ataque había tenido éxito. [...] Le mentí con la verdad. Lo que era mentira entonces es la verdad ahora y viceversa. Eso fue todo. (218)

And in the end, that is all, as Anabela makes very clear to the narrator: "Y adelante con la colección de héroes y logros del milagro mexicano. Pero nada de eso tiene que ver con la verdad, ni con la justicia [...]. Eso tiene que ver estrictamente con la seguridad y la tranquilidad pública" (234).

Anabela's angry lament divorces the Revolutionary promise from any necessary association with national reality, let alone progress. Significantly, her observation follows the narrator's description of Pizarro's funeral, where not only the union leader is mourned, but also the totalizing force he represented. The narrator describes the public mourning of Pizarro as the swan song of sublime totality. The funeral is a totalizing spectacle, recognized at first by the narrator as little more than political theater, "la correa eficiente de la vida corporativa mexicana" (222).

> Ahí estaba intercalada efectivamente, con antigua sabiduría escenográfica, a lo largo del camino, toda la población escolar de la ciudad, niños y niñas de las escuelas primarias [...] ahí [...] los miembros de las organizaciones sindicales de la ciudad, las meseras con claveles rojos en las manos, los telegrafistas y carteros [...]. Habían traído a campesinos y danzantes de la sierra; los quinientos taxis de Poza Rica

> esperaban también, montados uno tras otro sobre el camellón de una avenida, junto al despliegue gemelo de la maquinaria del sindicato, pipas y revolvedoras, tractores y trascavos, aplanadoras y grúas portátiles. (222)

Though he is conscious of the theatrical display taking place before his eyes, the narrator cannot completely resist its power, which he describes in terms that coincide with Kant's description of the mathematically sublime. Notably, both the narrator and Kant employ the emblematic figure of the pyramid. Distinguishing mathematical from aesthetic judgment, Kant writes regarding magnitude, "where it is considered an absolute measure beyond which no greater is possible subjectively (i.e. for the judging Subject), it then conveys the idea of the sublime" (99). He relates this to the aesthetic effect produced by the pyramids of Egypt, the appreciation of which cannot be performed all at once but must proceed step by step—"in this interval the first tiers [of the pyramid] always in part disappear before the imagination has taken in the last, and so the comprehension is never complete" (100). This necessarily gradual comprehension produces a feeling in the observer "of the inadequacy of his imagination for presenting the idea of a whole within which that imagination attains its maximum, and, in its fruitless efforts to extend this limit, recoils upon itself, but in so doing succumbs to an emotional delight" (100).

Cárdenas's ecstatic vision as parodied by the narrator's description of how the latter was photographed "looking toward the infinite" represents the novel's containment of the sublime as experienced by the Mexican president who represented perhaps more than any other national leader the hope for national economic independence. The narrator himself experiences a similar feeling at Pizarro's funeral. Describing the crowd, he writes:

> Conocía el esqueleto interno de esa abundancia [...] su orquestación administrativa [...]. Pero nunca dejaba de sorprenderme la vivacidad y la fuerza del efecto logrado sumando los escalones vivos de la pirámide, esa pirámide en cuya cúpula Pizarro había imperado [...]. Podía imaginar perfectamente el tumulto impenetrable en torno a la sede del sindicato [...] Una mancha viva de vehículos y personas

> [...]. Tras el movimiento de esa red [...] un resplandor fijo de reflectores perfilaba el movimiento instintivo de la multitud, cruzada por un torrente más poderoso que ella. (223)

A sublime totality, incomprehensible yet understood through the faith in the supersensible as organizing force, shapes and propels the crowd at Pizarro's funeral. Yet the source of this power is Pizarro's death, and the pyramid of people who gather for his funeral is portrayed by the narrator in much more glorious and totalizing terms than the pyramid that symbolizes his living strength at La Mesopotamia. This eulogy for Pizarro is thus also a eulogy for the Revolutionary state as fueled by the economic model of autonomous national development that Cárdenas inaugurated spectacularly on March 18, 1938, and that ended in equally dramatic terms with the oil bust of 1982.

Furthermore, the fact that the appraisal of sublime totality in Aguilar Camín's novel is filtered temporally and narratively provides yet another framing device that enables parody. The reader knows the narrator is describing the funeral years after the fact, years defined by what was, by many accounts, post-Revolutionary Mexico's worst economic crisis. With the death of Pizarro, the petroleum mystique dies too. Shortly thereafter, the promise of Mexico's oil wealth is revealed to the nation as yet another mirage with nothing substantial underpinning it except for a negative force, a quantity of debt as incomprehensible as the size of the crowd that gathered for Pizarro's funeral.

IX

Morir en el golfo provides no solution to the national crisis that began in the 1980s. Its parody of national-popular, developmentalist, Revolutionary discourse and its concomitant economic model empties out the rhetoric, revealing its hollowness and replacing it with nothing but a critique. Its negative emphasis is appropriate to the times. Consider, for example, the solution that López Portillo implemented in one of his last official acts as president when he nationalized the Mexican banks in September 1982, which, according to economist Judith Gentleman, was "billed in some quarters as the most significant assertion of state power since the Cárdenas period" (219).[17] But it was an assertion of state power that amounted to a perverse negative print of Cárdenas's 1938 expropriation, since it was enacted in order to help Mexico pay the enormous debt it owed to foreign banks. In 1938, Mexico nationalized oil. In 1982, it nationalized debt:

> Respecto a la nacionalización de la banca [...] señalamos que lo que se dio en México fue una estatización de la banca con una nacionalización de sus deudas, lo que equivale a decir que el Estado mexicano, celosamente supervisado por el FMI, surgía como garante último de las deudas del sector público y del sistema financiero privado, ante los acreedores internacionales, entre los cuales los bancos privados norteamericanos eran los predominantes. (Álvarez 106–07)[18]

High interest rates, increasing numbers of investments in dollars, rampant inflation, and the concomitant weakness of the peso—which the state devalued three times in 1982, and which produced more capital flight (Gentleman 221)—made it impossible for private Mexican financial interests to pay their share of the foreign debt. Returning to the idea that nationalizing the bank was an assertion of state power, it is important to note what Álvarez explains about the foreign pressures that forced the state to make this move, thus revealing how its "power" was little more than a reaction to external demands: "la cancelación de concesiones privadas para operar servicios financieros [...] fue un duro golpe a la otrora fracción hegemónica del bloque en el poder, la burguesía financiera mexicana" (94–95). Instead of an assertion of political dominance on the part of the State, nationalizing the bank was actually a symptom of its desperation in the context of the severe economic crisis faced by the nation.

Miguel de la Madrid, who became Mexico's president in December 1982, inherited the crisis, and servicing foreign debt quickly became the primary preoccupation of the initial years of his administration.[19] In his first month as president, de la Madrid instituted a set of reforms known as the Programa Inmediato de Reordenación Económica (PIRE). The reforms were outlined in ten points, which included among other things austerity measures to limit public spending, tax reform, salary regulation, and the promotion of savings (Álvarez 97). Furthermore, de la Madrid's reforms were designed to produce greater "integración de las economías de México y Estados Unidos" (Álvarez 97), and thus set the stage for the implementation of the North American Free Trade Agreement (NAFTA) in 1994. While de la Madrid's measures succeeded in reducing Mexico's debt (Mota 47), and regaining the political stability that teetered on the edge in the early 1980s (Mota 97), persistent social problems remained, notably, poverty and marginalization (Mota 105).[20] As Mota summarizes, "a los rezagos sociales ancestrales y a los acumulados durante la anterior fase de crecimiento [las décadas de la posguerra] se agregaron las secuelas de la crisis de los años ochenta" (105).[21]

The economic reforms of the 1980s signaled the official beginning of a neoliberal model of economic development in Mexico, which was most clearly embodied early on in the PIRE under de la Madrid, and later by the implementation of NAFTA during the presidency of Salinas de Gortari (1988–94). Clearly, however, the grounds for the economic reforms of the 1980s had been gradually established over the course of the Revolutionary state's development. For example, the long-term consequences of economic dependency were becoming clear to González Casanova in 1968 and Sergio Zermeño in 1978, as is evident in their publications on the subject.[22] Thus the oil boom of the late 1970s and its dependence upon foreign investment can be seen as both the last gasp of national-popular developmentalism and a paradigmatic example of its unsustainability.

The narrator of Aguilar Camín's novel never solves a single murder. What his detective work does uncover, however, is the lack of any solid basis for the optimism of the oil boom. His searches through the basements of Mexico's political power provide no satisfactory, coherent means of comprehending the social totality. Instead, his investigations indicate how *Morir en el golfo* completes a cycle of Mexican novels that construct totalizing visions of national community. This cycle began with Carlos Fuentes's *La región*, published at the height of Mexico's "economic miracle," when the dream of national autonomy remained valid, and when future economic growth could still be perceived as eventually containing all Mexicans, providing everyone with an opportunity for social advancement. The totalizing discourse that grounded Fuentes's novel slowly deteriorated over the course of this cycle. In the world of Aguilar

Camín's narrator and his shady informant, totality becomes a cynical veil. The notion of a supersensible force, the origin and destiny of a meaningful collective history capable of shaping national experience, is doomed to become nothing but a parody of itself.

Conclusion

The totalizing novel is the product of a centralized society whose goal is coherent, self-contained autonomy. Carlos Fuentes's *La región más transparente* represents this ideal in its exhaustive effort to contain all of Mexico's history within its pages and to present itself—and by extension the genre of the totalizing novel—as uniquely capable of transmitting that history, thereby setting the stage for a more promising future based on national self-knowledge and an epistemology that is able to produce that knowledge and reproduce itself. Yet the exclusive foundations of totalizing thought stubbornly make themselves known, at the limit of Fuentes's novel in its construction of Gladys García as the subaltern, and at the impasse that the narrator of *José Trigo* reaches when he mourns the loss of the historical, and historiographical, space once embodied by the train yards of Nonalco-Tlatelolco. The ultimately self-destructive attempt to preserve itself that the national-popular state made in 1968 changed the literary as well as the political landscape. Any totalizing novel written afterward could not avoid addressing Tlatelolco, and Mendoza's and Aguilar Mora's novels are thus paradigmatic. Their representations of Tlatelolco are also explicit critiques of the way in which the political power of the state based itself on an exclusive claim to the authorized ability of constructing national history as a guiding force. *Con Él* and *Si muero* undermine the originary thinking that structures that claim and test the limits of totalizing thought by recognizing and struggling with its inevitably violent consequences. The parodied instances of totality in *Morir en el golfo* are a far cry from Ixca Cienfuegos's triumphant transformation at the conclusion of *La región*. The national-popular dream as configured in the novel's characterization of López Portillo's petroleum policy and Pizarro's parallel political economy is hence removed from any productive association with historical reality or means of imagining the nation and its trajectory.

In July 2000, the PRI lost its first presidential election since its predecessor party was founded in 1929. The last three presidents who belonged to the party—de la Madrid, Salinas, and Ernesto Zedillo—promoted economic policies that intensified and expanded the neoliberal reforms introduced in the early 1980s. The most significant reform was the implementation of NAFTA on January 1, 1994. When the Ejército Zapatista de Liberación Nacional, or EZLN, made its explosive appearance on the same day, it began a strong, sustained challenge to both neoliberalism and traditional party-politics in Mexico. Though the Zapatistas flirted briefly with their own political party, the FZLN (Frente Zapatista de Liberación Nacional), they are now firmly anti-party, a position exemplified by Subcomandante Marcos's "Otra campaña," which he organized as the EZLN's response to the bitterly contested 2006 presidential race. The Zapatista insurgency and the accession to power of Vicente Fox in December 2000 posed the two most significant challenges to the single-party system that structured Mexican politics for more than two-thirds of the twentieth century. The Zapatistas' anti-party nationalism calls for inclusiveness but rejects ultimately exclusive governmental hierarchies. Fox's positions on the economy were generally a continuation of the neoliberal policies of the national leaders who preceded him, but his election ended the automatic association between the state and the PRI. The economic transition that culminated in the dissolution of the national-popular state in the 1980s was paralleled by an equally significant political transition that reached its defining moment in 2000. Both transitions are characterized by decentralization, a process whose impact on Mexican cultural production has produced notable tendencies that differ significantly from the trajectory of the totalizing novel during the national-popular period.

Two recent phenomena in Mexican literature help explain how decentralization frames the history of the totalizing novel. They are, first, the predominance of the chronicle, practiced most famously not only by Poniatowska and Monsiváis but also by Subcomandante Marcos; and, second, the most recent identifiable generation of Mexican writers, known as "el Crack." The chronicle's open-ended style and its immediate timeliness work against the self-contained synthesis desired by totalizing thought and the totalizing novel. The chronicle is germane to a historical age that lacks a clear, grand narrative like those constructed and sustained by national-popular ideology and mid-century Mexicanism.

The Crack, a movement founded explicitly as such in a 1996 manifesto presented by its practitioners Eloy Urroz, Ricardo Chávez, Ignacio Padilla, Jorge Volpi, and Pedro Ángel Palou, has condemned what its members consider an unproductive obsession with national culture. For example, the content of two of the movement's most celebrated works, Volpi's *En busca de Klingsor* (1999) and Ignacio Padilla's *Amphitryon* (2000), focus entirely on German historical themes, specifically the Nazi period. The Crack's anti-nationalist stance attests, negatively, to the insistent need to address the question of the nation. The refusal to write about Mexico results paradoxically in turning this question into an important motivation of the Crack's writers. Representing the nation thus remains as a repressed task no longer addressed in positive terms. The increasing prominence of the open-ended chronicle and the emergence of the ostensibly anti-nationalist Crack must be understood in relation to the dissolution of the national-popular state and the totalizing thought it fostered.

Notes

Chapter One
The Revolution Will Be Novelized: Carlos Fuentes's *La región más transparente* Constructs a Compensatory Totality

1. See Boldy for an exceptional close reading of the novel's opening pages, especially notable for its discussion of the philosophical and literary influences on Fuentes's work and the themes that occur in these pages that prefigure career-long preoccupations (16–29).

2. Rosario Castellanos casts Cienfuegos in the role of "inquisidor universal," the character who compares all others' actions with "las necesidades nacionales y con las exigencias históricas" ("Juventud" 178). Van Delden provides the most detailed analysis of Cienfuegos in the chapter dedicated to *La región* in his outstanding volume on Fuentes's career. For useful discussions of Cienfuegos, see also Boldy (16–18), Foster (35–36, 41), Franco ("*La región*" 65–71), Goldenberg (15), Leal (216), Manzo-Robledo (7–8), and Sánchez (167–68).

3. Zamacona has been analyzed by many critics of *La región*, who accurately compare his ideas to those of either Octavio Paz (see Sommers 137–52), Carlos Fuentes (see Sánchez 172–76, 211–24; and Goldenberg 22–33), or both (see Van Delden 31). See also Boldy (40).

4. Mexicanism refers, in general, to the effort to discover and define unique, authentically Mexican traits that define the national community. Schmidt notes that the term *lo mexicano*, or "the properly Mexican," was already in common use by the first decade of the twentieth century (39). See Gyurko for a discussion of Mexicanism's influence on the Mexican novel (243–44). Ochoa argues that *La región* parodies Mexicanism (196n6). While Manuel Zamacona, the character most explicitly aligned with Mexicanism, indeed dies an absurd death that challenges and even mocks his Mexicanist pieties, the novel's conclusion, I argue, represents an earnest mobilization of central ideas of Mexicanist thought.

5. Moreiras acknowledges that the term *narrative fissure* comes from the work of Michael Geyer and Charles Bright, "World History in a Global Age," *American Historical Review* 100 (1995): 1034–69.

6. For examples of this interpretation of the Revolution, see Paz (*Laberinto* 294), and Fuentes (*Tiempo* 11). Amidst a number of very positive reviews, an early negative review of *La región* went so far as to accuse Fuentes of plagiarizing Paz. See Reeve (14–15). For studies of the Mexicanist influence on *La región*, see Boldy (2–3, 9, 12–15), Labastida (14–15), and Sánchez (199–207).

7. I refer to the post-Revolutionary state in the past tense because it is a political system whose validity was bankrupt by the 1980s, when the nationalist ideologues of the PRI were vanishing as they yielded to the party's neoliberal technocrats, who began to gain power following the presidency of Luis Echeverría Álvarez (1970–76). I discuss this in greater detail in chapter 5. See also: Aguilar Camín, "Sólo cenizas"; Aguilar Camín, *Después del milagro*; and Álvarez, *La crisis global.*

8. In his "Notes on the Difficulty of Studying the State" (1977/1988), Philip Abrams warns social scientists against treating the state as an object of study because such an approach reinforces the idea that the state is coherent and autonomous, an illusion that helps legitimize the state's authority, coercion, and domination. I am referring here to Laclau's notion of "communitarian fullness," which refers to a non-existent, ideal state of community whose attainability becomes the battleground of political forms competing for hegemony. See Laclau's *Emancipation(s).*

9. In "La encrucijada" (1994), Lorenzo Meyer details how this period witnessed accelerated processes of urbanization, industrialization, and political centralization. See also Alan Knight, "The Peculiarities of Mexican History" (1992).

10. Teleological and centralized representational structures include intense and varied—and often state-sponsored—cultural production, such as the work produced by the Escuela mexicana de pintores [Mexican School of Painters] and Mexico City's National Museum of Anthropology.

11. National unity became one of the Mexican state's ideological hallmarks during the height of national-populism. It is often noted that one of the important rhetorical shifts that took place when Ávila Camacho succeeded Cárdenas is that references to socialism and to class conflict disappeared from official discourse, replaced by persistent calls to national unity. A telling example of this shift is the change in mottos of the increasingly powerful Confederación de Trabajadores Mexicanos (CTM) that took effect when Cárdenas left office. The former motto, "por una sociedad sin clases," became "por la emancipación de México." For further discussion of this broad rhetorical shift, see Lorenzo Meyer ("La encrucijada" 1303) and Zermeño (*México* 72–88).

12. Bartra develops these ideas most thoroughly in *Las redes imaginarias del poder político* (1981) and *La jaula de la melancolía* (1987).

13. The two most famous of such defects are the inferiority complex that Samuel Ramos outlines in *El perfil del hombre y la cultura en México* (1934) and the solitude that Octavio Paz contemplates in *Laberinto.*

14. Néstor García Canclini's analysis of the National Museum of Anthropology, a cultural institution completed with significant government support in 1964, is an informative illustration of how the state's construction and mobilization of national history presupposes and reinforces its privileged access to totality. For additional telling analyses of how the Mexican post-Revolutionary state mobilized history to bolster its legitimacy, see Mallon (*Peasant and Nation*) and Aguilar Camín ("Desde").

15. The Lázaro Cárdenas presidency of 1934–40 intensified the role of the state in Mexico's economic activity, most dramatically in the cases of land reform, banking, and, in 1938, the nationalization of the oil industry, an industry that, until then, was dominated by British, Dutch, and US capital, with investments by national capital that "fluctuó entre el 1 por ciento y 3 por ciento del total" (Lorenzo Meyer, "El primer tramo" 1202). Although Cárdenas's expropriation of the oil industry reduced Mexico's access to foreign oil markets, it eventually proved to be an economically wise decision because of the development of a domestic market for oil, which grew from 39 percent in 1937 to 90 percent by the end of the 1940s (Meyer, "El primer tramo" 1242). State-run banks and lending agencies gained prominence during the 1930s, compensating for the inability of private financial institutions to support Mexico's growing economy (Meyer, "El primer tramo" 1244–45). For an informative look at how popular political participation was discouraged, see Aguilar Camín's analysis of presidential discourse in "Desde."

16. Cárdenas dedicated 37.6 percent of the national budget to economic development, Ávila Camacho (1940–46) 39.2 percent, and Miguel Alemán (1946–52) more than 50 percent (Lorenzo Meyer, "La encrucijada" 1278).

17. See Phelan 310–11.

18. For diverse studies of the Mexicanist tradition, see Schmidt, Miller, Loyo, and Phelan. The persistence of the Mexicanist tradition in literary criticism is evident in Ocampo (7, 12) and Cresta de Leguizamón (150–53).

19. Schmidt describes Gamio's book as the text that "launched social anthropology in Mexico" (77), and as emblematic of the Revolutionary period of Mexicanism (69). Uranga's essay was published in the third issue of the Colegio de México's journal, *Historia Mexicana*, an important source for the formation and dissemination of mid-century Mexicanist thought.

20. See Miller (139–42). Gamio's work on Teotihuacán, published by the Secretaría de Educación Pública in 1924, is titled *Introducción, síntesis y conclusión a la población del Valle de Teotihuacán*.

21. See Schmidt 77–79.

22. An allusion to an earlier writer's thoughts on Mexican identity, Fuentes's title forms part of a chain of references similar to the way *La región* juxtaposes stories to form a unique historical totality. The phrase "La región más transparente," which appears in Reyes's text, is originally attributed to von Humboldt (Boldy 27). The date in Reyes's title refers, of course, to the year when Cortés arrived in what came to be known as New Spain, and it is also an anagram of the year when Reyes's book was published. The principal action of Fuentes's novel begins in 1951, another anagram, this time of the date of Reyes's text and the beginning of the Conquest of New Spain.

23. Regarding boom criticism, Rama's "El 'Boom' en perspectiva" stands out as an exceptionally good critical analysis. It appears in the anthology titled *Más allá del Boom*, which includes several other valuable essays on the boom. Significant recent works on the boom include those by Martin, Avelar, and Levinson.

24. Sommers (108–11) and Franco ("*La región*" 65–66) emphasize the importance of Dos Passos on *La región,* while Labastida highlights Faulkner's influence (16).

25. Paradigmatic examples include Mario Vargas Llosa's *La casa verde* (1961), Julio Cortázar's *Rayuela* (1963), and Gabriel García Márquez's *Cien años de soledad* (1967). See Boldy for a discussion of *La región*'s importance as a boom novel (7).

26. Mejía Duque contrasts different writers' opinions regarding the relationship between narrative expression and revolution, identifying what he determines as an exaggerated optimism in the case of Fuentes. Mejía Duque compares Fuentes's position to those of Vargas Llosa and Cortázar, who emphasize the limitations of a literary revolution, positing as a realistic goal radical changes only within the scope of narrative (123–33).

27. Mejía Duque also succinctly defines the boom as a pioneering moment, arguing that "Cuando el escritor latinoamericano toma la pluma no se siente clausurando ni decorando una Historia, sino inaugurándola" (88).

28. The inaugural quality of boom literature is still sustained by recent critical reflections. In reference to *La región*, for example, Labastida writes in 2002 about the end of the 1950s, "Empezaba a nacer otro país, abierto al mundo" (19); see also Franco ("*La región*" 62–63). The universalizing tendency of Mejía Duque's words—obviously not the only ones to note that the boom placed Latin American literature on the world stage—are echoed more recently by Labastida, who says of *La región*, "La escritura de Fuentes fue decisiva en el derrumbe de la Cortina de Nopal; ayudó a incorporar al país en el concierto universal" (19).

29. See Boldy for a description of the two women that emphasizes their contrasts (47).

30. In his analysis of *La región*, Van Delden elaborates on the existentialist characteristics of Zamacona's death—which Van Delden concludes is distinct from the *acte gratuit* of the French existentialist tradition—and Pola's professional trajectory within the context of the influence of existentialism on Fuentes's work and thought (12–26). Boldy mentions Zamacona's death in his discussion of Fuentes's career-long preoccupation with the theme of redemption (2, 15). He also associates Zamacona's death with the redemption of Robles in his specific analysis of *La región* (15, 49–52).

31. In her study of the prostitute in modern German literature, Christiane Schönfeld makes an observation also relevant to García's appearance in Fuentes's novel: "This figure [...] opposes all that is complete, finished, and polished" (24). As I argue below, García stands in *La región* as the final obstacle toward completing the representation of social totality the novel constructs.

32. Bary also analyzes the discrepancies between narrative perspectives that structure this episode, arguing that they represent an aesthetic shortcoming of Fuentes's novel (910).

33. The italics designate García's thoughts, as opposed to her words.

34. Van Delden's interpretation of Cienfuegos's final transformation brought this characteristic of it to my attention (27).

35. See Blanco 256–57 and Sánchez 217–18.

Chapter Two
Animating the Popular: Fernando del Paso's *José Trigo* and the Ruins of Totalizing Thought

1. These dates are repeated throughout the novel. Notably, they appear as the opening and closing dates of the two chapters titled "Cronologías" (127, 407).

2. The actual labor dispute took place from the summer of 1958 to the spring of 1959, and it was characterized by a series of victories and defeats for the railroad workers, who struck on a number of separate occasions, first in June 1958 and lastly in March 1959. Del Paso's fictional portrayal of the strike transposes its events to 1960. Soto argues that this transposition is due to the importance, in Aztec mythology, of numbers divisible by four (141).

3. José Trigo's role in the narrator's education has not escaped critics' attention. See Chávarri (399–400), Dessau (512), and Rodríguez Lozano ("Hacia una poética" 98).

4. Clear parallels exist between Ixca Cienfuegos and José Trigo and between Gladys García and Buenaventura. Both Cienfuegos and Trigo serve as tour guides of sorts, and both García and Buenaventura are women who play important roles in fulfilling the narrative desire for an integrated and integrating history. Yet Trigo and Buenaventura remain more elusive than the characters who help structure Fuentes's novel, and del Paso's text ultimately rejects the idea of capturing popular knowledge and its production. See Fiddian for a comparison of Fuentes's and del Paso's novels that posits more continuity between the two texts than I see in my readings of them (*Novels* 32–35).

5. In an early assessment of *José Trigo*, Dotorri laments that the novel conceals history behind myth (295). Soto provides an outstanding analysis of the Aztec mythology underpinning the novel's central chapter, "Puente" (125–39); Fiddian's reading of the novel's incorporation of Aztec mythology also analyzes the text's Christian references (*Novels* 36–47).

6. See Davis (158, 185), Pani, and García Cortés.

7. Jean Meyer describes how Cristeros and their families set up camps around the Volcano of Colima very similar to the one described in del Paso's novel (147).

8. Soto's analysis of *José Trigo* outlines thoroughly the historical and mythical meanings associated with place names in the train yards (136–37).

9. Del Paso wrote *José Trigo* between 1959 and 1966. His efforts were supported by a scholarship from the Centro Mexicano de Escritores from 1964 to 1965 (Dessau 510). See Dessau and Chávarri for two early scholarly articles on *José Trigo*. Both critics are helpful because they contextualize the novel's production and introduce topics that will continue to be the focus of later critiques of *José Trigo*, including the novel's cyclical structure, its portrayal of the railroad workers' strike, and the testimonial role played by its title character. Dessau notes that del Paso was awarded the Villaurrutia Prize in 1966, and that the novel's first print run of 6,000 was a commercial success (510). Although published in 1989, Borgman's article provides the best overview to date of the novel's critical reception. Later analyses by Fiddian (*Novels*), López Gónzalez ("Obra clave"), and Rodríguez Lozano ("Crítica literaria" and "Hacia una poética") contribute significantly to the discussions surrounding the text. For a recent summary of the literary and historical context of del Paso's fiction, see Fiddian (*Novels* 1–8).

10. Gareth Williams maintains that "the formation of the modern nation-state in Latin America [...] was for the most part predicated on the active integration and institutionalization of the notion of the people" (4).

11. After years of simmering conflict, the Cristero Rebellion began in earnest in August 1926, when, in response to "Calles's Law," which obliged priests to register their names with the federal government, the Mexican Episcopate declared the cessation of public worship throughout Mexico (Jean Meyer 48). This move, in turn, gradually led to an armed conflict that consumed the Western Central region of Mexico for three years. The war resulted in about 100,000 military casualties, an indeterminate but significant loss of civilian life, and the utter disruption of entire villages, towns, and regions.

12. For religiously based motivation, see also Butler (208–10). See Armando Bartra for a detailed analysis of the Cristero Rebellion in the context of the Revolutionary government's land-reform policies of the 1920s, specifically in terms of how such policies divided Mexico's rural communities (36–57); Jean Meyer also discusses land distribution as a factor that exacerbated the military conflict (106–10).

13. Butler concurs with Jean Meyer on the question of the record of the Cristero Rebellion, writing that studying the Cristero Rebellion presents challenges to the historian because "the regime was only interested in exterminating the Cristeros, not documenting them" (196).

14. In Alan Knight's words, "the Cristiada taught the Church—that is to say the hierarchy—a hard lesson. Urged by Rome, the bishops sold out the rank-and-file Cristeros, cut a deal with the state, and traded institutional survival for political reticence" ("Peculiarities" 135).

15. Recent analyses of the relationship between the Mexican popular classes and the state tend to be more nuanced. See, for example, the essays in Gilbert and Nugent; and, for the Cristero Rebellion, see Purnell, who criticizes Jean Meyer's rather homogenous view of "the people" (7).

16. In Thomas Benjamin's words, the Revolution was "perceived as permanent and ongoing," and "unified by a 'revolutionary family' in which feuds would be forgotten if not entirely forgiven" (68).

17. Arnaldo Córdova's work is an important reference for scholars interested in the formation of the Revolutionary state. For historical, sociological, and anthropological analyses of the Revolution and its socio-political consequences, see also Knight, Lomnitz-Adler, Mallon, and Gilbert and Nugent. For a study that focuses on Mexico's rural populations and their uneven and often violent integration into the Revolutionary state, see Roger Bartra, *Campesinado*.

18. Óscar Mata argues that *José Trigo* is too heterogeneous to be considered a novel. Attesting to their coherence and less experimental style, the chapters titled "La Cristiada" represent, for Mata, "la novela dentro de la obra que no es novela" (54).

19. Ángel Arias calls *José Trigo*'s portrayal of the Cristero Rebellion, not inaccurately, "una recreación paródica" (27).

20. Jean Meyer translated this quotation for the English edition of his book, from which I cite here.

21. Jean Meyer's research into the Cristero Rebellion determines that only about five priests fought alongside the Cristeros, while a larger number served as military chaplains or supported combatants in other ways (69–75). Considering that the number of combatants who supported the Rebellion numbered around 50,000 (Jean Meyer 114–18), the number of actively militant priests is statistically irrelevant. See also Butler's analysis of who fought in the Cristiada, which focuses on the state of Michoacán (179).

22. Economically speaking, the Cristeros tended to be manual laborers who owned no property. A far smaller fraction owned land of any quantity (Jean Meyer 85–94).

23. The Cristero Rebellion actually forced Calles's Federal Army into a military stalemate, compelling the government to negotiate with the Church (Jean Meyer 64–65).

24. Alonso cites Rosendo (390) as his source for this speech delivered by Portes Gil to workers in Nuevo León on September 23, 1929.

25. See Aguilar Camín (*Después* 62–75).

26. *Charrismo* refers to a system within which labor leaders protect state, corporate, and personal interests more than they defend the interests of the workers at large. For example, the Secretary General of the STFRM before Vallejo was elected, Samuel Ortega Hernández, was also candidate for senator from Tlaxcala in 1958 (Alonso 116). Thus it was in his interest to appease those in power. Alonso offers the following general definition of *charrismo*: "la intervención de la fuerza pública para apoyar o imponer la determinada dirección sindical" (177). For additional perspectives on the 1958–59 movement of the STFRM, see the publication titled *Los ferrocarrileros hablan*, which emerged from a roundtable discussion that took place in Puebla in 1980. Many participants of the 1958–59 movement participated, including Mexican Communist Party leader Valentín Campa. See also Vallejo.

27. See Zermeño, whose sociological analysis of the Student Movement of 1968 provides important insights into its long- and short-term causes and its sociopolitical consequences (*México*).

28. After all, as the novel's third-person narrator observes, even Buenaventura has forgotten all about the Rebellion: "ya no recuerda la Guerra de los Cristeros, los muertos, los hijos perdidos" (439–40).

29. See especially Soto (137–39) and Fiddian (*Novels* 44–47).

30. Soto describes the conclusion to the strike narrative as a "profecía poética" of the massacre that actually took place at the Plaza of Tlatelolco on October 2, 1968 (143).

31. In one of the few previous analyses of this enigmatic scene, Nora Dotorri explains Luciano's appearance on the handcar as a moment of magical realism (274, 294). This fits with Dotorri's broader argument that del Paso mythifies the railroad strike, removing it from an explanatory historical context (295). Regarding the appearance of the handcar, I prefer López González's explanation: "el automóvil azul [...] se convierte por obra del deseo en un carro triunfal, un armón azul donde el líder viene sentado" (132).

32. See Fiddian for a reading of how the novel's symbolism and biblical references reinforce the notion that Luciano appears as a saint (*Novels* 36–37).

33. López González analyzes this scene in detail (*Obra clave* 131–34), defining it as an example of how the narrator is able to "contar la historia de un país y de un sector social desde la perspectiva del oprimido" (133). I contend that, in the end, the novel rejects the sustainability of communicating such a perspective.

34. In his reading of Kant's "Analytic of the Sublime," Jean-François Lyotard elaborates on the sudden, dramatic appearance of the sublime (54–56).

Chapter Three
The Stained Plaza: María Luisa Mendoza's *Con Él, conmigo, con nosotros tres* and the Origins of the Mestizo Nation

1. Even though it is subtitled a *cronovela*, I call Mendoza's text a novel throughout my analysis because, like novels traditionally do, it absorbs other genres into its structure as it tells an ultimately fictional tale. By the time Mendoza received support to write *Con Él* from the Center of Mexican Writers during that organization's 1968–69 scholarship period, she was already a successful journalist, having published a regular column titled *La O por lo redondo* in the newspaper *El Día* since 1961 (see Mendoza, *La O*). Mendoza also discusses the publication of *Con Él* in her autobiography. Of particular interest is the fact that her publisher asked her to change its title from "Tiniebla Tlatelolca" for political reasons (*De cuerpo entero* 37–38). For summaries of her career, see Domínguez Cuevas (237–40) and Robles (1: 325–41). See Young for a discussion of the similarities between Mendoza's "cronovela" and US New Journalism (76–78).

2. Paz wrote "Intermitencias" immediately after the massacre and mailed it along with his letter of resignation to the Cultural Committee of the Olympic Games. He was scheduled to serve as a judge in the Committee's poetry competition. "Intermitencias" would have to wait for publication, however, and it did not appear publicly until late October, after the Games were completed. It then appeared in Paz's collection titled *Ladera este*. Paz's resignation from the Cultural Committee was not as well-known or significant as his simultaneous resignation from his post as ambassador to India. See Volpi (369–80).

3. Castillo's work is a valuable resource for understanding the feminist literary tradition in Latin America. See also López González ("Justificación").

4. In a relevant observation that challenges traditional ideas that link motherhood exclusively with domesticity and reproduction of the social order, Jean Franco's analysis of the Mothers of the Plaza de Mayo in Argentina concludes that their activism "show[s] that mothering is not simply tied to anatomy but is a position involving a struggle over meanings and the history of meanings" ("Beyond Ethnocentrism" 514). Adding to the novel's autobiographical quality is the fact that Mendoza is, like Delfina, also unable to have children. In her 1991 autobiography, Mendoza reflects on what it means for her to be a woman without children (*De cuerpo entero* 27, 30–31, 42, 44).

5. See Domínguez Cuevas (239). For an interesting analysis of why Latin American women writers and academics have often refused to consider themselves feminists, see Kaminsky.

6. See Aguayo (*1968*) for the estimates of how many demonstrators and members of security forces were at Tlatelolco (219–21).

7. Aguayo's careful reconstruction of what happened on October 2 is the most detailed to date, and it makes a persuasive case for the existence of snipers around the Plaza who had been ordered to fire on the Army in order to provoke a bloodbath. See especially the chapters in his *1968: Archivos de la violencia* titled "Tlatelolco potosino" and "Máquina sin control" (205–33).Two more-recent, detailed analyses of the massacre are the film *Tlatelolco: Las claves de la masacre* (Carlos Mendoza, 2003), and Carlos Montemayor's outstanding analysis of film footage and military documents titled *Rehacer la historia*.

8. The deceitful accounts in the press have been a focal point of representations of the Student Movement since at least 1969. Ramón Ramírez's remarkably comprehensive *El movimiento estudiantil de México* contextualizes newspaper headlines within a vast array of documents, belying their narrow, partisan perspective. Elena Poniatowska's *La noche de Tlatelolco* compiles the headlines of the dominant Mexican dailies from the days following Tlatelolco, whose attributions of guilt to the students appear in ironic contrast to the testimonies that comprise her work (200–02). More recently, Jorge Volpi's *La imaginación y el poder* covers the press and its representation of the massacre (327–40).

9. See Ramírez, especially the official proclamations of the *Cámara de diputados* (2: 400–01, 405–07); see also Aguayo (*1968* 261–79); also relevant are Volpi's observations on the elaboration of conspiracy theories that were initiated and fostered by official sources and coerced participants in the Student Movement (340–53).

10. See Aguayo (*1968* 189–202); see also Volpi (367–69).

11. In 1993, the government assembled a Truth Commission. See Aguayo, who was a participant in this investigation, for a description of its limitations (*1968* 13–15). Aguayo's book *1968: Los archivos de la violencia* serves as his corrective to what he considered to be the sorely underfunded and hobbled Commission.

12. To date, the most thorough investigations have been unofficial publications, such as Aguayo's *1968* and the works co-written by Monsiváis and Scherer García. Echeverría has managed to elude prosecution despite recent efforts to hold him officially accountable for Tlatelolco and the Jueves de Corpus massacre of June 10, 1971. See Aranda, Carrillo Prieto, Castillo García, Dresser, Hilares, and Poy Solano.

13. See Aguayo for a consideration of how the notion that foreign interests had corrupted the Student Movement was a central delegitimization strategy (*1968* 91–105). The compulsion to protect "national security" is not only a domestic interest. In fact, it reveals Mexico's political dependence on the United States, which exported the doctrine of national security throughout Latin America during the latter half of the twentieth century. For a broader discussion of this topic, see chapter 4, where I analyze in greater detail the combination of factors that contributed to the weakening of the Mexican state's hegemony.

14. Aguayo provides useful insight into this president's belligerence (*1968* 11–12).

15. The most thorough interpretation of the Plaza's symbolic importance appears in Paz's "Posdata." Gyurko emphasizes how literary representations of 1968 often reinforced the simultaneous history embodied by Tlatelolco Plaza (269).

16. From the first days of the Student Movement, its declarations tended to call for democracy and respect for the Constitution as the best response to the government's abuses of power. See for example: the statements of the *Partido Comunista Mexicano*, the *Profesores de la Escuela Nacional de Ciencias Biológicas*, the *Profesores de la Escuela Nacional de Economía*, and the *Profesores de la Facultad de Ciencias Políticas y Sociales*, compiled and reprinted in Ramírez (2: 15–24). José Revueltas stood out as one of the most sophisticated ideologues of the Student

Movement. See for example, *"Nuestra bandera,"* his statement written on August 26, 1968, on behalf of the *Comité de Lucha de la Facultad de Filosofía y Letras* (Revueltas and Cheron 49–52). See also the bitterly ironic and often humorous self-defense that Revueltas read at his sentencing trial in 1970 (Revueltas and Cheron 257–79). Examples of democratic and pro-constitutional rhetoric abound in collected statements from the Student Movement. To my knowledge, Ramírez's collection of documents is the most complete compilation in print. In his analysis of the Student Movement's guiding ideology, Zermeño identifies its support of the Constitution as a counter-position to the government's inability to live up to the Constitution that supposedly guided the state: "La crítica del orden político no implicaba, en este caso, la crítica a la Constitución sino más bien se orientaba a mostrar la distancia entre los principios constitucionales y el funcionamiento efectivo del sistema político mexicano" (*México* 52).

17. See Zermeño for an analysis of the Student Movement's first days and immediate causes (*México* 11–23), as well as for an analysis of the extremely restrictive political atmosphere of the late 1960s, which made any protest against the ruling party a significant and dangerous oppositional act (41–54).

18. The entire speech is reprinted in Ramírez 2: 189–211.

19. For a similar reading of Tlatelolco's inaugural violence, within the context of an analysis of Paz's "Posdata" and Poniatowska's *Massacre*, see Sorensen.

20. See Aguayo for a convincing, definitive account of how top government officials, including Díaz Ordaz and Echeverría, plotted the massacre (*1968* 205–13).

21. Of course, not everyone was in agreement about how to respond to Tlatelolco. A handful of prominent intellectuals, like Salvador Novo and Martín Luis Guzmán, supported the government's actions. See Volpi 410–13.

22. For filmmakers like Jorge Fons (*Rojo amanecer*, 1989) and Leobardo López Aretche (*El Grito*, 1968), getting their works distributed was much more complicated, since film was perceived by the government to be a more dangerous medium because of its accessibility to a wider audience than those who read print media. Not only did Fons's film appear twenty years after 1968, but it was also censored upon its original release, the ending cut out. An interesting document, though of much poorer production-value than Fons's film, López Aretche's film is practically lost to obscurity.

23. Arguably the best-known textual representations of the Student Movement are *Días de guardar* (1970) by Carlos Monsiváis, *La noche de Tlatelolco* (1971) by Elena Poniatowska, and *Los días y los años* by Luis González de Alba. Their lack of emphasis on the coherence, unity, and self-sufficiency of the traditional novel enabled them to mount a particularly effective resistance to the official portrayal of the events of 1968. For an analysis of how the events of 1968 transformed boundaries of genre in contemporary Mexican narrative, see Steele. See Corona and Jörgensen for a good recent anthology of studies of the growing prominence of the chronicle in Mexico. Monsiváis's work has been reprinted more than a dozen times; *Los días y los años* almost twenty. Elena Poniatowska's collective testimonial is the only one of the three to be translated into English and it has been reprinted more than fifty times. Regarding analyses of post-1968 literature in general, Kohut's edited anthology stands out as exceptionally thorough and presents a number of perspectives from writers and critics alike. Cynthia Steele's monograph is one of the best single-authored analyses of post-1968 narrative. Especially important is her focus on gender. Her analysis of Fernando del Paso's *Palinuro de México* (1977) is a particularly interesting look at how a fictional representation of 1968 employs different narrative styles. And, though *Palinuro* is also a totalizing novel, it is less thoroughly structured by Tlatelolco than is *Con Él*. Good anthologies of 1968 literature include: the collection that focuses on José Revueltas by Andrea Revueltas and Philippe Cheron; the collection edited by Marco Antonio Campos and Alejandro Toledo; and the collection edited by Ivonne Gutiérrez. Most recently, Claire Brewster has published an important book that focuses on the post-1968 journalistic output of Carlos Fuentes, Carlos Monsiváis, Octavio Paz, and Elena Poniatowska.

24. See Mendoza's column from *El día* titled "Tiniebla Tlatelolca" (*La O* 112–13), which is also the name of the first chapter of *Con Él*.

Chapter Four
Totality in Post-Tlatelolco Mexico: Subjectivity and Interpellation in Jorge Aguilar Mora's *Si muero lejos de ti*

1. *Halcones*, which translates into English as "hawks," were groups of young men the governments of Díaz Ordaz and Echeverría hired to disrupt protest movements. They were not officially connected to the government, and thus committed acts of violence against dissenters in a paramilitary capacity. Their most notorious murders occurred on what has come to be known as the "Jueves de Corpus" massacre of June 10, 1971, in which dozens of students were killed.

2. Martini was not the sole painter. He received help from his brother-in-law Lippo Memmi (Cole 81–82).

3. Other critics of the novel do not provide nearly as detailed or developed critiques as Biron does. See, for example, Brushwood (76), Sefchovich (214), Trejo Fuentes (62), Domínguez Michael (263), and Martré (83–89).

4. For discussions of the state's increased support of cinematic production under Echeverría, see Pérez Turrent. The *apertura*'s limitations indeed revealed themselves, especially in the "Jueves de Corpus" massacre, the ferocious counterinsurgency efforts against urban and rural guerrilla movements, the censorship of any meaningful cinematic representation of 1968, and the government-backed takeover of Julio Scherer García's *Excelsior* in 1976. For an interesting, contradictory, and controversial (for being overly optimistic) discussion of the "apertura," see Fuentes (*Tiempo* 178–93). See also Aguilar Camín and Lorenzo Meyer (247–49).

5. The critique of the Revolution's practical effects mounted by *La región más transparente* is a significant example. Going farther back, Martín Luis Guzmán's 1929 novel, *La sombra del caudillo*, advances a scathing attack on the political class that consolidated itself in the decade following the Revolution. Of course, events like the Cristero Rebellion and the STFRM strike of 1958–59 provide additional examples of dissatisfaction with the Revolutionary regime.

6. L. Meyer identifies a dramatic increase in foreign investment between 1940 and 1970, due in part to weak domestic industry: "De alguna manera, el grupo industrial nacional empezó a ser relegado a un puesto secundario por falta de capacidad técnica. La inversión extranjera directa que en 1940 era de 411 millones de dólares, y que para 1950 había subido apenas a 566 millones, ascendió a casi 3 000 millones en 1970" ("La encrucijada" 1292). See also Castellanos Suárez 222–36.

7. For additional studies of how economic growth limited national sovereignty, see Zermeño ("Los intelectuales" 225–29; "Estado" 97–99).

8. Castellanos Suárez briefly discusses the development of rural insurgency in Guerrero (233–36). For a historically contextualized discussion of how the events of 1968 produced specific guerrilla movements, see Fernández Gómez (277–82). For the observations of student leaders regarding the connections between the Student Movement and the urban and rural insurgencies in the early 1970s, see: Guevara Niebla (151–53), Álvarez Garín (157), and Trejo Delarbre (159–60). Fernández Gómez's study of insurgency in Mexico is notably thorough and comprehensive, and stands out among the scattered works about insurgency in the 1970s. Armando Bartra's study of insurgency in Guerrero is also exceptional. Though works of fiction, Carlos Montemayor's trio of novels about *La guerrilla* provide useful historical perspectives on Mexican insurgency and counterinsurgency of the 1960s and 1970s. They are titled *Guerra en el paraíso* (1991), *Los informes secretos* (2000), and *Las armas del alba* (2003). Salvador Castañeda, who was a militant in the MAR (Movimiento de Acción Revolucionaria), has published fiction on the *Guerrilla* as well, including *¿Por qué no dijiste todo?* (1980) and *La patria celestial* (1992).

9. See Alejandro Álvarez for an economic focus on Mexico's strategic regional importance (29–36). For a broad historical study of how the United States has combined political and economic influence on Latin America, see Smith.

10. In addition to Brewster's study, see Corona Gutiérrez and Jörgensen for a contextualized analysis of the Mexican chronicle. See Egan for a study that focuses solely on Monsiváis and his trajectory. For English translations of a number of Monsiváis's chronicles, see Kraniauskas.

11. Elena Poniatowska's *Noche de Tlatelolco* served as a foundational moment in the tradition of critical testimonial in Mexico, and it was followed up by her later publications *Fuerte es el silencio* (1980) and *Nada, nadie: Las voces del temblor* (1988). For Monsiváis's critical texts that accompanied this opening, see, most notably *Días de guardar* (1971) and *Entrada libre* (1987). His chronicle about the 1994 Zapatista Convención Nacional Democrática is also important for its emphasis on the diverse nature of Mexican civil society; see "Crónica." Regarding literature, works that challenge norms and treat sensitive topics include Montemayor's and Castañeda's novels, cited above, and, among many other examples, the novels of Ángeles Mastretta and Brianda Domecq, and the plays and screenplays of Sabina Berman.

12. See Carrillo Prieto, Dresser, and Hilares.

13. Many clues in the 13th chapter, where this scene appears, suggest that Yoris's assault occurs on the same night that the army besieged the Preparatoria Nacional, destroying its door with a bazooka. The 13th chapter presents the first clear references to the events of 1968 in the novel.

14. See the passage where exile is described as a desire for recuperation and continuity (17) and the description of old neighborhoods in Mexico City that suggest a decadent continuity (64). Elsewhere, Yoris laments the succession of events, places, and people that he cannot place in any meaningful order (278, 300, 337, 365).

15. See additional references to the "aletazos de murciélago" (285, 369, 465). Significantly they also appear when Uchelo dies (394).

16. An earlier reference to a destructive surface also explains how it disorients and divides the orphans from one another (400–01).

17. Repetition of entire passages, sometimes slightly modified, occurs at other moments in the text (130–34, 402). The repetition of the passage about the train, praxis, and hope occurs four times, but, in another of the novel's rejections of continuity, the passages are numbered I–V, which suggests that one piece of the series will always be missing.

Chapter Five
The "Machine of Savage Stories": State, Fiction, and Totality in Héctor Aguilar Camín's *Morir en el golfo*

1. *Marxism and Form*, *The Political Unconscious*, *The Geopolitical Aesthetic*, and *Postmodernism* all exemplify this aspect of Jameson's work.

2. See especially Bakhtin's essays, compiled in *The Dialogic Imagination.*

3. Moreiras's study of *Morir en el golfo* focuses on this distance ("Ethics and Politics").

4. This is the conclusion that Moreiras reaches in his convincing analysis of the novel.

5. The concept of the "ethical state" is developed by Gramsci, whose description of it illustrates why the concept is helpful for understanding the Mexican populist state: "Every State is ethical in as much as one of its most important functions is to raise the great mass of the population to a particular cultural and moral level, a level (or type) which corresponds to the needs of the productive forces for development" (258).

6. Writing in his diary a few days before he officially nationalized Mexican oil production and distribution on March 18, 1938, Cárdenas connected this historic opportunity for Mexico to "deshacerse del yugo político y económico" of foreign oil companies with the ability to fulfill more completely "el programa de reforma social establecido en la Constitución" (qtd. in Beltrán Mata 22–23).

7. Mota also considers the long term impacts of capital flight: "La fuerte transferencia de recursos al exterior limitó la producción y comprometió el crecimiento futuro: a fines de la década de los noventa todavía vivimos sus efectos" (33).

8. When Grayson describes his interview with the petroleum workers' union leader Joaquín Hernández Galicia, known as "La Quina," he recounts a situation remarkably similar to the narrator's encounter with Pizarro: "While waiting there on May 31, 1978, for an interview, I witnessed scenes reminiscent of an episode from *The Godfather* unfold outside his gate. Men gathered to plead for work or a handout; women came to have unfaithful husbands disciplined [...]" (90).

9. See Lustig for a discussion of the failures of the national-developmentalist program that was based on ISI. See also Székely (*Economía* 33–51).

10. The essay in question is titled "Third-World Literature in the Era of Multinational Capitalism." See Aijaz Ahmad's equally famous, critical response to Jameson's text and Jameson's rebuttal.

11. Grayson's description of Villahermosa also focuses on the inequality of the city and the precarious employment situation of at least two-thirds of the population of Tabasco during the oil boom (77–78).

12. Grayson's chapter on the oil workers' union provides a useful and detailed history and description of the STPRM from its foundation to 1980 (81–102).

13. See the remainder of Grayson's description of La Quina for more similarities between him and Pizarro, which include, among other things, the actual union leader's vast landholdings and company stores and his recurrence to violence (89–93).

14. See Székely, who notes that the failed natural-gas-exportation plan was "la primera señal de que factores internacionales que no están bajo el control del régimen mexicano podrían obstaculizar la ejecución exitosa del programa de desarrollo petrolero" (*Economía* 101).

15. Buendía was in fact very critical of López Portillo's oil policy. See the collection of his columns titled *Los petroleros*. For a history of the Buendía murder and hobbled government investigation, see the Article 19 report titled *In the Shadow of Buendía* (1–4).

16. See Álvarez for a discussion of the influence of international finance capital on the Mexican oil bust and debt crisis (81–84).

17. See Gentleman for a discussion of the specific reforms undertaken during the nationalization (222–23). The bank was privatized again in 1990. See Mota (45) and Lustig (89).

18. As Gentleman notes, "According to one report, Citibank, Chase Manhattan and Bank of America had 40% of their capital tied up in Mexico" (221–22).

19. See Lustig for a brief but good summary of how the debt crisis of the 1980s led to significant changes in Mexican economic policy that fueled recent globalization and typified neoliberal reforms. As Lustig writes in 2001, "Gone is the import-substitution industrialization model that had characterized Mexico since the 1930s. Instead, Mexico has become a fairly open economy in which state intervention is limited by a new legal and institutional framework. Under the new model, the tendency has been for the market to replace regulation, private ownership to replace public ownership, and competition, including that from foreign goods and investors, to replace protection" (85). See also Mota, esp. chapter 2.

20. A sign of the gravity of the situation is de la Madrid's well-known pledge: "No permitiré que la Patria se nos deshaga entre las manos" (qtd. in Mota 45).

21. See also Lustig, who summarizes in 2001, "despite the widespread economic reforms, Mexico's per capita output grew by only 0.45 percent per year between 1980 and 1999. This is disappointing, particularly for the roughly 20 million Mexicans who live on less than $2 a day" (86).

22. González Casanova, "Aritmética contrarrevolucionaria" and Zermeño, *México: Una democracia utópica*, respectively.

Works Cited

Abrams, Philip. "Notes on the Difficulty of Studying the State." *Journal of Historical Sociology* 1.1 (1988): 58–89.

Aguayo Quezada, Sergio. *1968: Los archivos de la violencia*. México, DF: Grijalbo, 1998.

———. "The Uses, Abuses and Challenges of Mexican National Security: 1946–1990." *México: In Search of Security*. Ed. Bruce Michael Bagley and Sergio Aguayo Quezada. Miami: U of Miami North-South Center, 1993. 97–142.

Aguilar Camín, Héctor. "Desde la alta tribuna espiritual: Cultura presidencial." *Saldos de la Revolución*. Ed. Aguilar Camín. México, DF: Océano, 1985. 79–105.

———. *Después del milagro*. México, DF: Cal y Arena, 1988.

———. *Morir en el golfo*. México, DF: Océano, 1986.

———. "Sólo cenizas hallarás (1968–1976)." *Saldos de la Revolución*. Ed. Aguilar Camín. México, DF: Océano, 1985. 107–33.

Aguilar Camín, Héctor, and Lorenzo Meyer. *A la sombra de la Revolución Mexicana*. México, DF: Cal y Arena, 1989.

Aguilar Mora, Jorge. *Si muero lejos de ti*. México, DF: Joaquín Mortiz, 1979.

Ahmad, Aijaz. "Jameson's Rhetoric of Otherness and the 'National Allegory.'" *Social Text* 17 (1987): 3–25.

Alewyn, Richard. "The Origin of the Detective Novel." Trans. Glenn W. Most. *The Poetics of Murder: Detective Fiction and Literary Theory*. Ed. Glenn W. Most and William W. Stowe. New York: Harcourt, Brace, Jovanovich, 1983. 62–78.

Alonso, Antonio. *El movimiento ferrocarrilero en México, 1958–1959: De la conciliación a la lucha de clases*. México, DF: Era, 1972.

Althusser, Louis. "Ideology and Ideological State Apparatuses (Notes towards an Investigation)." Trans. Ben Brewster. *Lenin and Philosophy and Other Essays*. Ed. Althusser. New York: Monthly Review, 1971. 127–86.

Álvarez, Alejandro. *La crisis global del capitalismo en México: 1968/1985*. México, DF: Era, 1987.

Álvarez Garín, Raúl. "La Dispersión." *Pensar el 68*. Ed. Hermann Bellinghausen. México, DF: Cal y Arena, 1988. 155–58.

Amin, Shahid. "Ghandi as Mahatma." *Selected Subaltern Studies*. Ed. Ranajit Guha and Gayatri Chakravorty Spivak. Oxford: Oxford UP, 1988. 288–346.

Anadón, José. "Entrevista a Carlos Fuentes (1980)." *Revista Iberoamericana* 49.123–24 (1983): 621–30.

Anderson, Benedict. *Imagined Communities.* London: Verso, 1983.

Anderson, Mark. "A Reappraisal of the 'Total Novel': Totality and Communicative Systems in Carlos Fuentes's *Terra nostra.*" *Symposium* 57.2 (2003): 59–79.

Aranda, Jesús. "Proscribe el delito de genocidio si se cometió antes del 1982: SCJN." *La Jornada* 24 Feb. 2005. 7 June 2005 <http://www.jornada.unam.mx/2005/feb05/050224/003n1pol>.

Arias, Ángel. *Entre la cruz y la sospecha: Los Cristeros de Revueltas, Yáñez y Rulfo.* Madrid: Iberoamericana, 2005.

Article 19. *In the Shadow of Buendia: The Mass Media and Censorship in Mexico.* London: Article 19, 1989.

Avelar, Idelber. *The Untimely Present: Postdictatorial Latin American Fiction and the Task of Mourning.* Durham: Duke UP, 1999.

Bagley, Bruce Michael, and Sergio Aguayo Quezada, eds. *Mexico: In Search of Security.* Miami: U of Miami North-South Center, 1993.

Bakhtin, M. M. *The Dialogic Imagination.* Trans. Caryl Emerson and Michael Holquist. Austin: U of Texas P, 1981.

Bartra, Armando. *Los herederos de Zapata: Movimientos campesinos posrevolucionarios en México.* México, DF: Era, 1985.

Bartra, Roger. *Campesinado y poder político en México.* México, DF: Era, 1982.

———. "Cultura y poder político." *La democracia ausente.* Ed. Bartra. México, DF: Grijalbo, 1986. 71–83.

———. *La jaula de la melancolía: Identidad y metamorfosis del mexicano.* México, DF: Grijalbo, 1987.

———. *Las redes imaginarias del poder político.* México, DF: Era, 1981.

———. "Revolutionary Nationalism and National Security in México." *México: In Search of Security.* Ed. Bruce Michael Bagley and Sergio Aguayo Quezada. Miami: U of Miami North-South Center, 1993. 143–72.

Bary, David. "Poesía y narración en cuatro novelas mexicanas." *Revista Iberoamericana* 55 (1989): 903–14.

Beltrán Mata, José Antonio. *México: Crónica de los negros intereses del petróleo.* México, DF: Grupo Editorial Diez, 2005.

Benjamin, Thomas. *La Revolución: Mexico's Great Revolution as Memory, Myth, and History.* Austin: U of Texas P, 2000.

Benjamin, Walter. "Critique of Violence." Trans. Edmund Jephcott. *Reflections: Essays, Aphorisms, Autobiographical Writings*. Ed. Peter Demetz. New York: Schocken, 1986. 277–300.

Bermúdez, Antonio J. *La política petrolera mexicana*. México, DF: Joaquín Mortiz, 1976.

Beverley, John. *Against Literature*. Minneapolis: U of Minnesota P, 1993.

———. *Subalternity and Representation: Arguments in Cultural Theory*. Durham: Duke UP, 1999.

Biron, Rebecca. "Death in el D.F.: Urban Fantasy in Aguilar Mora, Ramirez, Fuentes, and Blanco." *Discourse* 26.1–2 (2004): 58–85.

Blanco, José Joaquín. "Fuentes: De la pasión por los mitos al polyforum de las mitologías." *La paja en el ojo: Ensayos de crítica*. Ed. José Joaquín Blanco. Puebla: Editorial Universidad Autónoma de Puebla, 1980. 243–70.

Boldy, Steven. *The Narrative of Carlos Fuentes: Family, Text, Nation*. Durham, UK: U of Durham, 2002.

Borges, Jorge Luis. "Las ruinas circulares." *Obras completas*. Ed. Carlos V. Frías. Vol. 1. Barcelona: Emecé, 1989. 451–55.

Borgman, Patricia D. "Fernando del Paso's *José Trigo*: A Literary Enigma?" *Romance Languages Annual* 1 (1989): 390–94.

Brewster, Claire. *Responding to Crisis in Contemporary Mexico: The Political Writings of Paz, Fuentes, Monsiváis, and Poniatowska*. Tucson: U of Arizona P, 2005.

Brushwood, John S. *La novela mexicana (1967–1982)*. México, DF: Grijalbo, 1985.

Buendía, Manuel. *Los petroleros*. México, DF: Fundación Manuel Buendía, Océano, 1985.

Butler, Matthew. *Popular Piety and Political Identity in Mexico's Cristero Rebellion: Michoacan, 1927–29*. Oxford: Oxford UP, 2004.

Campos, Marco Antonio, and Alejandro Toledo, eds. *Poemas y narraciones sobre el movimiento estudiantil de 1968*. México, DF: UNAM, 1996.

Carrillo Prieto, Ignacio. "Recuperar la memoria y procurar la justicia." *Nexos* July 2004: 17–20.

Castellanos, Rosario. "La juventud: Un tema, una perspectiva, un estilo." *La crítica de la novela mexicana contemporánea*. Ed. Aurora M. Ocampo. México, DF: UNAM, 1981. 175–90.

Castellanos, Rosario. *Mujer que sabe latín.* México, DF: Fondo de Cultura Económica, 1973.

Castellanos Suárez, José Alfredo. "Expansión del capitalismo monopolista en México 1940 a 1970." *Los días sin tregua: 1876–1970, centuria de luchas populares.* Ed. Genaro A. Figueroa Ruiz. Chapingo: Universidad Autónoma de Chapingo, 1994. 206–36.

Castillo, Debra. *Talking Back: Toward a Latin American Feminist Literary Criticism.* Ithaca: Cornell UP, 1992.

Castillo García, Gustavo. "La FEMOSPP pedirá la detención de Echeverría por la matanza de Tlatelolco." *La Jornada* 16 May 2005. 7 June 2005 <http://www.jornada.unam.mx/2005/may05/050516/007n1pol.php>.

Centro de Investigaciones del Movimiento Obrero, ed. "Los ferrocarrileros hablan." *Foro y exposición sobre el movimiento ferrocarrilero.* México, DF: Centro de Investigaciones Históricas del Movimiento Obrero, 1983.

Chávarri, Raúl. "El personaje en la moderna novela mejicana." *Cuadernos Hispanoamericanos* 215 (1967): 395–400.

Cole, Bruce. *Sienese Painting: From Its Origins to the Fifteenth Century.* New York: Harper and Row, 1980.

Córdova, Arnaldo. *La ideología de la Revolución mexicana: La formación del nuevo régimen.* México, DF: Era, 1973.

Corona Gutiérrez, Ignacio. *Después de Tlatelolco: Las narrativas políticas en México, 1976–1990: Un análisis de sus estrategias retóricas y representacionales.* Guadalajara: Universidad de Guadalajara, 2001.

Corona Gutiérrez, Ignacio, and Beth Jörgensen, eds. *The Contemporary Mexican Chronicle: Theoretical Perspectives on the Liminal Genre.* Albany: SUNY P, 2002.

Corral, Wilfrido. "Novelistas sin timón: Exceso y subjetividad en el concepto de 'Novela total.'" *Modern Language Notes* 116.2 (2001): 315–49.

Cresta de Leguizamón, María Luisa. "Los caminos de la narrativa mexicana de hoy." *La crítica de la novela mexicana contemporánea.* Ed. Aurora M. Ocampo. México, DF: UNAM, 1981. 145–56.

Davis, Diane E. *Urban Leviathan: Mexico City in the Twentieth Century.* Philadelphia: Temple UP, 1994.

Deleuze, Gilles, and Felix Guatarri. *A Thousand Plateaus: Capitalism and Schizophrenia.* Trans. Brian Massumi. Minneapolis: U of Minnesota P, 1987.

del Paso, Fernando. *José Trigo.* México, DF: Siglo XXI, 1966.

de Luna, Andrés, and Norma Patiño. "Una pantalla que rasgar: Una conversación con Jorge Aguilar Mora." *Revista de la Universidad de México* 34.2 (1979): 21–24.

Derrida, Jacques. "Force of Law: The 'Mystical Foundation of Authority.'" *Cardozo Law Review* 11.919 (1990): 921–1045.

———. *Of Grammatology*. Trans. Gayatri Chakravorty Spivak. Baltimore: Johns Hopkins UP, 1976.

———. *The Truth in Painting*. Trans. Geoff Bennington and Ian McLeod. Chicago: U of Chicago P, 1987.

Dessau, Adalbert. "*José Trigo*: Notas acerca de un acontecimiento literario en la novela mexicana." *Bulletin Hispanique* 70 (1968): 510–19.

Domínguez Cuevas, Martha, ed. *Los becarios del Centro Mexicano de Escritores (1952–1997)*. México, DF: Aldus, 1999.

Domínguez Michael, Christopher. *Servidumbre y grandeza de la vida literaria*. México, DF: Joaquín Mortiz, 1998.

Dottori, Nora. "*José Trigo*: El terror a la historia." *Nueva novela latinoamericana*. Ed. Jorge Lafforgue. Vol. 1. Buenos Aires: Paidos, 1972. 262–99.

Dresser, Denise. "Cuentas por saldar." *Nexos* July 2004: 31–36.

Egan, Linda. *Carlos Monsiváis: Culture and Chronicle in Contemporary Mexico*. Tucson: U of Arizona P, 2001.

Fernández Gómez, Raúl. "Jeu politique et guerrilla rural au Mexique." Diss. École des Hautes Études en Sciences Sociales, 1980.

Fiddian, Robin William. "James Joyce and Spanish-American Fiction: A Study of the Origins and Transmission of Literary Influence." *Bulletin of Hispanic Studies* 66.1 (1989): 23–39.

———. *The Novels of Fernando Del Paso*. Gainesville: UP of Florida, 2000.

Foster, David William. "*La región más transparente* and the Limits of Prophetic Art." *Hispania* 56 (1973): 35–42.

Fowler, Don D. "Uses of the Past: Archaeology in the Service of the State." *American Antiquity* 52.2 (1987): 229–48.

Franco, Jean. "Beyond Ethnocentrism: Gender, Power, and the Third-World Intelligentsia." *Marxism and the Interpretation of Culture*. Ed. Cary Nelson and Lawrence Grossberg. Urbana and Chicago: U of Illinois P, 1988. 503–15.

———. "*The Critique of the Pyramid* and Mexican Narrative after 1968." *Latin American Fiction Today*. Ed. Rose S. Minc. Upper Montclair, NJ: Hispamérica, 1979. 49–60.

Franco, Jean. *The Decline and Fall of the Lettered City: Latin America in the Cold War*. Cambridge: Harvard UP, 2002.

Franco, Jean. "*La región más transparente* de Carlos Fuentes: Entre el orden y el desorden." *Carlos Fuentes: Perspectivas críticas*. Ed. Pol Popovic Karic. México, DF: Siglo XXI, 2002. 61–78.

Frank, Joseph. *The Widening Gyre: Crisis and Mastery in Modern Literature*. New Brunswick, NJ: Rutgers UP, 1963.

Fuentes, Carlos. *La nueva novela hispanoamericana*. México, DF: Joaquín Mortiz, 1969.

———. *La región más transparente*. México, DF: Fondo de Cultura Económica, 1958.

———. *Tiempo mexicano*. México, DF: Joaquín Mortiz, 1971.

Gamio, Manuel. *Forjando patria*. México, DF: Porrúa, 1916.

García Canclini, Néstor. *Hybrid Cultures: Strategies for Entering and Leaving Modernity*. Trans. Christopher L. Chiappari and Silvia L. López. Minneapolis: U of Minnesota P, 1995.

García Cortés, Adrián. *La reforma urbana de México: Crónicas de la comisión de planificación del Distrito Federal*. México, DF: Bay Gráfica y Ediciones, 1971.

Gentleman, Judith. *Mexican Oil and Dependent Development*. New York: Peter Lang, 1984.

Gilbert, Joseph, and Daniel Nugent, eds. *Everyday Forms of State Formation: Revolution and the Negotiation of Rule in Modern Mexico*. Durham: Duke UP, 1994.

Goldenberg, Isaac. "Perspectivismo y mexicanidad en la obra de Carlos Fuentes." *Cuadernos Hispanoamericanos* 271 (1973): 15–33.

González Casanova, Pablo. *Aritmética contrarrevolucionaria*. Puebla: Universidad Autónoma de Puebla, 1976.

González de Alba, Luis. *Los días y los años*. México, DF: Era, 1971.

Gramsci, Antonio. *Prison Notebooks*. Trans. Quintin Hoare and Geoffrey Nowell. Ed. Quintin Hoare and Geoffrey Nowell. New York: International Publishers, 1971.

Grayson, George W. *The Politics of Mexican Oil*. Pittsburgh: U of Pittsburgh P, 1980.

Guevara Niebla, Gilberto. "Secuelas en la izquierda." *Pensar el 68*. Ed. Hermann Bellinghausen. México, DF: Cal y Arena, 1988. 151–54.

Gugelberger, Georg M., ed. *The Real Thing: Testimonial Discourse and Latin America*. Durham: Duke UP, 1996.

Guha, Ranajit. *Dominance without Hegemony*. Cambridge: Harvard UP, 1997.

Gutiérrez, Ivonne, ed. *Entre el silencio y la estridencia: La protesta literaria del 68*. México, DF: Aldus, 1998.

Gutiérrez de Velasco, Luz Elena. "La nada como herencia." *Sin imágenes falsas, sin falsos espejos: Narradoras mexicanas del Siglo XX*. Ed. Aralia López González. México, DF: Colegio de México, 1995. 315–27.

Gyurko, Lanin A. "Twentieth-Century Fiction." *Mexican Literature: A History*. Ed. David William Foster. Austin: U of Texas P, 1994. 243–303.

Hernández Martín, Jorge. "Paco Ignacio Taibo II: Post-Colonialism and the Detective Story in Mexico." *The Post-Colonial Detective*. Ed. Ed Christian. New York: Palgrave, 2001. 159–75.

Hilares, Gustavo. "Los avatares de una justicia propuesta." *Nexos* July 2004: 22–28.

Hirsch, Marianne. *Family Frames: Photography, Narrative and Postmemory*. Cambridge: Harvard UP, 1997.

Holquist, Michael. "Whodunit and Other Questions: Metaphysical Detective Stories in Post-War Fiction." *New Literary History* 3.1 (1971): 135–56.

Jameson, Fredric. "A Brief Response." *Social Text* 17 (1987): 26–27.

———. *The Geopolitical Aesthetic: Cinema and Space in the World System*. Bloomington and London: Indiana UP and the British Film Institute, 1992.

———. *Marxism and Form: Twentieth-Century Dialectical Theories of Literature*. Princeton: Princeton UP, 1971.

———. "On Raymond Chandler." *The Poetics of Murder: Detective Fiction and Literary Theory*. Ed. Glenn W. Most and William W. Stowe. New York: Harcourt, Brace, Jovanovich, 1983. 122–48.

———. *The Political Unconscious: Narrative as a Socially Symbolic Act*. Ithaca: Cornell UP, 1981.

———. *Postmodernism, or, the Cultural Logic of Late Capitalism*. Durham: Duke UP, 1991.

———. "Third-World Literature in the Era of Multinational Capitalism." *Social Text* 15 (1986): 65–88.

Kaminsky, Amy. "Lesbian Cartographies: Body, Text, and Geography." *Cultural and Historical Grounding for Hispanic and Luso-Brazilian Feminist Literary Criticism*. Ed. Hernán Vidal. Minneapolis: Institute for the Study of Ideologies and Literature, 1989. 223–56.

Kant, Immanuel. *The Critique of Judgment*. Trans. James Creed Meredith. Oxford: Oxford UP, 1952.

Knight, Alan. "The Peculiarities of Mexican History: Mexico Compared to Latin America, 1821–1992." *Journal of Latin American Studies* 24. Quincentenary Supplement (1992): 99–144.

———. "The Politics of the Expropriation." *The Mexican Petroleum Industry in the Twentieth Century*. Ed. Jonathan C. Brown and Alan Knight. Austin: U of Texas P, 1992. 90–128.

Kohut, Karl, ed. *Literatura mexicana hoy: Del 68 al ocaso de la Revolución*. Frankfurt: Vervuert, 1991.

Kraniauskas, John. *Mexican Postcards*. London: Verso, 1997.

Kristeva, Julia. *Revolution in Poetic Language*. 1974. Trans. Margaret Waller. New York: Columbia UP, 1984.

Labastida, Jaime. "Introducción." *Carlos Fuentes: Perspectivas críticas*. Ed. Pol Popovic Karic. México, DF: Siglo XXI, 2002. 11–20.

Lacan, Jacques. *The Four Fundamental Concepts of Psychoanalysis*. Trans. Alan Sheridan. New York: Norton, 1978.

Laclau, Ernesto. *Emancipation(s)*. London: Verso, 1996.

Leal, Luis. "Nuevos novelistas mexicanos." *La crítica de la novela mexicana contemporánea*. Ed. Aurora M. Ocampo. México, DF: UNAM, 1981. 215–23.

Levinson, Brett. *The Ends of Literature: The Latin American "Boom" in the Neoliberal Marketplace*. Stanford: Stanford UP, 2001.

Lomnitz-Adler, Claudio. *Exits from the Labyrinth: Culture and Ideology in the Mexican National Space*. Berkeley: U of California P, 1992.

López González, Aralia. "Justificación teórica." *Sin imágenes falsas, sin falsos espejos: Narradoras mexicanas del Siglo XX*. Ed. López González. México, DF: Colegio de México, 1995. 13–48.

———. "Una obra clave en la narrativa mexicana: *José Trigo*." *Revista Iberoamericana* 56.150 (1990): 117–41.

Loyo, Aurora. "Balances optimistas sobre *La cultura en México*: La visión de los intelectuales 'consagrados.'" *Historias* 21 (1988–89): 149–63.

Lustig, Nora. "Life Is Not Easy: Mexico's Quest for Stability and Growth." *Journal of Economic Perspectives* 15.1 (2001): 85–106.

Lyotard, Jean-François. *Lessons on the Analytic of the Sublime*. Trans. Elizabeth Rottenberg. Palo Alto: Stanford UP, 1994.

Macherey, Pierre. *A Theory of Literary Production*. Trans. Geoffrey Wall. London: Routledge, 1978.

Mallon, Florencia. *Peasant and Nation: The Making of Postcolonial México and Peru*. Berkeley: U of California P, 1995.

Manzo-Robledo, Francisco. "La segmentación de los grupos sociales en el espacio urbano: *La región más transparente* (1958) de Carlos Fuentes y *Las reinas de Polanco* de Guadalupe Loaeza (1988)." *Espéculo: Revista de Estudios Literarios* 23 Mar.–June 2003. 28 July 2005 <http://www.ucm.es/info/especulo/>.

Marks, Elaine, and Isabelle de Courtivron, eds. *New French Feminisms*. New York: Schocken, 1981.

Martin, Gerald. *Journeys through the Labyrinth: Latin American Fiction in the Twentieth Century*. London: Verso, 1989.

Martré, Gonzalo. *El movimiento popular estudiantil de 1968 en la novela mexicana*. México, DF: UNAM, 1986.

Masiello, Francine. *The Art of Transition: Latin American Culture and Neoliberal Crisis*. Durham: Duke UP, 2001.

Mata, Óscar. *Un océano de narraciones: Fernando del Paso*. Puebla: Universidad Autónoma de Puebla, 1991.

Mejía Duque, Jaime. *Narrativa y neocoloniaje en América Latina*. Buenos Aires: Crisis, 1974.

Mendoza, Carlos. *Tlatelolco: Las claves de la masacre*. 2003. Canal seis de julio.

Mendoza, María Luisa. *Con Él, conmigo, con nosotros tres*. México, DF: Joaquín Mortiz, 1971.

———. *De cuerpo entero*. México, DF: UNAM, 1991.

———. *La O por lo redondo*. México, DF: Grijalbo, 1971.

Meyer, Jean. *The Cristero Rebellion: The Mexican People between Church and State 1926–1929*. Trans. Richard Southern. Cambridge: Cambridge UP, 1976.

Meyer, Lorenzo. "La encrucijada." *Historia general de México*. Ed. Centro de Estudios Históricos. México, DF: Colegio de México, 1994. 1275–355.

———. "El primer tramo del camino." *Historia general de México*. Ed. Centro de Estudios Históricos. México, DF: Colegio de México, 1994. 1183–271.

Miller, Nicola. *In the Shadow of the State: Intellectuals and the Quest for National Identity in Twentieth-Century Spanish America*. London: Verso, 1999.

Monsiváis, Carlos. "1968: Dramatis personae." *México: Una democracia Utópica: El movimiento estudiantil del '68*. Ed. Sergio Zermeño. México, DF: Siglo XXI, 1978. xi–xxiv.

———. "Crónica de una convención (Que no lo fue tanto) y de un acontecimiento muy significativo." *EZLN: Documentos y comunicados*. Ed. EZLN. México, DF: Era, 1994. 313–23.

———. *Días de guardar*. México, DF: Era, 1971.

———. *Entrada libre: Crónicas de la sociedad que se organiza*. México, DF: Era, 1987.

———. "Homenaje a la indiferencia moral." *La cultura en México* 17 Apr. 1968: viii.

———. "No con un sollozo, sino entre disparos (Notas sobre cultura mexicana 1910–1968)." *Revista Iberoamericana* 55.148–49 (1989): 715–35.

———. "Notas sobre la cultura mexicana en el Siglo XX." *Historia general de México*. Ed. Centro de Estudios Históricos. México, DF: Colegio de México, 1994. 1375–548.

———. "La pasión de la historia." *Historia ¿Para qué?* Ed. Carlos Pereyra, Luis Villoro, et al. México, DF: Siglo XXI, 1980. 171–93.

Montemayor, Carlos. *Rehacer la historia: Análisis de los nuevos documentos del 2 de octubre de 1968 en Tlatelolco*. México, DF: Planeta, 2000.

Moreiras, Alberto. "Ethics and Politics in Héctor Aguilar Camín's *Morir en el golfo* and *La guerra de Galio*." *South Central Review* 21.3 (2004): 70–84.

———. *The Exhaustion of Difference: The Politics of Latin American Cultural Studies*. Durham: Duke UP, 2001.

———. *Tercer espacio: Literatura y duelo en América Latina*. Santiago: LOM Ediciones / Universidad Arcis, 1999.

Mota, Sergio. *México: Estabilización y cambio estructural 1982–1988*. Monterrey: Castillo, 1998.

Ocampo, Aurora M. Prólogo. *La crítica de la novela mexicana contemporánea*. Ed. Ocampo. México, DF: UNAM, 1981. 7–17.

Ochoa, John A. *The Uses of Failure in Mexican Literature and Identity*. Austin: U of Texas P, 2004.

Pani, Mario. *Nonoalco Tlaltelolco Urban Development Scheme: The Urban Regeneration of Mexico City*. México, DF: Banco Nacional Hipotecario y de Obras Públicas, 1961.

Paz, Octavio. "Intermitencias del oeste (3)." *Poemas y narraciones sobre el movimiento estudiantil de 1968*. Ed. Marco Antonio Campos and Alejandro Toledo. México, DF: UNAM, 1996. 40.

———. *El laberinto de la soledad*. Ed. Enrico Mario Santi. Madrid: Cátedra, 1993.

———. *Ladera este*. México, DF: Joaquín Mortiz, 1969.

———. "Posdata." *El laberinto de la soledad*. Ed. Enrico Mario Santi. Madrid: Cátedra, 1993. 363–415.

Pérez Turrent, Tomás. "Crises and Renovations (1965–91)." Trans. Ana M. López. *Mexican Cinema*. Ed. Paulo Antonio Paranagua. London: British Film Institute and IMCINE, 1995. 94–115.

Phelan, John. "México y lo mexicano." *Hispanic American Historical Review* 36.3 (1956): 309–18.

Poniatowska, Elena. *Fuerte es el silencio*. México, DF: Era, 1980.

———. *Nada, nadie: Las voces del temblor*. México, DF: Era, 1988.

———. *La noche de Tlatelolco*. México, DF: Era, 1971.

Poy Solano, Laura. "Podría la corte convertir a México en refugio de genocidas: Comité 68." *La Jornada* 5 June 2005. 7 June 2005 <http://www.jornada.unam.mx/2005/jun05/050605/003n1pol.php>.

Purnell, Jennie. *Popular Movements and State Formation in Revolutionary Mexico: The Agraristas and Cristeros of Michoacan*. Durham: Duke UP, 1999.

Rama, Ángel. "El 'Boom' en perspectiva." *Más allá del Boom: Literatura y mercado*. Ed. David Viñas. México, DF: Marcha, 1981. 51–110.

———. *La ciudad letrada*. Hanover, NH: Ediciones del Norte, 1984.

Ramírez, Ramón. *El movimiento estudiantil de México (Julio/diciembre de 1968)*. México, DF: Era, 1969.

Ramos, Samuel. *El perfil del hombre y la cultura en México*. México, DF: Planeta, 1998.

Reeve, Richard M. "The Making of *La region más transparente*: 1949–1974." *Carlos Fuentes: A Critical View*. Ed. Robert Rossman and Charles Brody. Austin: U of Texas, 1982.

Revueltas, Andrea, and Philippe Cheron, eds. *México 68: Juventud y revolución*. México, DF: Era, 1978.

Robles, Martha. *La sombra fugitiva: Escritoras en la cultura nacional*. 2 vols. México, DF: UNAM, 1985.

Rodríguez Lozano, Miguel G. "José Trigo: Hacia una poética." *Literatura Mexicana* 7.1 (1996): 79–104.

Rodríguez Lozano, Miguel G. "*José Trigo* y la crítica literaria." *Literatura Mexicana* 5.2 (1994): 479–95.

Rosendo, Salazar. *Historia de las luchas proletarias de México.* México, DF: Talleres Gráficos de la Nación, 1956.

Sánchez, Marta Ester. "Three Latin American Novelists in Search of lo Americano: A Productive Failure." PhD Diss. U of California, San Diego, 1977.

Scherer García, Julio, and Carlos Monsiváis. *Parte de guerra, Tlatelolco 1968: Documentos del general Marcelino García Barragán.* México, DF: Nuevo Siglo/Aguilar, 1999.

———. *Los patriotas: De Tlatelolco a la guerra sucia.* México, DF: Aguilar, 2004.

Schmidt, Henry C. *The Roots of Lo Mexicano: Self and Society in Mexican Thought, 1900–1934.* College Station: Texas A & M UP, 1978.

Schönfeld, Christiane. *Commodities of Desire: The Prostitute in Modern German Literature.* Rochester, NY: Camden House, 2000.

Sefchovich, Sara. *México: País de ideas, país de novelas.* México, DF: Grijalbo, 1987.

Smith, Robert Freeman. "The United States and International Politics in Latin America." *The United States and Latin American Sphere of Influence:* Vol. 1—*The Era of Caribbean Intervention, 1890–1930.* Ed. Smith. Malabar, FL: Robert E. Krieger Publishing, 1981. 1–34.

Sommer, Doris. *Foundational Fictions.* Berkeley: U of California P, 1991.

Sommers, Joseph. *After the Storm: Landmarks of the Modern Mexican Novel.* Albuquerque: U of New Mexico P, 1968.

Sorensen, Diana. "Tlatelolco 1968: Paz and Poniatowska on Law and Violence." *Mexican Studies /Estudios Mexicanos* 18.2 (2002): 297–321.

Soto, Lilvia. "Tres aproximaciones a *José Trigo.*" *Revista Chilena de Literatura* 30 (1987): 125–54.

Spivak, Gayatri Chakravorty. *A Critique of Postcolonial Reason: Toward a History of the Vanishing Present.* Cambridge: Harvard UP, 1999.

———. "Who Claims Alterity?" *Remaking History.* Ed. Barbara Kruger and Phil Marianai. Seattle: Bay, 1989. 269–92.

Stavans, Ilan. *Antiheroes: Mexico and Its Detective Novel.* Madison and Teaneck, NJ: Fairleigh Dickinson UP, 1997.

Steele, Cynthia. *Politics, Gender, and the Mexican Novel, 1968–1988: Beyond the Pyramid.* Austin: U of Texas P, 1992.

Székely, Gabriel. *La economía política del petróleo en México, 1976–1982.* México, DF: Colegio de México, 1983.

———. "The Oil Industry and Mexico's Relations with the Industrial Powers." *The Mexican Petroleum Industry in the Twentieth Century.* Ed. Jonathan C. Brown and Alan Knight. Austin: U of Texas P, 1992. 256–79.

Taibo II, Paco Ignacio. *68.* México, DF: Planeta, 1991.

Trejo Delarbre, Raúl. "Del campus a la nación." *Pensar el 68.* Ed. Hermann Bellinghausen. México, DF: Cal y Arena, 1988. 159–61.

Trejo Fuentes, Ignacio. "La novela mexicana de los setentas y los ochentas." *Literatura mexicana hoy: Del 68 al ocaso de la Revolución.* Ed. Karl Kohut. Frankfurt: Vervuert, 1991. 55–65.

Uranga, Emilio. "Optimismo y pesimismo del mexicano." *Historia mexicana* 1.3 (1952): 395–410.

Vallejo, Demetrio. *Las luchas ferrocarrileras que conmovieron a México.* México, DF: Sin nombre, 1967.

Van Delden, Maarten. *Carlos Fuentes, Mexico and Modernity.* Nashville: Vanderbilt UP, 1998.

Van Dijk, Ann. "The Angelic Salutation in Early Byzantine and Medieval Annunciation Imagery." *Art Bulletin* 81.3 (1999): 420–36.

Vargas Llosa, Mario. *Carta de batalla por Tirant lo Blanc.* 1969. Barcelona: Seix Barral, 1991.

————. *García Márquez: Historia de un deicidio.* Barcelona and Caracas: Seix Barral, 1971.

Volpi, Jorge. *La imaginación y el poder: Una historia intelectual de 1968.* México, DF: Era, 1998.

Williams, Gareth. *The Other Side of the Popular: Neoliberalism and Subalternity in Latin America.* Durham: Duke UP, 2002.

Williams, Raymond L. *Vargas Llosa: Otra historia de un deicidio.* México, DF: Taurus, 2000.

Williamson, R. "Novela nacional y marginación sociopolítica en la trayectoria novelística de Carlos Fuentes." *Canadian Journal of Latin American and Caribbean Studies* 14.28 (1989): 117–28.

Young, Dolly J., and William D. Young. "The New Journalism in Mexico: Two Women Writers." *Chasqui* 12.2–3 (1983): 72–80.

Zermeño, Sergio. "Estado y sociedad en el capitalismo tardío." *Revista Mexicana de Sociología* 77.1 (1977): 61–117.

Zermeño, Sergio. "Los intelectuales y el estado en la década perdida." *Revista Mexicana de Sociología* 52.3 (1990): 213–35.

———. *México: Una democracia Utópica: El movimiento estudiantil del '68*. México, DF: Siglo XXI, 1978.

Zizek, Slavoj. *The Puppet and the Dwarf: The Perverse Core of Christianity*. Cambridge: MIT, 2003.

Index

About the Author

Ryan F. Long, University of Oklahoma, researches culture and politics in Mexico, especially the late twentieth century. He has published articles on a range of topics, including the conflict in Chiapas, Mexican cinema, and a number of writers, such as Ignacio Manuel Altamirano, Álvaro Mutis, and Luis González de Alba.